The Least You Should Know about English

ELEVENTH EDITION

form A

WRITING SKILLS

titles: italicise or underline

The Least You Should Know about English

ELEVENTH EDITION

form A

WRITING SKILLS

PAIGE WILSON
PASADENA CITY COLLEGE

TERESA FERSTER GLAZIER
LATE, WESTERN ILLINOIS UNIVERSITY

WADSWORTH
CENGAGE Learning

Australia • Brazil • Japan • Korea • Mexico • Singapore • Spain • United Kingdom • United States

The Least You Should Know about English: Writing Skills, Form A, Eleventh Edition
Paige Wilson and Teresa Ferster Glazier [late]

Senior Publisher: Lyn Uhl

Director of Developmental English and College Success: Annie Todd

Development Editor: Karen Mauk

Assistant Editor: Melanie Opacki

Editorial Assistant: Matthew Conte

Media Editor: Amy Gibbons

Senior Marketing Manager: Kirsten Stoller

Marketing Coordinator: Ryan Ahern

Marketing Communications Manager: Courtney Morris

Content Project Manager: Aimee Chevrette Bear

Art Director: Jill Ort

Print Buyer: Susan Spencer

Rights Acquisition Specialist: Shalice Shah-Caldwell

Production Service: PreMediaGlobal

Cover Designer: Hanh Luu

Cover Image: Veer/Corbis

Compositor: PreMediaGlobal

For product information and technology assistance, contact us at **Cengage Learning Customer & Sales Support, 1-800-354-9706**

For permission to use material from this text or product, submit all requests online at **www.cengage.com/permissions.** Further permissions questions can be emailed to **permissionrequest@cengage.com.**

Library of Congress Control Number: 2010941196

ISBN 13: 978-0-495-90633-9

ISBN 10: 0-495-90633-6

Wadsworth
20 Channel Center Street
Boston, MA 02210
USA

Cengage Learning is a leading provider of customized learning solutions with office locations around the globe, including Singapore, the United Kingdom, Australia, Mexico, Brazil and Japan. Locate your local office at **international.cengage.com/region**

Cengage Learning products are represented in Canada by Nelson Education, Ltd.

For your course and learning solutions, visit **www.cengage.com.**

Purchase any of our products at your local college store or at our preferred online store **www.cengagebrain.com.**

Printed in the United States of America
2 3 4 5 6 7 14 13 12 11

CONTENTS

This book is for students who need to review basic English skills and who may profit from a simplified "least you should know" approach. Parts 1 to 3 cover the essentials of word choice and spelling, sentence structure, punctuation and capitalization. Part 4 on writing teaches students the basic structures of the paragraph and the essay, along with the writing skills necessary to produce them, and provides samples by both student and professional writers.

The "least you should know" approach attempts to avoid the use of linguistic terminology whenever possible. Students work with words they know instead of learning a vocabulary they may never use again.

Abundant exercises prompt students to identify structures, correct errors, write sentences, and proofread paragraphs. Diligent students learn to use these new skills automatically and begin to *apply them to their writing*. Most exercises consist of sets of ten thematically-linked, informative sentences on both timely and timeless subjects—anything from the world's oldest tree to its newest form of "thought-controlled" robot. Such exercises reinforce the need for coherence of details in student writing. With answers provided at the back of the book, students can correct their own work and progress at their own pace—in class and at home.

Changes to the eleventh edition continue the "Least You Should Know" tradition, with updated explanations, examples, and exercises throughout the text. Part 1 now presents "Spelling" before "Word Choice," discusses dictionary use throughout, and includes new ways to distinguish between "Words Often Confused." Part 2 on "Sentence Structure" further clarifies the use of first-person, second-person, and third-person pronouns. Part 3's coverage of "Punctuation" now cross-references Part 4's completely new section on "Choosing and Using Quotations." This comprehensive new section offers "Guidelines for Including Quotations," complete with explanations and samples of signal phrases and punctuation practices unique to quoting. Finally, Part 4 now includes discussions and examples of first-person and third-person approaches to writing, and a total of fourteen updated Writing Exercises follow key discussions throughout the Writing section.

The Least You Should Know about English functions equally well in the classroom and at home as a self-tutoring text. The clear explanations, ample exercises, and answers at the back of the book provide students with everything they need to progress on their own. Students who have previously been overwhelmed by the complexities of English should, through mastering simple skills and through writing and rewriting basic papers, gain the ability to succeed in further composition courses.

A **Test Booklet**, available only to instructors, corresponds directly to the book's content and includes both single-sentence and paragraph-length tests/exercises within each section.

ACKNOWLEDGMENTS

For their extremely helpful commentary on the book, I would like to thank the following reviewers:

Jacen Alexander, *Bakersfield College*
Michelle Christopherson, *Modesto Junior College*
Natalie S. Daley, *Linn-Benton Community College*
Lisa Moreno, *Los Angeles Trade-Technical College*
Marjory Thrash, *Pearl River Community College, Poplarville*

In addition, thanks to my publishing team for their expertise and hard work: Annie Todd, Melanie Opacki, Karen Mauk, Aimee Chevrette Bear, and Trish O'Kane.

For their specific contributions and helpful suggestions, I extend my gratitude to the following students: Jacqueline Castro, Frances Castanar, Alex DeLaTorre, Carlos Falcon, Christine Foy, Nicholas Velez, and Maggie Wong.

As always, I am especially indebted to my family, friends, students, and colleagues for their ongoing support and encouragement.

Paige Wilson
Pasadena City College

This book is dedicated to Teresa Ferster Glazier (1907–2004). In creating *The Least You Should Know about English*, she discovered a way to teach grammar and writing that students and teachers have actually enjoyed for over thirty years. Her original explanations and approaches have been constant sources of inspiration for this and all previous coauthored editions, as they will be for all future editions of her text.

What Is the Least You Should Know?

Most English textbooks try to teach you more than you need to know. This book will teach you the least you should know—and still help you learn to write clearly and acceptably. You won't have to learn grammatical terms like *gerund, auxiliary verb,* or *demonstrative pronoun.* You can get along without knowing such technical labels if you understand a few key concepts. You *should* know about the parts of speech and how to use and spell common words; you *should* be able to recognize subjects and verbs; you *should* know the basics of sentence structure and punctuation—but rules, as such, will be kept to a minimum.

The English you'll learn in this book is sometimes called Standard Written English, and it may differ slightly or greatly from the English you use when speaking. Standard Written English is the form of writing accepted in business and the professions. So no matter how you speak, you will communicate better in writing when you use Standard Written English. For instance you might *say,* "That's a whole nother problem," but you would probably want to *write,* "That's a completely different problem." Knowing the difference between spoken English and Standard Written English is essential in college, in business, and in life.

Until you learn the least you should know, you may have difficulty communicating in writing. Look for the misused word in the following sentence, for example:

I hope that the university will except my application for admission.

The writer probably relied on the sound, not the meaning, of the word *except* to choose it. The two words *except* and *accept* sound similar but have completely different meanings. (See page 8.) The writer should have used the one that means approve the application (*accept* it):

I hope that the university will *accept* my application for admission.

Then all of the words would have communicated clearly. Here's another example, this time with missing punctuation:

The manager fired Kevin and Chloe and I received a promotion.

This sentence needs a comma to separate its two independent clauses:

The manager fired Kevin and Chloe, and I received a promotion.

But perhaps the writer meant the following:

The manager fired Kevin, and Chloe and I received a promotion.

Punctuation changes the meaning of the sentence, especially for Chloe. With the help of this text, we hope that your writing will become so clear that no one will misunderstand it.

As you make your way through the book, it's important to remember information after you learn it because many concepts and structures build upon others. For example, once you can identify subjects and verbs, you'll be better able to recognize fragments, understand subject-verb agreement, and use correct punctuation. Explanations and examples are brief and clear, and it shouldn't be difficult to learn from them—*if you want to*. But you have to want to!

HOW TO LEARN THE LEAST YOU SHOULD KNOW

1. Read each explanatory section carefully (aloud, if possible).

2. Do the first exercise. Compare your answers with those at the back of the book. If they don't match, study the explanation again to find out why.

3. Do the second exercise and correct it. If you miss a single answer, go back once more to the explanation. You must have missed something. Be tough on yourself. Don't just think, "Maybe I'll get it right next time." Reread the examples, and *then* try the next exercise. It's important to correct each group of ten sentences before moving on so that you'll discover your mistakes early.

4. You may be tempted to quit after you do one or two exercises perfectly. Instead, make yourself finish another exercise. It's not enough to *understand* a concept or structure. You have to *practice* using it.

5. If you're positive that you've learned a concept or structure after doing several exercises, move on to the proofreading and sentence composing exercises, where you can apply that knowledge to your writing.

Learning the basics of spelling and word choice, sentence structure, and punctuation does take time. Generally, college students should study a couple of hours outside of class for each hour in class. You may need to study more. Undoubtedly, the more time you spend, the more your writing will improve.

P A R T   1

Spelling and Word Choice

Anyone can learn to spell better and use words more effectively. You can eliminate most of your spelling and word choice errors if you want to. It's just a matter of deciding you're going to do it.

THE IMPORTANCE OF A GOOD DICTIONARY

A current, full-featured dictionary is a basic but commonly underused resource for many writers. College-level print dictionaries provide the spelling, pronunciation, definitions, usage, and sources of words, as well as foreign phrases, famous names, and geographical locations. The latest dictionaries also offer online resources, including audio and video features that bring words, people, and places to life. Of course, most computers and word-processing programs have built-in dictionaries and spell-check capabilities. However, the automatic "corrections" they suggest may at times cause more damage to your meaning than your original mistakes would. The good news is that dictionaries of all kinds will become more useful once you learn the "least you should know" about spelling and word choice.

If you really intend to improve your spelling and choice of words, study each of the following sections until you make no mistakes in the exercises.

Your Own List of Misspelled Words

Words That Can Be Broken into Parts

Guidelines for Doubling a Final Letter

Words Often Confused (Set 1)

Words Often Confused (Set 2)

The Eight Parts of Speech

Adjectives and Adverbs

Contractions

Possessives

Your Own List of Misspelled Words

You can create your own personal dictionary on the inside cover of your English notebook or in some other obvious place by making a corrected list of all the misspelled words from your graded papers. Review and practice using the correct spellings until you're sure of them, and edit your papers to find and fix repeated errors.

Words That Can Be Broken into Parts

Breaking words into their parts will often help you spell them correctly. Each of the following words is made up of two shorter words. Note that the word then contains all the letters of the two shorter words.

chalk board	. . .	chalkboard	room mate	. . .	roommate
over due	. . .	overdue	home work	. . .	homework
super market	. . .	supermarket	under line	. . .	underline

Becoming aware of prefixes such as *dis, inter, mis,* and *un* is also helpful. When you add a prefix to a word, note that no letters are dropped, either from the prefix or from the word.

dis appear	disappear	mis represent	misrepresent
dis appoint	disappoint	mis spell	misspell
dis approve	disapprove	mis understood	misunderstood
dis satisfy	dissatisfy	un aware	unaware
inter act	interact	un involved	uninvolved
inter active	interactive	un necessary	unnecessary
inter related	interrelated	un sure	unsure

Have someone dictate the preceding list for you to write and then mark any words you miss. Memorize the correct spellings by noting how each word is made up of a prefix and a word.

Guidelines for Doubling a Final Letter

Most spelling rules have so many exceptions that they aren't much help. But here's one worth learning because it has very few exceptions.

Double a final letter (consonants only) when adding an ending that begins with a vowel (such as *ing, ed, er*) if all three of the following are true:

1. The word ends in a single consonant,

2. which is preceded by a single vowel (the vowels are *a, e, i, o, u*),

3. and the accent is on the last syllable (or the word only has one syllable).

We'll try the rule on a few words to which we'll add *ing, ed,* or *er*.

begin
    1. It ends in a single consonant—*n,*
    2. preceded by a single vowel—*i,*
    3. and the accent is on the last syllable—be *gín.*
    Therefore, we double the final consonant and write *beginning, beginner.*

stop
    1. It ends in a single consonant—*p,*
    2. preceded by a single vowel—*o,*
    3. and the accent is on the last syllable (there is only one).
    Therefore, we double the final consonant and write *stopping, stopped, stopper.*

filter
    1. It ends in a single consonant—*r,*
    2. preceded by a single vowel—*e,*
    3. But the accent isn't on the last syllable. It's on the first—*fíl* ter.
    Therefore, we *don't* double the final consonant. We write *filtering, filtered.*

keep
    1. It ends in a single consonant—*p,*
    2. but the *p* isn't preceded by a single vowel. There are two *e*'s.
    Therefore, we *don't* double the final consonant. We write *keeping, keeper.*

NOTE 1—Be aware that *qu* is treated as a consonant because *q* is almost never written without *u*. Think of it as *kw*. In words like *equip* and *quit*, the *qu* acts as a consonant. Therefore, *equip* and *quit* both end in a single consonant preceded by a single vowel, and the final consonant is doubled in *equipped* and *quitting*.

> **NOTE 2**—The final consonants *w, x,* and *y* do not follow this rule and are not doubled when adding *ing, ed,* or *er* to a word (as in *bowing, fixing,* and *enjoying*).

E X E R C I S E S

Add *ing* to these words. Correct each group of ten before continuing so you'll catch any errors early.

Exercise 1

1. tint
2. dress
3. tow
4. steal
5. discover

6. split
7. sand
8. quiz
9. box
10. squint

Exercise 2

1. shout
2. mix
3. drip
4. deploy
5. refer

6. display
7. dig
8. enjoy
9. hem
10. tax

Exercise 3

1. get
2. trust
3. trip
4. plan
5. play

6. miss
7. read
8. occur
9. skim
10. scream

Exercise 4

1. creep
2. subtract
3. abandon
4. droop
5. say
6. weed
7. fog
8. drop
9. refer
10. submit

Exercise 5

1. interpret
2. fix
3. bet
4. stoop
5. flip
6. infer
7. guess
8. bug
9. jog
10. build

Words Often Confused (Set 1)

Learning the difference between often-confused words will help you overcome many of your spelling problems. We've divided the most commonly confused words into two sets. Study the pairs of words in Set 1 carefully, with their helpful memory tips and examples, before trying the exercises. Then move on to Set 2. If you practice each set thoroughly, your spelling should improve.

a, an

Use *an* before a word that begins with a vowel sound (*a, e, i,* and *o,* plus *u* when it sounds like *uh*) or silent *h*. Note that it's not the letter but the *sound* of the letter that matters.

an apple, *an* essay, *an* inch, *an* onion

an umpire, *an* ugly design (The *u's* sound like *uh*.)

an hour, *an* honest person (The *h's* are silent.)

Use *a* before a word that begins with a consonant sound (all the sounds except the vowels, plus *u* or *eu* when they sound like *you*).

a chart, *a* pie, *a* history book (The *h* is not silent in *history*.)

a union, *a* uniform, *a* unit (The *u's* sound like *you*.)

a European vacation, *a* euphemism (*Eu* sounds like *you*.)

accept, except

Accept means "to receive or agree to take." Think of the two *c's* in *accept* as two arms curling up to receive something.

I *accept* this award on my mother's behalf.

Except means "excluding" or "but." Think of the *x* in *except* as two arms crossed to block something or someone.

The airline upgraded everyone *except* Stanley.

advise, advice

Advise is a verb. (Pronounce the *s* like a *z*.)

I *advise* you to take your time finding the right job.

Advice is a noun. (It rhymes with *rice*.)

I took my doctor's *advice* to eat more brown rice.

affect, effect

Affect is a *verb* that means "to alter or influence someone or something." Try substituting another *verb* that starts with *a*—like *alter* or *amaze* or *astound*—to see if one of them works. If it does, then use this verb that starts with *a*: *affect*.

> All quizzes will *affect* the final grade. (All quizzes will *alter* the final grade.)

> That story *affected* everyone who heard it. (That story *amazed* everyone who heard it.)

Effect is most commonly used as a *noun* and means "a result." Focus on the *e* sound in *effect* and *result*, and try substituting *result* for *effect* as a test.

> The strong coffee had a powerful *effect*. (The strong coffee had a powerful *result*.)

> We studied the *effects* of sleep deprivation in my psychology class. (We studied the *results*. . . .)

all ready, already   If you can leave out the *all* and the sentence still makes sense, then *all ready* is the form to use.

> We're *all ready* for our trip. (*We're ready for our trip* makes sense.)

> The banquet is *all ready*. (*The banquet is ready* also makes sense.)

But if you can't leave out the *all* and still have a sentence that makes sense, use *already*.

> They've *already* eaten dinner. (*They've ready eaten dinner* doesn't make sense.)

> We have seen that movie *already*. (*We have seen that movie ready* doesn't make sense either.)

are, our   *Are* is a present form of the verb "to be."

> We *are* going to Colorado Springs.

Our is a pronoun that shows we possess something.

> We painted *our* fence to match the house.

brake, break   *Brake* used as a verb means "to slow or stop motion." It's also the name of the device that slows or stops motion.

> I had to *brake* quickly to avoid an accident.

> Luckily I just had my *brakes* fixed.

Break used as a verb means "to shatter" or "to split." It's also the name of an interruption, as in "a coffee break."

She never thought she would *break* a world record.

Enjoy your spring *break*.

choose, chose

The difference here is one of time. Use *choose* for present and future; use *chose* for past.

I will *choose* a new major this semester.

They *chose* the wrong time of year to travel to India.

clothes, cloths

Clothes are garments people wear; *cloths* are pieces of material you might clean or polish something with.

I love the *clothes* that characters wear in old movies.

Workers at car washes use special *cloths* to dry the cars.

coarse, course

Coarse describes a rough texture.

I used *coarse* sandpaper to smooth the surface of the board.

Course is used for all other meanings.

Of *course* we visited the golf *course* at Pebble Beach.

complement, compliment

Complement, spelled with an *e,* means to complete something or bring it to perfection.

Use a color wheel to find a *complement* for purple.

Juliet's personality *complements* Romeo's: she is practical, and he is a dreamer.

Compliment, spelled with an *i,* has to do with praise. Remember the *i* in "*I* like compliments," and you'll remember to use the *i* spelling when you mean praise.

My recent evaluation included a nice *compliment* from my new boss.

We *complimented* them on their new home.

conscious, conscience

Conscious means "awake" or "aware."

They weren't *conscious* of any problems before the accident.

Conscience means that inner voice of right and wrong. The extra *n* in *conscience* should remind you of "No," which is what your conscience often says to you.

My *conscience* told me not to keep the money I found.

dessert, desert	*Dessert* is the sweet one, the one people like two helpings of. So give it two helpings of *s*. Remember also that "stressed" spelled backwards is *desserts*.
	When I'm stressed, I can eat two *desserts* in a row.
	The other one, *desert,* is used for all other meanings and has two pronunciations.
	I promise that I won't *desert* you at the party.
	The snake slithered slowly across the *desert*.
do, due	*Do* is a verb, an action. You *do* something.
	I *do* most of my homework on the weekends.
	But a payment or an assignment is *due;* it is scheduled for a certain time.
	Our first essay is *due* tomorrow.
	Due also comes before *to* in a phrase that means *because of.*
	The outdoor concert was canceled *due to* rain.
feel, fill	*Feel* describes *feel*ings.
	Whenever I stay up late, I *feel* sleepy in class.
	Fill is the action of pouring into or packing a container fully.
	Why did he *fill* the pitcher to the top?
fourth, forth	The word *fourth* has *four* in it. But note that *forty* does not. Remember the word *forty-fourth* to help you spell both of these words related to numbers.
	This is our *fourth* quiz in forty-eight hours.
	My grandparents celebrated their *forty-fourth* anniversary.
	If you don't mean a number, use *forth*.
	The ship's passengers walked back and *forth* on deck.
have, of	*Have* is a verb. Sometimes, in a contraction, it sounds like *of.* When you say *could've,* the *have* may sound like *of,* but it is not written that way. Always write *could have, would have, should have, might have.*
	We should *have* planned our vacation sooner.
	Then we could *have* used our coupon for a free ticket.

Use *of* only in a prepositional phrase. (See p. 63.)

She sent me a box *of* chocolates for my birthday.

hear, here

The last three letters of *hear* spell "ear." You *hear* with your ear.

When I listen to a seashell, I *hear* ocean sounds.

The other spelling *here* tells "where." Note that the three words indicating a place or pointing out something all have *here* in them: *here, there, where.*

I'll be *here* for three more weeks.

it's, its

It's is a contraction and means "it is" or "it has."

It's hot. (*It is* hot.)

It's been hot all week. (*It has* been hot all week.)

Its is a possessive. Pronouns such as *its, yours, hers, ours, theirs,* and *whose* are already possessive forms and never need an apostrophe. (See p. 48.)

The jury had made *its* decision.

The dog pulled at *its* leash.

knew, new

Knew has to do with *knowledge;* both start with a silent *k.*

New means "not old."

Her friends *knew* that she wanted a *new* bike.

know, no

Know has to do with *knowledge;* both start with a silent *k.*

By Friday, I must *know* all the state capitals.

No means "not any" or the opposite of "yes."

My boss has *no* patience. *No,* I am not exaggerating.

EXERCISES

Circle the correct words in parentheses. Don't guess! If you aren't sure, turn back to the explanatory pages. When you've finished one exercise, compare your answers with those at the back of the book. Correct each set of ten sentences before continuing so you'll catch your mistakes early.

Exercise 1

1. Dog and cat lovers have (a, an) unbelievable (knew, new) tool to help them talk with their animals.

2. (It's, Its) a translating device for a dog or a cat that turns (it's, its) barks or meows into words.

3. These animal translators have (all ready, already) been (accepted, excepted) in Japan, where the products were invented and recently updated.

4. The Bowlingual translator works in the same way as the Meowlingual translator, (accept, except) that a dog wears half of the device on (it's, its) collar.

5. The cat translator is (a, an) one-piece unit that the curious cat owner places near the cat while (it's, its) purring, meowing, or hissing.

6. Once (a, an) pet's sounds (are, our) recorded, the machine analyzes them, links them with (a, an) emotion, and translates them into messages that humans will understand.

7. Many pet owners wonder what their pets (due, do) and how they (feel, fill) while the owners (are, our) at work or away on short trips.

8. To ease the (conscious, conscience) of these pets' companions, the Bowlingual and Meowlingual devices can record their pets' sounds for the whole day and translate the results later.

9. Makers claim that these devices can (hear, here) the difference between a bark or meow that means "I'm hungry" and one that means "My collar is too tight."

10. A pet's happiness can strongly (affect, effect) the well-being of (it's, its) human companion.

Source: PC World, July 18, 2003 and *www.macworld.co.uk,* July 16, 2009

Exercise 2

1. Most people have (all ready, already) tasted salsa and love (it's, its) spicy, fresh taste.

2. Salsa is a (coarse, course) mixture of tomatoes, onions, green chilies, and cilantro.

3. Of (coarse, course), salsa is the perfect (complement, compliment) to eggs, chicken, or chips.

4. Many people don't (know, no) that salsa can help prevent food poisoning.

5. (A, An) study of fresh salsa juice has found that (it's, its) twice as powerful as man-made medicine at killing Salmonella bacteria.

6. (It's, Its) mainly the cilantro in the salsa that has (a, an) antibacterial (affect, effect).

7. The disinfecting chemical in salsa might even become (a, an) ingredient in (are, our) cleaning products in the future.

8. After they (hear, here) about salsa's power to kill bacteria, people might (choose, chose) to (feel, fill) their plates with it to avoid food poisoning.

9. That would be a good idea, (accept, except) that (a, an) normal serving of salsa has only (a, an) small amount of the antibacterial ingredient.

10. Therefore, experts still (advise, advice) people to cook their food thoroughly and store their food safely.

Source: Science News, June 19, 2004

Exercise 3

1. I've been reading that (are, our) individual dreams say (a, an) awful lot about us but that some dreams (are, our) common to us all.

2. (It's, Its) strange, for example, that many people (feel, fill) as though they are falling or flying in a dream.

3. In another common dream experience, we realize suddenly that we are not wearing any (clothes, cloths), and we don't (know, no) why.

4. Or we dream that we have missed a deadline when a test or a paper was (do, due), but we have forgotten to (do, due) it.

5. Whether we are (conscious, conscience) of it or not, our dream lives can have (a, an) (affect, effect) on (are, our) real lives.

6. If in a dream we (brake, break) the heart of someone we love, we might wake up the next morning with a guilty (conscious, conscience).

7. Of (coarse, course), we may dream of eating (a, an) entire gallon of chocolate ice cream for (dessert, desert) and (feel, fill) another kind of guilt.

8. Dream experts give the following (advise, advice) to those who want to call (fourth, forth) the dreams that slip away from the (conscious, conscience) mind once we are awake.

9. They suggest that dreamers put paper and a pencil by the bed before going to sleep in order to write down a dream as soon as (it's, its) over.

10. We all (know, no) that (know, no) amount of coaxing will bring back a dream that our brain (all ready, already) (choose, chose) to forget.

Exercise 4

1. I took my sister's (advice, advise) and (accepted, excepted) (are, our) mutual friends' invitation to have dinner with them last night.

2. Both Caroline and Tim (are, our) studying to be professional chefs.

3. She plans to be (a, an) all-purpose cook, and he will specialize in (desserts, deserts).

4. As a final project for their latest cooking (coarse, course), they (choose, chose) a four-(coarse, course) menu with a spectacular (dessert, desert), and they invited me to help them judge the results.

5. I didn't have to (hear, here) more than that to make me (feel, fill) hungry.

6. I arrived with a guilty (conscious, conscience), however, because I (knew, new) I was more interested in the food than the company at first.

7. The (affect, effect) of the whole experience was a pleasant surprise: the tasty dishes (complemented, complimented) our lively conversations about movies, sports, and cooking techniques.

8. After the meal's (fourth, forth) (coarse, course), I was (all ready, already) for dessert, and the individual soufflés with soft chocolate centers fulfilled everyone's expectations.

9. Having dinner with Caroline and Tim was a nice (brake, break) from my normal routine.

10. Looking back, I would (have, of) enjoyed the evening even if we had called out for pizza.

Exercise 5

1. (It's, Its) not often that a company buys back (it's, its) own product (a, an) hundred years after selling it.

2. That's just what Levi Strauss & Co. (choose, chose) to (do, due) in May of 2001 after (a, an) anonymous person sold the company a pair of Levi's jeans dating back to the 1880s.

3. (Do, Due) to a rich 130-year history, the Levi Strauss company wanted to add the (knew, new) discovery to the archive of antique jeans the company (all ready, already) had.

4. The pair recently discovered was older than any found before and would therefore (fill, feel) a gap in the company's archive of historically accurate (clothes, cloths).

5. Adding to (it's, its) rarity, the 1880s pair was designed with (a, an) unique left-thigh pocket for tools, as well as other special features.

6. Before the auction, no one (knew, new) exactly how much the rare jeans would fetch, but their worth was estimated at approximately $30,000.

7. (Conscious, Conscience) of the jeans' incredible value, two different auction services participated in gathering the bids.

8. Collectors of vintage denim (clothes, cloths) from around the world bid for the privilege of owning this oldest surviving pair of Levi's, and they could (have, of) easily gone to someone other than the Levi Strauss company.

9. But the jeans' original maker really wanted them to (complement, compliment) the younger pairs in the archive, so the company made (it's, its) final bid and got the 120-year-old pants for $46,532.

10. While the company's high bid did not surprise anyone involved in the auction, it did (brake, break) the record for the highest amount ever paid for a pair of jeans.

Source: Levi Strauss & Co. Press Release (May 15, 2001)

PROOFREADING EXERCISE

Find and correct the ten errors contained in the following paragraph. All of the errors involve Words Often Confused (Set 1).

I've always wanted to no what makes a person want to set or brake a Guinness world record. For example, if someone all ready has a record for collecting more than 2,500 rubber ducks, does another person really need to beat that record? Also, the objects that people chose to collect our often strange. There are records for collecting the highest number of erasers from all over the world, tags from designer cloths, and labels from water bottles, to name just a few. Of coarse, it's nice to receive complements and recognition for a impressive collection. Maybe I should of kept all those take-out menus I just threw away and tried to set a new record myself.

SENTENCE WRITING

The surest way to learn these Words Often Confused is to use them immediately in your own writing. Choose the five pairs of words that you most often confuse from Set 1. Then use each of them correctly in a new sentence. No answers are provided at the back of the book, but you can see if you are using the words correctly by comparing your sentences to the examples in the explanations.

Words Often Confused (Set 2)

Study this second set of words as carefully as you did the first. Read the short explanations, helpful hints, and sample sentences before attempting the exercises. By learning all of the word groups in both sets, you can eliminate many basic spelling problems.

lead, led	*Lead* is the metal that rhymes with *head*.

Old paint is dangerous because it often contains *lead*.

The past form of the verb "to lead" is *led*.

What factors *led* to your decision?

I *led* our school's debating team to victory last year.

If you don't mean past time, use *lead,* which rhymes with *seed*.

I will *lead* the debating team again this year.

loose, lose   *Loose* means "not tight." Note how *l o o s e* that word is. It has plenty of room for two *o*'s. Remember that *loose* and *tooth* both have two *o*'s in the middle.

My sister has a *loose* tooth.

Lose is the opposite of win. Pronounce the *s* like a *z*.

If we *lose* the next game, we will be out for the season.

passed, past   *Passed* is a form of the verb "to pass."

Nanette easily *passed* her math test.

The runner *passed* the baton to her teammate.

I *passed* your house on my way to the store.

Use *past* when you mean "*by*" or to refer to the time that came before the present.

I drove *past* your house. (Meaning "I drove *by* your house." The verb in the sentence is *drove*.)

It's best to learn from *past* experiences.

In the *past,* he worked for a small company.

personal,   Pronounce these two correctly, and you won't confuse
personnel   them—*pérsonal, personnél*.

She shared her *personal* views as a parent.

Personnel means "a group of employees."

I had an appointment in the *personnel* office.

piece, peace   Remember "a *piece* of *pie*." The word meaning "a *piece*" always begins with *pie*.

Some students asked for an extra *piece* of scratch paper.

The other word, *peace,* means "the opposite of war."

The two sides finally signed a *peace* treaty.

principal, principle   *Principal* means "main." Both words have *a* in them: princip*a*l, m*a*in.

The *principal* concern is safety. (main concern)

We paid both *principal* and interest. (main amount of money)

Also, think of a school's "princi*pal*" as your "*pal*."

An elementary school *principal* must be kind. (main administrator)

A *principle* is a "rule." Both words end in *le*: princip*le*, ru*le*.

I am proud of my *principles*. (rules of conduct)

We value the *principle* of truth in advertising. (rule)

quiet, quite   Pronounce these two correctly, and you won't confuse them. *Quiet* means "free from noise" and rhymes with *diet*.

Golfers often ask spectators to be *quiet*.

Quite means "really" or "very" and ends with the same three letters as *white*.

The bleach made my towels *quite* white.

right, write   *Right* means "correct," "proper," or "the opposite of left. "

You will find your keys if you look in the *right* place, on the *right* side of the coffee table.

It also means "in the exact location, position, or moment."

Your keys are *right* where you left them.

Let's go *right* now.

Write means "to compose sentences, poems, essays. . . ."

> I *write* in my journal every day.

than, then   *Than* is used to compare. Remember that both *than* and *compare* have an *a* in them.

> I am taller *than* my sister.

Then tells when. *Then* and *when* rhyme, and both have an *e* in them.

> I always write a rough draft of a paper first; *then* I revise it.

their, there, they're   *Their* is a possessive, meaning "belonging to them."

> They read *their* essays out loud.

There points out something. Remember that the three words indicating a place or pointing out something all have *here* in them: *here, there, where.*

> I know that I haven't been *there* before.

> In Hawaii, *there* is always a rainbow in the sky.

They're is a contraction and means "they are."

> *They're* living in Canada now. (*They are* living in Canada now.)

threw, through   *Threw* is the past form of "to throw."

> The students *threw* snowballs at each other.

> I *threw* away my application for a scholarship.

If you don't mean "to throw something," use *through.*

> We could see our beautiful view *through* the new curtains.

> They worked *through* their differences.

two, too, to   *Two* is a number.

> We have written *two* papers so far in my English class.

Too means "very" or "also," and so it also has an extra *o*.

> The movie was *too* long and *too* violent. (very)

> They are enrolled in that biology class, *too*. (also)

Use *to* for all other meanings.

> They like *to* ski. They're going *to* the mountains.

weather,
whether

Weather refers to conditions of the atmosphere.

Snowy *weather* is too cold for me.

Whether means "if."

I don't know *whether* it is snowing there or not.

were, wear,
where

These words are pronounced differently but are often confused in writing.

Were is a past form of the verb "to be."

We *were* interns at the time.

Wear usually means "to have on," as in wearing clothes.

I always *wear* a scarf in winter.

Where refers to a place. Remember that the three words indicating a place or pointing out something all have *here* in them: *here, there, where.*

Where are the teachers' mailboxes?

who's, whose

Who's is a contraction and means "who is" or "who has."

Who's responsible for signing the checks? (*Who is* responsible?)

Who's been reading my e-mail? (*Who has* been reading my e-mail?)

Whose is a possessive. Words such as *whose, its, yours, hers, ours, and theirs* are already possessive forms and never need an apostrophe. See p. 48.

Whose keys are these?

woman,
women

The difference here is one of number: wo*man* refers to one adult female; wo*men* refers to two or more adult females.

I know a *woman* who has bowled a perfect game.

I bowl with a group of *women* from my work.

you're, your

You're is a contraction and means "you are."

You're as smart as I am. (*You are* as smart as I am.)

Your is a possessive meaning "belonging to you."

I borrowed *your* lab book.

E X E R C I S E S

Circle the correct words in parentheses. When you've finished one exercise, compare your answers with those at the back of the book. Do only ten sentences at a time so that you will catch your mistakes early.

Exercise 1

1. I just learned that Mother's Day was started by a schoolteacher (who's, whose) mother was very important to her.

2. Anna Jarvis is the name of the (woman, women) who created the special day (two, too, to) celebrate mothers.

3. Jarvis's mother (passed, past) away on a second Sunday in May early in the twentieth century.

4. She began to give flowers for other people's mothers to (were, wear, where) on the day her own mother died.

5. Jarvis (lead, led) the movement to recognize mothers with a holiday in (their, there, they're) honor.

6. In 1914, Congress (passed, past) a resolution to make Mother's Day an official celebration in America.

7. Since (than, then), people have used the second Sunday in May to pay extra attention to the (woman, women) who have raised them.

8. Some people (right, write) loving messages in cards.

9. Others send gifts of flowers or candy (threw, through) the mail.

10. (Weather, Whether) it's a card, a gift, or just a (quiet, quite) dinner at home or in a restaurant, a Mother's Day gesture means a lot.

Source: The Writer's Almanac, May 12, 2007

Exercise 2

1. If the UniverSoul Circus has ever come to (you're, your) town, you may know that (their, there, they're) the only traveling circus company that is owned and operated by black Americans.

2. (Their, There, They're) ringmaster is "Casual Cal" Dupree, (who's, whose) (lead, led) this "hip hop big top" since it began in 1993.

3. Dupree cofounded the group in Atlanta with his partner Cedric Walker (two, too, to) offer the public a more interactive experience (than, then) was available from circuses in the (passed, past).

4. (Their, There, They're) is dancing and singing (threw, through) most of the UniverSoul Circus show—and not just by the performers.

5. Audience members are encouraged to get out of (their, there, they're) seats from the beginning and (two, too, to) continue participating until the end.

6. Like all circuses, the (principal, principle) aim of this show is to entertain the audience with animal acts, comedy routines, and daring acrobatics.

7. The musicians and performers in this troupe offer (quiet, quite) a mixture of cultures.

8. In addition to the acts from America, (their, there, they're) are performers from China, Chile, Africa, South America, and Colombia.

9. The atmosphere of the UniverSoul Circus is (loose, lose) and light-hearted; for instance, one of the acts is a double-Dutch jump-rope exhibition.

10. No matter (were, wear, where) you live in the United States, the UniverSoul Circus will likely be coming (two, too, to) a town nearby soon; don't miss it!

Source: www.universoulcircus.com

Exercise 3

1. Vehicle names often reveal (their, there, they're) number of wheels, such as the unicycle—a one-wheeler—and the quadricyle, a four-wheeled precursor to the automobile.

2. The bicycle, with its (two, too, to) wheels, continues to be one of the most popular methods of transportation around the world.

3. In the (passed, past), bicycles' wheels (were, wear, where) not always the same size.

4. One wheel was often much larger (than, then) the other; the front wheel might have been six feet high, or the back wheel twice as tall as the front.

5. At first, bikes (were, wear, where) so difficult to ride that doctors named a condition "bicycle face" for the facial expression of a person (who's, whose) trying to balance on one.

6. (Threw, Through) the years, the bicycle has played a fascinating part in history.

7. In the late 1800s, (woman, women) started to (were, wear, where) pants partly because of bicycles.

8. Susan B. Anthony, the famous advocate for (woman, women), gave the bicycle credit for many of (their, there, they're) new-found freedoms: greater comfort in clothes, increased mobility, and more choices for employment.

9. Bicycles have also been used in wars when other means of travel (were, wear, where) hazardous due to bad (weather, whether) or in places (were, wear, where) roads (were, wear, where) impassable.

10. Bicycles are still so coveted that more (than, then) a million and a half bikes are stolen in America every year.

Source: Kids Discover, July 2004

Exercise 4

1. Test (you're, your) knowledge of animal history by answering the following question: which came first, sharks or dinosaurs?

2. (You're, Your) (right, write) if you answered sharks; they have been around for millions of years, and (their, there, they're) really (quiet, quite) amazing creatures.

3. Most sharks travel (through, threw) the water constantly without stopping, but some appear (two, too, to) sleep (right, write) on the bottom of the ocean.

4. (Their, There, They're) teeth never have a chance to (were, wear, where) down because each tooth is designed to come (loose, lose) easily, and (their, there, they're) is always another tooth waiting to take its place.

5. Sharks range in size from the six-inch cigar shark (two, too, to) the sixty-foot whale shark, and most of them are (quiet, quite) harmless (two, too, to) humans if they are left in (piece, peace).

6. More people die each year from being stung by bees (than, then) from being attacked by sharks, so (their, there, they're) reputation as killers is perhaps exaggerated.

7. Sharks can sense the movements of a fish in trouble or a swimmer (who's, whose) bleeding, and that's when (their, there, they're) likely to attack.

8. A shark doesn't chew its food, but bites off and swallows one big (piece, peace) at a time.

9. Baby sharks are called pups, and different species of sharks have different numbers of pups at a time—from (two, too, to) to close to a hundred.

10. A few sharks lay (their, there, they're) eggs in pouches with descriptive names like "mermaid's purses" and "devil's wheelbarrows"; these pouches are then laid on the ocean floor, and they stay (their, there, they're) until the shark pups hatch.

Source: 1996 Aqua Facts (Vancouver Aquarium)

Exercise 5

1. Some people will go (threw, through) almost anything to look better.

2. Cosmetic surgeries for men and (woman, women) are more popular (than, then) ever.

3. A person (who's, whose) eyelids sag or someone (who's, whose) not happy with a "spare tire" can just get an eye-lift or a lunchtime liposuction job.

4. In the (passed, past), we could read people's ages on (their, there, they're) faces.

5. Now we can't tell (weather, whether) (their, there, they're) young or old except by a close look at (their, there, they're) elbows.

6. A man or a (woman, women) who chooses to (were, wear, where) makeup can even have it permanently applied by a tattoo artist.

7. One must be (quiet, quite) sure before getting makeup tattoos because (their, there, they're) irreversible.

8. Cosmetic surgery candidates should consider this (principal, principle): "If (you're, your) not absolutely certain, (than, then) don't do it."

9. Knowing (weather, whether) a surgical option is (right, write) or wrong is a (personal, personnel) decision.

10. (Their, There, They're) may be more to (loose, lose) (than, then) (their, there, they're) is to gain.

PROOFREADING EXERCISE

See if you can correct the ten errors in this paragraph. All errors involve Words Often Confused (Set 2).

When I was in high school, I past all my classes but didn't learn as much as I wanted too. All of my teachers did they're best, and the principle was an enthusiastic women who's love of education was contagious. Their was no shortage of school spirit; I just wasn't paying enough attention to make the hard information stick. Since I lead a carefree life at the time, I goofed off more then I should have. If I had those high school years to live over again, I would listen in class, do my homework carefully, and make sure that I knew all of the write answers on tests and that I didn't just forget the answers once the test was over.

SENTENCE WRITING

Choose ten words from Words Often Confused (Set 2) and write a new sentence using each one correctly. No answers are provided at the back of the book, but you can compare your sentences to the examples in the explanations.

The Eight Parts of Speech

Choosing the right word is an important aspect of writing. As we've explained, some words sound alike but are spelled differently and have different meanings (*past* and *passed,* for instance), and some words are spelled the same but sound different and mean different things (*lead,* for the action of "leading," and *lead,* for the stuff inside pencils). Besides learning to spell better, it is important to understand the roles that words play in sentences.

Just as one actor can play many different parts in movies (a hero, a villain, a humorous sidekick), single words can play different parts in sentences (a noun, a verb, an adjective). These are called the *eight parts of speech,* briefly defined with examples below.

1. **Nouns** name *people, places, things,* or *ideas* and are used as subjects and objects in sentences. **Proper nouns** that name *specific people, places, things,* or *ideas*—such as *Marie Curie, New York City, Kleenex,* and *Freemasonry*— are capitalized and can include more than one word. (See pp. 57, 63, and 133 for more about nouns as subjects and objects. See p. 191 for more about capitalizing specific nouns.)

   Ms. Kim and the other **librarians** are proud of the **success** of the new **library**.

2. **Pronouns** are special words—such as *I, she, him, it, they, who, that,* and *us*—that replace nouns to avoid repeating them. (See p. 150 for more about pronouns.)

   In fact, **they** (the librarians) are very proud of **it** (the new library's success).

3. **Adjectives** add description to nouns and pronouns—telling *which one, how many, what kind, color,* or *shape* they are. (See p. 33 for more about adjectives.)

   The **head** librarian designed the **new, state-of-the-art** facilities.

   The words *a, an,* and *the* are special forms of adjectives called **articles**. They always introduce a noun or a pronoun and are used so often that there is no need to label them.

4. **Verbs** show action or state of being. (See p. 57 and p. 91 for more about verbs.)

   She **was** an architect before she **retired** and **became** a librarian.

5. **Adverbs** add information—such as *when, where, why,* or *how*—to verbs, adjectives, and other adverbs. (See p. 34 for more about adverbs.)

   Now the library can **easily** accommodate thousands of students **daily**.

6. **Prepositions** show position in *space* and *time* and are followed by noun objects to form prepositional phrases. (See p. 63 for more about prepositions.)

   The computers lounges **in** the library are full **by** the middle **of** the morning.

7. **Conjunctions** are connecting words—such as *and, but,* and *or*—and words that begin dependent clauses—such as *because, since, when, while,* and *although.* (See p. 69 and p. 83 for more about conjunctions.)

> The library **and** its landscaping impress people **when** they first see the campus.

8. **Interjections** interrupt a sentence to convey a greeting or to show surprise or other emotions and are rarely used in Standard Written English.

> When they walk up or drive by, they say, "**Oh**, what a great building!"

To find out what parts of speech an individual word can play, look it up in a good, college-level dictionary. (See p. 3.) You'll find a list of definitions beginning with an abbreviated part of speech (*n, adj, prep,* and so on) that identifies its possible uses. However, seeing how a word is used in a particular sentence is the best way to identify its part of speech. Look at these examples:

> Our **train** arrived at exactly three o'clock.
>
> (*Train* is a noun in this sentence, naming the vehicle we call a "train.")
>
> Sammy and Helen **train** new employees at Sea World.
>
> (*Train* is a verb in this example, showing the action of "training.")
>
> Doug's parents drove him to the **train** station.
>
> (*Train* is an adjective here, adding description to the noun *station.*)

All of the words in a sentence work together to create meaning, but each one serves its own purpose by playing a part of speech. Think about how each of the words in the following sentence plays the particular part of speech labeled:

>   n   prep   adj   n   adv   v   adj   n   prep n conj v
> Students at community colleges often attend several classes in a day and are
>
>   adv   adj   conj pro   adv   v   adv
> very tired when they finally go home.

Below, you'll find an explanation for each label:

Students	n (*names the people* who are the subject of the sentence)
at	prep (*begins a prepositional phrase* showing position in space)
community	adj (*adds description* to the noun *colleges,* telling what kind)
colleges	n (*names the place* that is the object of the preposition *at*)
often	adv (*adds to the verb,* telling when students *attend* classes)
attend	v (*shows an action,* telling what the students do)

several	adj (*adds description* to the noun *classes*, telling how many)
classes	n (*names the things* that the students *attend*)
in	prep (*begins a prepositional phrase* showing position in time)
a	no label (an article that *points to the noun day*)
day	n (*names the thing* that is the object of the preposition *in*)
and	conj (*joins* the two verbs *attend* and *are*)
are	v (*shows a state of being*, linking the subject *students* with the descriptive word *tired*)
very	adv (*adds to the adjective* that follows, telling how *tired* the students are)
tired	adj (*describes the noun* subject *students*)
when	conj (*begins a dependent clause*)
they	pro (*replaces* the word *students* as a new subject to avoid repetition)
finally	adv (*adds to the verb*, telling when they *go* home)
go	v (*shows an action*, telling what they do)
home.	adv (*adds to the verb*, telling where they *go*)

Familiarizing yourself with the parts of speech will help you spell better now and understand phrases and clauses better later. Each of the eight parts of speech has characteristics that distinguish it from the other seven, but it takes practice to learn them.

EXERCISES

Label the parts of speech above all of the words in the following sentences using the abbreviations **n**, **pro**, **adj**, **v**, **adv**, **prep**, **conj**, and **interj**. Remember that proper nouns can include more than one word and that you may ignore the words *a*, *an*, and *the*. Refer back to the definitions and examples of the parts of speech whenever necessary. When in doubt, leave a word unmarked until you check the answers at the back of the book after each set of ten sentences.

Exercise 1

1. Bette Nesmith Graham invented correction fluid in the 1950s.

2. She originally called her invention Mistake Out.

3. Later, she changed its name to Liquid Paper.

4. Originally, Graham worked as a typist, and she often made mistakes.

5. She brought white paint to work and covered her typos with it.

6. Soon everyone wanted a bottle of Graham's correction paint.

7. She mixed the product in her kitchen and bottled it like fingernail polish.

8. Single-handedly, Graham developed a product that made millions of dollars.

9. Her son, Michael Nesmith, also benefited from her success.

10. He was a member of The Monkees, a popular band in the 1960s.

Source: Invention and Technology, Fall 2009

Exercise 2

1. Adults exercise in many different ways.

2. Some people walk around the neighborhood or run in the park.

3. Others ride their bikes to and from work or school.

4. Many people join programs at their local fitness centers.

5. These centers have the latest exercise equipment.

6. Treadmills and weight machines are very popular.

7. People can listen to music while they exercise.

8. Exercise should always be fun.

9. One secret to a good exercise program is flexibility.

10. A schedule that is too strict often leads to failure.

Exercise 3

1. Plants need water and sunlight.

2. Sometimes house plants die unexpectedly.

3. Often people give them too much water or not enough water.

4. I saw an experiment on a television show once.

5. It involved two plants.

6. The same woman raised both plants with water and sunlight.

7. The plants grew in two different rooms.

8. She yelled at one plant but said sweet things to the other.

9. The verbally praised plant grew beautifully.

10. The verbally abused plant died.

Exercise 4

1. Wow, pigeons have a built-in compass in their brains!

2. This compass points them in the right direction as they fly.

3. Recently, pigeon experts in England conducted a study of these birds.

4. The study tracked the flights of certain pigeons for two years.

5. The results were very surprising.

6. Modern pigeons usually ignored their inner compasses.

7. They navigated by other methods instead.

8. The pigeons simply looked down and followed human highways.

9. They remembered roads from previous flights and took the same roads home again.

10. The pigeons even traced the roads' turns, curves, and roundabouts as they flew.

Source: The Daily Telegraph, February 6, 2004

Exercise 5

1. Wild Quaker parrots are also interesting birds.

2. They originally came from Argentina.

3. They are noisy inhabitants of neighborhoods across North America.

4. These birds live in large nests at the top of tall trees.

5. Only Quaker parrots build nests.

6. These nests have three compartments.

7. The back part offers protection for the eggs.

8. The middle section houses the adults.

9. Parrots in the front compartment guard the entrance to the nest.

10. Some people raise Quaker parrots as pets.

PARAGRAPH EXERCISE

Here is a brief excerpt from the book *The Pact: Three Young Men Make a Promise and Fulfill a Dream* by Drs. Sampson Davis, George Jenkins, and Rameck Hunt. Their dream was for all three of them to become doctors, and they did. Label the parts of speech above as many of the words as you can before checking your answers at the back of the book.

When I look back over my life and the lives of my friends, I also see that involvement in school and community activities helped us [when we felt] the negative pull of our peers. I joined the Shakespeare Club in elementary school and the Police Athletic League in junior high school, and I played baseball in high school. Sam took karate lessons from grade school through his early years in high school and also played on our high-school baseball team. And Rameck took drama lessons in junior high school, and in high school he joined the drama club. . . .

SENTENCE WRITING

Write ten sentences imitating those in Exercises 1–5. Keep your sentences short (under 10 words each), and avoid using to _____ forms of verbs. Label the parts of speech above the words in your imitation sentences.

Adjectives and Adverbs

English has only two kinds of modifiers: adjectives and adverbs. "To modify" means to change or improve something, usually by adding to it. Two of the eight parts of speech, adjectives and adverbs, are used to *add* information to other words. Try to remember that both *adj*ectives and *adv*erbs *add* information.

ADJECTIVES

- Adjectives *add to nouns and pronouns* by answering these questions: *Which one? What kind? How much or how many? What size, what color, or what shape?*

adj   n   adj   n   adj adj adj

She bought a *new* textbook with *multicolored* tabs. It has *one large blue*

n   adj   adj   adj   n   adj   adj adj pro

tab, *two medium yellow* tabs, and *three small red* ones.

- Adjectives usually come *before the nouns they modify.*

adj   n   adj   n   adj adj   adj   n

The *new* library stands on the *north* side of *our big beautiful* campus.

- However, adjectives can also come *after the nouns they modify.*

n   ad   adj   adj   n   adj   n

The land, *flat* and *accessible,* was the perfect location for the new building.

- Adjectives may also come *after linking verbs* (is, am, are, was, were, feel, seem, appear, taste . . .) to add description to the subject. For further discussion of these special verbs, see page 133.

n   lv   adj   adj

The trees are *lush* and *plentiful.*

n   lv   adj   adj   n   lv   adj   adj

The juice tasted *fresh* and *delicious.* (or) The juice was *fresh* and *delicious.*

- Adjectives can be *forms of nouns and pronouns* that are used to add information to other nouns.

adj   n   adj   n   adj   adj   n

The *tree's* owner always trims *its* branches during *his summer* vacation.

adj   n   adj   n

I love *chocolate* cake for *my* birthday.

ADVERBS

- Adverbs *add to verbs, adjectives, and other adverbs* by answering these questions: *How? When? Where? Why? In what way?*

      adv   v   adv   v   adv adv
I *quickly* typed my paper and *reluctantly* turned it *in late*.

      v   adv   v
She did *not* accept my paper at first.

     adv   adj
I was *very* nervous about it.

       adv   adj   n
She had an *extremely* disappointed look on her face.

      adv adj   adv   adj
The deadline was *very* clear and *quite* reasonable.

     adv   adv adv
Students *often* work *really hard* at the end of the term.

- Unlike adjectives, some adverbs can move around in sentences without changing the meaning.

   adv
Now I have enough money for a vacation.

   adv
I *now* have enough money for a vacation.

           adv
I have enough money *now* for a vacation.

                adv
I have enough money for a vacation *now*.

Notice that many—but not all—adverbs end in *ly*. Be aware, however, that adjectives can also end in *ly*. Remember that a word's part of speech is determined by how the word is used in a particular sentence. For instance, in the old saying "The early bird catches the worm," *early* adds to the noun, telling which bird. *Early* is acting as an adjective. However, in the sentence "The teacher arrived early," *early* adds to the verb, telling when the teacher arrived. *Early* is an adverb.

     Now that you've read about adjectives and adverbs, try to identify the question that each modifier (adj or adv) answers in the example below. Refer back to the questions listed under Adjectives and Adverbs.

   adj   n   adj   n   adv   adv   v
My family and I went to the farmer's market yesterday. There we watched the

           adj   adj   n   adv   v   adv adj
decoration of a huge wedding cake. The baker skillfully squeezed out colorful

       n   adj   n   adv adj adj   n   adj   adj

flowers, leaf patterns, and pale pink curving letters made of smooth, creamy

     n

frosting.

> **NOTE**—Although we discuss only single-word adjectives and adverbs here, phrases and clauses can also function as adjectives and adverbs following similar patterns.

CHOOSING BETWEEN ADJECTIVES AND ADVERBS

Knowing how to choose between adjectives and adverbs is important, especially in certain kinds of sentences. See if you can make the correct choices in these three sentences:

> We did (good, well) on that test.
>
> I feel (bad, badly) about quitting my job.
>
> Your friend speaks (really clear/really clearly).

Did you choose *well, bad,* and *really clearly?* If you missed *bad,* you're not alone. You might have reasoned that *badly* adds to the verb *feel,* but *feel* is acting in a

                                                                    v

special way here—not naming the action of feeling with your fingertips (as in "I *feel*

            adv   n   adj

the fabric *carefully*"), but describing the feeling of it (as in "The *fabric* feels *smooth*"). To understand this concept, try substituting "I feel (happy, happily)" instead of "I feel (bad, badly)" and note how easy it is to choose.

    Another way that adjectives and adverbs work is to compare two or more things by describing them in relation to one another. The *er* ending is added to both adjectives and adverbs when comparing two items, and the est ending is added when comparing three or more items.

         adj   n   adj   adj   n   adj   adj   n

The first group was *big*. The second group was *bigger*. The third group was

        adj   pro

the *biggest* one of all.

        v   adv   v   adv   v   adv

You work *hard*; he works *harder*; I work *hardest*.

In some cases, such comparisons require the addition of a word (*more* or *most, less* or *least*) instead of a change in the ending from *er* to *est*. Longer adjectives and adverbs usually require these extra adverbs to help with comparisons.

adj   adv   adj   adv   adj

Food is *expensive*; gas is *more expensive*; rent is *most expensive*.

adv   adv   adv   adv   adv

He dances *gracefully*; you dance *less gracefully*; I dance *least gracefully*.

E X E R C I S E S

Remember that adjectives add to nouns and pronouns, while adverbs add to verbs, adjectives, and other adverbs. If you learn the difference between adjectives and adverbs, your word choice will improve. Check your answers frequently.

Exercise 1

Identify whether each *italicized* word is used as an adjective or an adverb in the sentence.

1. The "New Books" displays at bookstores *always* attract me. (adjective, adverb)

2. These displays usually stand right next to the *front* entrance. (adjective, adverb)

3. They hold everything from *tiny* paperbacks to huge reference works. (adjective, adverb)

4. The books are brand new and cover *various* topics. (adjective, adverb)

5. *Yesterday,* I discovered a whole book about flowers. (adjective, adverb)

6. The book's title was *very* straightforward: <u>Flowers.</u> (adjective, adverb)

7. I loved its *intriguing* subtitle: <u>How They Changed the World.</u> (adjective, adverb)

8. The *bright* pink tulip on its cover also appealed to me. (adjective, adverb)

9. I had *never* considered the effects of flowers on the world. (adjective, adverb)

10. Therefore, I bought the book and took it *home* to read. (adjective, adverb)

Exercise 2

Identify whether the word *only* is used as an adjective or an adverb in the following sentences. In each sentence, try to link the word *only* with another word to figure out if *only* is an adjective (adding to a noun or pronoun) or an adverb (adding to a verb, adjective, or other adverb). Have fun with this exercise!

1. I reached into my wallet and pulled out my *only* dollar. (adjective, adverb)
2. I had *only* one dollar. (adjective, adverb)
3. *Only* I had a dollar. (adjective, adverb)
4. One company *only* paints buildings. (adjective, adverb)
5. That company paints *only* buildings, not houses. (adjective, adverb)
6. Another company replaces *only* shingles, not clapboards. (adjective, adverb)
7. In my French class, we speak in French *only*. (adjective, adverb)
8. In my French class, we *only* speak in French. (adjective, adverb)
9. I was happy as an *only* child. (adjective, adverb)
10. She was the *only* one with a car. (adjective, adverb)

Exercise 3

Choose the correct adjective or adverb form required to complete each sentence.

1. I have a (close, closely) relative in show business.
2. I am (close, closely) related to someone in show business.
3. I feel (close, closely) to my family at the holidays.
4. My boss suffered (bad, badly) with a cold for several weeks.
5. He felt really (bad, badly) because of his fever.
6. Then he had a (bad, badly) reaction to a prescription drug and felt even worse.
7. The students jogged (very happy, very happily) in the cool morning mist.
8. They were (very happy, very happily) with their choice of P.E. class.
9. The whole class received (good, well) grades on the test.
10. The whole class performed (good, well) on the test.

Exercise 4

Choose the correct adjective or adverb form required to complete each sentence.

1. Kylie rents the (large, larger, largest) apartment in the whole building.

2. Josh's apartment is (large, larger, largest) than her parents' house.

3. Everyone needs a space that is (large, larger, largest) enough for the essentials.

4. Many of the apartments in my favorite building had very (ugly, uglier, ugliest) carpeting.

5. The carpet in the second apartment was (ugly, uglier, ugliest) than in the first.

6. But the (ugly, uglier, ugliest) carpet of all had medallion shapes in bright yellow and green all over it.

7. I've never seen a carpet pattern (ugly, uglier, ugliest) than that.

8. Unfortunately, the (friendly, friendlier, friendliest) people lived in the ugly-carpet building.

9. The tenants of the other buildings were (friendly, friendlier, friendliest), too.

10. They were all (friendly, friendlier, friendliest) than my current neighbors.

Exercise 5

Label all of the adjectives (adj) and adverbs (adv) in the following sentences. Mark the ones you are sure of; then check your answers at the back of the book and find the ones you missed.

1. I took a helpful class online in the spring.

2. An Internet specialist taught me research skills.

3. I discovered very useful tools for Web research.

4. The instructor clearly explained various kinds of online resources.

5. She gave me several optional topics for each assignment.

6. I especially enjoyed the articles from my two projects about world music.

7. Now I fully understand the benefits of online classes.

8. They are fun and rewarding because students work at their own pace.

9. I am definitely less confused about online sources.

10. I can do research online and enjoy the process completely.

PROOFREADING EXERCISE

Correct the five errors in the use of adjectives and adverbs in the following paragraph. Then try to label all of the adjectives (adj) and adverbs (adv) in the paragraph for practice.

My most favorite movie of all time is <u>The Matrix</u>. This movie is intenser than any other movie about the future. Neo, the main character, is smart and creative. He feels badly about the emptiness of his life. He has a dull, unsatisfying job, and he wants some excitement. Eventually, a team of real people from outside the Matrix find Neo and try repeated to recruit him. Neo joins their team and fights against the agents in the Matrix. <u>The Matrix</u> may be just the first part of a trilogy, but in my opinion, it is still the better movie of the three.

SENTENCE WRITING

Write a short paragraph (five to seven sentences) describing your favorite type of music, or favorite song, at the moment. Then go back through the paragraph and label your single-word adjectives and adverbs.

Contractions

When two words are shortened into one, the result is called a *contraction*:

is not   ·····➤   isn't   you have   ·····➤   you've

An apostrophe marks the spot where the letter or letters are left out in most contractions:

I am	I'm
I have	I've
I shall, I will	I'll
I would	I'd
you are	you're
you have	you've
you will	you'll
she is, she has	she's
he is, he has	he's
it is, it has	it's
we are	we're
we have	we've
we will, we shall	we'll
they are	they're
they have	they've
are not	aren't
cannot	can't
do not	don't
does not	doesn't
have not	haven't
let us	let's
who is, who has	who's
where is	where's
were not	weren't

would not	wouldn't
could not	couldn't
should not	shouldn't
would have	would've
could have	could've
should have	should've
that is	that's
there is	there's
what is	what's

Remember that one contraction does not follow this rule: *will not* becomes *won't.*

In all other contractions that you're likely to use, the apostrophe goes exactly where the letter or letters are left out. Note especially that *it's, they're, who's,* and *you're* are contractions. Use them when you mean *two* words. (See p. 48 for more about the possessive forms—*its, their, whose,* and *your*—which *don't* need apostrophes.)

EXERCISES

Add the missing apostrophes to the contractions in the following sentences. A few of the sentences do not include any contractions. Be sure to correct each exercise before going on to the next so you'll catch your mistakes early.

Exercise 1

1. College tuition and living expenses arent easy to afford.

2. Many high school and community college students havent considered entering an essay contest as a method of raising money for college.

3. Most people dont even know that such contests exist.

4. Every academic year, hundreds of essay competitions take place around the country, and theyre all different.

5. In 2003, Morghan Transue was awarded five thousand dollars for the essay shed submitted to the National Endowment for the Humanities' "Idea of America" Contest.

6. In her essay, Transue focused on the system of "checks and balances" between the government's three branches and how theyd achieved their balancing powers.

7. Politics and history are common topics for these essay contests, but they arent the only topics.

8. Some contests call for essays by students whove read famous works of literature.

9. For instance, theres the contest run by the Ayn Rand Institute with a $10,000 prize for the best essay on *The Fountainhead*.

10. For someone whos read widely and thought deeply, essay contests might help supplement other ways of raising money for a college education.

Source: Newsweek, April 12, 2004

Exercise 2

1. Whats a strong natural substance that might save thousands of lives in the future?

2. Youre right if youre thinking of bamboo.

3. Engineers from around the world have recently tested its strength and flexibility.

4. Experts found that its equally impressive when its used in its natural state and when its mixed with more traditional building materials, such as concrete.

5. Structures made from bamboo-based products are clearly safer when theres an earthquake.

6. They dont crack or crumble, even when theyre shaken violently by powerful earthquake simulators.

7. Theres a long list of factors that make bamboo a promising building material of the future.

8. It doesnt cost much and wont catch on fire.

9. Its lightweight but isnt brittle.

10. And although theyll be easy and quick to build, bamboo-reinforced buildings wont need repair for decades.

Source: Discover, August 2004

Exercise 3

1. Africanized or "killer" bees arent coming to the United States—theyre already here.

2. They arrived in Texas in 1990, and theyve continued to make their way into the country since then.

3. Theyre not any different in appearance than the bees youre used to seeing buzzing around flower gardens.

4. Yet weve probably all heard by now that theyre very different in their behavior.

5. Theyre more aggressive and more defensive than other bees.

6. People and animals are in the most danger when theyre near a hive.

7. Theres a good chance that the bees will warn someone whos too close to them, but theyve also been known to attack for no reason at all.

8. A person under attack shouldnt stand still or try to fight the bees off but should run as fast and as far away as possible.

9. The fact that the killer bees have arrived doesnt mean its time to panic.

10. After all, research shows that bee stings are one of the lowest ranked causes of death in the United States; thats the good news.

Source: Living with Killer Bees (Quick Trading Co., 1993)

Exercise 4

1. Im sure youve heard of Barbie and Ken, the famous toy couple.

2. These two may be dating in their doll lives, but they didnt start that way.

3. In real life, shes his sister, hes her brother, and theyre both the children of Ruth Handler, whos the inventor of the Barbie doll.

4. Handler named the dolls after her own daughter and son, but thats where the similarity ends.

5. The idea for the Barbie doll came when Handler noticed that her young daughter Correct the five errors in the with traditional dolls but with realistic, grown-up looking dolls instead.

6. Thats where the Barbie weve all seen got her start, and shes got lots of accessories and outfits that dont fit any other doll.

7. When Barbie was first introduced at the 1959 New York Toy Show, the reaction wasnt positive at all.

8. Handler's idea didnt need any help in the stores, however; Barbie made $500 million by the late 1960s, and shes been extremely popular ever since.

9. Handler's husband Elliot co-founded the Mattel company before Barbie came along, and was responsible for the success of its toy furniture and musical instruments.

10. Ruth Handler didnt take anything for granted; shes used her life experiences in another positive way by helping design a more natural-looking artificial breast after her own bout with breast cancer.

Source: Mothers of Invention, From the Bra to the Bomb: Forgotten Women and their Unforgettable Ideas (Quill, 1989)

Exercise 5

1. Classrooms have predictable shapes; theyre either square or rectangular.

2. Student desks can usually be moved around, unless theyve been bolted to the floor.

3. Some students prefer to sit in the front so that theyre near the teacher and the board.

4. Ive always liked to sit in the back of the classroom.

5. For me, its the perfect position to take notes and pay attention to everything thats happening.

6. When were asked to pull our chairs together into small groups, Im most comfortable with my back to the wall.

7. A friend of mine has a different idea; hes certain that the side of the room by the door is the best place to sit.

8. Of course, hes often late to class, so its the right spot for him to find a seat without disturbing the teacher.

9. Of course, the row near the windows isnt a good place to sit if theyre open.

10. It can be too noisy, too sunny, or too distracting if theres a view of anything interesting.

PROOFREADING EXERCISE

Correct the ten errors in the following paragraph. The mistakes could be from any of the areas covered so far.

I bought a knew car last week. It was the first time I had too deal with car salespeople. I did'nt believe all those stories about the pressure they make you feel. However, now that I have gone threw the experience, I no that its true. Whether I was alone or with my family, the salespeople were at my elbow the whole time. Even when I asked them to give me time to look around, they were still quiet persistent. The only one who's sales pitch wasn't annoying was a women. Out of all the salespeople, she was the calmer, so I bought my car from her.

SENTENCE WRITING

Doing exercises will help you learn a rule, but it is even more helpful to use what you've learned in writing. Write ten sentences using contractions. You might write about which you like better, working alone or working in groups. Try to use as many contractions as you can.

Possessives

Words that clarify ownership are called *possessives*. The trick in writing possessives is to ask the question "Who (or what) does the item belong to?" Modern usage has made *who* acceptable when it begins a question. More correctly, of course, the phrasing should be "*Whom* does the item belong to?" or even "*To whom* does the item belong?"

In any case, if the answer to this question does not end in *s* (as in *player, person, people, children, month*), simply add an *apostrophe* and *s* to show the possessive. Look at the first five examples in the chart below.

However, if the answer to the question already ends in *s* (as in *players and Brahms*), add only an apostrophe after the *s* to show the possessive. See these two examples in the chart and say them aloud to hear that their sound does not need to change when made possessive.

Finally, some *s*-ending words need another sound to make the possessive clear. If you need another *s* sound when you *say* the possessive (for example, *the office of my boss* becomes *my boss's office*), add the apostrophe and another *s* to show the added sound.

a player (uniform)	Whom does the uniform belong to?	a player	Add *'s*	a player's uniform
a person (clothes)	Whom do the clothes belong to?	a person	Add *'s*	a person's clothes
people (clothes)	Whom do the clothes belong to?	people	Add *'s*	people's clothes
children (games)	Whom do the games belong to?	children	Add *'s*	children's games
a month (pay)	What does the pay belong to?	a month	Add *'s*	a month's pay
players (uniforms)	Whom do the uniforms belong to?	players	Add *'*	players' uniforms
Brahms (Lullaby)	Whom does the Lullaby belong to?	Brahms	Add *'*	Brahms' Lullaby
my boss (office)	Whom does the office belong to?	my boss	Add *'s*	my boss's office

The trick of asking "Whom does the item belong to?" will always work, but you must ask the question every time. Remember that the key word is *belong*. If you ask the question another way, you may get an answer that won't help you. Also, notice that the trick does not depend on whether the answer is *singular* or *plural*, but on whether it ends in *s* or not.

TO MAKE A POSSESSIVE

1. Ask "Whom (or what) does the item belong to?"
2. If the answer doesn't end in *s*, add an *apostrophe* and *s*.
3. If the answer already ends in *s*, add just an *apostrophe* or an *apostrophe* and *s* if you need an extra sound to show the possessive (as in *boss's office*).

EXERCISES

Follow the directions carefully for each of the following exercises. Because possessives can be tricky, we include explanations in some exercises to help you understand them better.

Exercise 1

Cover the right column and see if you can write the following possessives correctly. Ask the question "Whom (or what) does the item belong to?" each time. Don't look at the answer before you try!

1. a teacher (assignments)	_____	a teacher's assignments
2. the women (soccer team)	_____	the women's soccer team
3. Nellie (essay)	_____	Nellie's essay
4. Jess (new job)	_____	Jess's or Jess' new job
5. the Smiths (house)	_____	the Smiths' house
6. a cat (whiskers)	_____	a cat's whiskers
7. dogs (reflexes)	_____	dogs' reflexes
8. Judge Malden (rulings)	_____	Judge Malden's rulings
9. students (textbooks)	_____	students' textbooks
10. a nation (resources)	_____	a nation's resources

(Sometimes you may have a choice when the word ends in *s*. *Jess's new job* may be written *Jess' new job*. Whether you want your reader to say it with or without an extra *s* sound, be consistent when given such choices.)

> **CAUTION—**Don't assume that every word that ends in *s* is a possessive. The *s* may indicate more than one of something, a plural noun. Make sure the word actually possesses something before you add an apostrophe.

A few commonly used words have their own possessive forms and don't need apostrophes added to them. Memorize this list:

our, ours	its
your, yours	their, theirs
her, hers, his	whose

Note particularly *its, their, whose,* and *your.* They are already possessive and don't require an apostrophe. (These words sound just like *it's, they're, who's,* and *you're,* which are *contractions* that use an apostrophe in place of their missing letters.)

Exercise 2

Cover the right column and see if you can write the required form; the answer might be a *contraction* or a *possessive.* If you miss any, go back and review the explanations.

1. Yes, (she) the one who received the scholarship.	she's
2. (You) applying to two schools, aren't you?	You're
3. Have you requested (you) transcripts?	your
4. (It) been raining for two days.	It's
5. These are my tax returns; are those (her)?	hers
6. (They) advice helped me a lot.	Their
7. Do you know (who) textbook that is?	whose
8. My phone is useless; (it) battery is worn out.	its
9. (He) my mentor and best friend.	He's
10. (Who) going with you on the field trip?	Who's

Exercise 3

Here's another chance to check your progress with possessives. Cover the right column again as you did in Exercises 1 and 2, and add apostrophes correctly to any possessives. Each answer is followed by an explanation.

1. The students went to their counselors offices.

   counselors' (You didn't add an apostrophe to *students*, did you? The students don't possess anything.)

2. The teams bus broke down with all the players on board.

   team's (Whom does the bus belong to? The players don't possess anything.)

3. I was invited to my friends graduation.

   friend's (if it belongs to one friend), friends' (to two or more friends)

4. That writers ideas are very clever.

   writer's (The ideas don't possess anything in the sentence.)

5. Gus opinion is similar to mine.

   Gus's (The *s* after the apostrophe adds the extra letter Gus' needs to *sound* possessive.)

6. Last semesters grades were the best yet.

   semester's (The grades belong to last semester.)

7. The Millers house is just outside of the city.

   The Millers' (Whom does the house belong to? No need to add an extra *s* to Millers'.)

8. I'm reading many books in my childrens literature class.

   children's (The literature belongs to children, but the books don't possess anything.)

9. The students handed the teacher their essays.

   No apostrophe. *Their* is already possessive, and the students don't possess anything in the sentence.

10. The sign on the door said, "Employees Entrance."

    Employees' (The entrance is for employees only.)

Exercises 4 and 5

Now you're ready to add apostrophes to the possessives that follow. But be careful. *First*, make sure the word really possesses something; not every word ending in *s* is a possessive. *Second*, remember that certain words already have possessive forms and don't use apostrophes. *Third*, even though a word ends in *s*, you can't tell where the apostrophe goes until you ask the question, "Whom (or what) does the item belong to?" The apostrophe or apostrophe and *s* should follow the answer to that question. Check your answers at the back of the book after the first set.

Exercise 4

1. Supermodel Jerry Hall has long been famous for being Mick Jagger's wife.
2. Since the couple's divorce, she has continued to work as a model and an actress.
3. On February 24, 2004, Hall's fame grew when she set a new world record in London.
4. A world record may take days, weeks, or even years to accomplish.
5. Jerry Hall's record-breaking activity took just three and a half hours.
6. During one of London's many organized events to promote theater and culture, Hall appeared as a character in six different musicals in one night.
7. All of her characters' parts were small, and none of them included lines.
8. The six theaters' audiences were unaware that the actress's brief appearances were contributing to a world record.
9. Although her shortest role's duration was just thirty seconds, the total for Hall's six performances added up to thirty-three minutes on stage.
10. Hall carefully followed the Guinness judge's rules by using various means of transportation between theaters and by changing each character's costume before moving on to the next.

Source: Visit London (*visitlondon.com*) press release, February 25, 2004

Exercise 5

1. David Mannings reputation as a movie reviewer was destroyed in the spring of 2001.
2. This critics words of praise had been printed on several of Columbia Pictures movie posters at the time and had helped to convince the public to see the films.
3. Mannings glowing quotations appeared on ads for *A Knights Tale, The Patriot,* and *Hollow Man.*

4. However, there was a problem with this particular writers opinions.

5. David Mannings praise was empty because David Manning didn't exist.

6. One of the movie studios employees had invented Manning and made up the quotations printed on the posters.

7. A news writer discovered that Mannings identity was a fake.

8. The publics reaction surprised both news people and entertainment industry executives.

9. Many moviegoers said that they expected movie poster quotations to be false and therefore weren't surprised when the studio admitted the truth.

10. The entertainment industry took the deception very seriously, however, and all of the films posters with phony quotes on them were reprinted.

Source: BBC News, August 3, 2005

PROOFREADING EXERCISE

Find the five errors in the following paragraph. All of the errors involve possessives.

The Martins are a family that has lived next door to me for eighteen years. I have grown up with the Martin's son, Milo, as my best friend. My family is smaller than Milo's family, but I've never been close to anyone but him. The funny thing about the Martins is their names. They all begin with the letter "M." Milos' parent's names are Michael and Maureen. His brother's names are Monty and Mike; his sister's name is Marie. Unlike the Martins, my family member's names all begin with different letters, and I'm glad.

SENTENCE WRITING

Write ten sentences using the possessive forms of the names of your family members or the names of your friends. You could write about a recent event that brought your friends or family together. Just tell the story of how the event came about and briefly what happened that day.

REVIEW OF CONTRACTIONS AND POSSESSIVES

Here are two review exercises. First, add the necessary apostrophes to the following sentences. Take your time, and try to get all of the correct answers.

1. *I Love Lucy's* chocolate factory episode is famous and fun to watch, but its premise is outdated by today's standards.

2. Lucy's husband, Ricky, and Ethel's husband, Fred, switch places with their wives.

3. Ricky and Fred can't wait to see what it's like to stay home and do all the housework.

4. They think it'll be much easier than working to support the family.

5. Lucy and Ethel's first step is to visit an employment agency and apply for a job that suits them; they take the employment agent's suggestion and start work at a candy factory.

6. One of the factory's best candy makers tries to teach Lucy the technique of pooling the chocolate, rolling the centers briefly around in it, and ending with a swirl of chocolate on the candies' tops.

7. But Lucy's candy centers get lost in her chocolate, and she can't find any pieces big enough to deserve a swirl; Ethel doesn't do much better in her area.

8. Eventually, Ethel and Lucy are stationed at the candy wrapping conveyor belt; at first, they do fine, but as its speed increases, they don't know what to do and end up hiding or eating as many chocolates as they wrap.

9. Meanwhile, at home, Ricky and Fred's experiences haven't been any more successful than Lucy and Ethel's, and they all decide that it's best to switch back again.

10. We've "come a long way" since men and women's roles were as limited as they seemed in *I Love Lucy's* time, but it's still a very funny show.

Second, add the necessary apostrophes to the following paragraph.

I consider my friend Alexis to be one of the smartest people I know. Alexis is a twenty-five-year-old film student at a nearby university. Shes presently in her senior year, but thats just the beginning for Alexis. She plans to take full advantage of her universitys resources to learn what she needs before starting her own filmmaking career. She has access to her fellow students talent, her different teachers equipment and experience, and the film schools many contacts. Alexis doesnt agree with a lot of the advice she gets from people in the film industry. They try to discourage her sometimes, but she wont let anything distract her from her goal of making great movies. Ive always been impressed by Alexis self-confidence, and its inspired me to believe in myself more than I ever have before.

PROGRESS TEST

This test covers everything we have covered so far. One sentence in each pair is incorrect. The other is correct. Read both sentences carefully before you decide. Then write the letter of the incorrect sentence in the blank. Try to isolate and correct the error if you can.

1. _____ **A.** Both of the candidate's speeches were too long.

   _____ **B.** They should have talked less and answered more questions.

2. _____ **A.** My older sister bought a hybrid car.

   _____ **B.** She's very satisfied with it's performance so far.

3. _____ **A.** My boss complimented me on my professional attitude.

   _____ **B.** I gave my supervisor credit for training me good.

4. _____ **A.** Last month, we found a abandoned cat in the alley.

   _____ **B.** At first, it was no bigger than a potato, but it's growing now.

5. _____ **A.** The coach didn't know where the plane tickets were.

   _____ **B.** The team members had to search threw all of their luggage.

6. _____ **A.** I recently learned how to ride an unicycle.

   _____ **B.** It's fun to ride, but it's not easy to stop.

7. _____ **A.** Our new satellite network has all ready gone out several times.

   _____ **B.** When we can, we enjoy watching TV shows from other countries.

8. _____ **A.** There are two teachers in my biology class.

   _____ **B.** One of them is a better lecturer then the other.

9. _____ **A.** Eating a snack before a quiz can have positive effects.

   _____ **B.** Sweets can effect the brain's ability to concentrate.

10. _____ **A.** It's hard for me to accept advise from most people.

   _____ **B.** My grandmother is an exception; she's very wise.

P A R T   2

Sentence Structure

Sentence structure refers to the way sentences are built using words, phrases, and clauses. Words are single units, and words link up in sentences to form clauses and phrases. Clauses are word groups *with* subjects and verbs, and phrases are word groups *without* subjects and verbs. Clauses are the most important because they make statements—they tell who did what (or what something is) in a sentence. Look at the following sentence for example:

We visited the Grand Canyon with our geology club over the summer.

It contains twelve words, each playing its own part in the meaning of the sentence. But which of the words together tell who did what? *We visited the Grand Canyon* is correct. That word group is a clause. Notice that *with our geology club* and *over the summer* also link up as word groups but don't include somebody (subject) doing something (verb). Instead, they are phrases to clarify *how* and *when* we visited the Grand Canyon.

Importantly, you could leave out one or both of the phrases and still have a sentence—*We visited the Grand Canyon*. However, you cannot leave the clause out. Then you would just have *With our geology club over the summer*. Remember, every sentence needs at least one clause that can stand by itself.

Learning about the structure of sentences helps you control your own. Once you know more about sentence structure, you can understand writing errors and learn how to avoid them.

Among the most common errors in writing are fragments, run-ons, and awkward phrasing.

Here are some fragments:

Wandering around the new library all afternoon.

Because I tried to handle too many responsibilities at once.

By tutoring the students in groups.

These groups of words don't make complete statements—not one has a clause that can stand by itself. Who was *wandering around the library?* What happened *because [you] tried to handle too many responsibilities at once?* What did someone gain *by tutoring the students in groups?* These incomplete sentence structures fail to communicate a complete thought.

In contrast, here are some run-ons:

Book prices are dropping they're still too high.

The forecast calls for rain tomorrow I think I'll drive to school.

A truck parked in front of my driveway and it made me late for work.

Unlike fragments, run-ons make complete statements, but the trouble is they make *two* complete statements; the first *runs on* to—or runs *into*—the second. Without the help of proper punctuation, the reader has to go back and find a break between the two ideas.

So fragments don't make any complete statements, and run-ons make too many complete statements without punctuating them. Another problem occurs when the phrasing in a sentence just doesn't make sense.

Here are a few sentences with awkward phrasing:

The problem from my grades started to end.

It was a great time at my sister's graduation.

She won me at chess every time we played.

Try to find the word groups that show who did what—that is, the clauses (*The problem started*, *It was*, and *She won*). Now try to put the clauses and phrases together to form a precise meaning. It's difficult, isn't it? You'll see that many of the words don't work together, such as *problem from my grades, started to end, it was a great time at,* and *won me at chess*. These sentences don't communicate clearly due to awkward phrasing.

Fragments, run-ons, and awkward phrasing confuse the reader. If you can learn to avoid these and other sentence structure errors, your writing will be stronger and easier to understand. Unfortunately, there is no quick, effortless way to strengthen your sentence structure. First, you need to understand how clear sentences are built. Then you can eliminate common errors in your own writing.

This section will describe areas of sentence structure one at a time and then explain how to avoid errors associated with the different areas. For instance, we start by helping you find subjects and verbs and understand dependent clauses; then we show you how to correct fragments. You can go through the whole section yourself to learn all of the concepts and structures. Or your teacher may assign only parts based on errors the class is making.

Finding Subjects and Verbs

The most important words in sentences are those that make up its independent clause—the subject and the verb. When you write a sentence, you write about a noun or pronoun (a person, place, thing, or idea). That's the *subject*. Then you write what the subject *does* or *is*. That's the *verb*.

Lightning strikes.

The word *Lightning* is the thing you are writing about. It's the subject, and we'll underline all subjects once. *Strikes* tells what the subject does. It shows the action in the sentence. It's the verb, and we'll underline all of them twice. Most sentences do not include only two words (the subject and the verb). However, these two words still make up the core of the sentence even if other words and phrases are included with them.

Lightning strikes back and forth from the clouds to the ground very quickly.

It often strikes people on golf courses or in boats.

When many words appear in sentences, the subject and verb can be harder to find. Because the verb often shows action, it's easier to spot than the subject. Therefore, always look for it first. For example, take this sentence:

The neighborhood cat folded its paws under its chest.

Which word shows the action? The action word is folded. It's the verb, so we'll underline it twice. Now ask yourself who or what folded? The answer is cat. That's the subject, so we'll underline it once.

Study the following sentences until you understand how to pick out subjects and verbs:

The college celebrates its fiftieth anniversary tomorrow. (Which word shows the action? The action word is celebrates. It's the verb, so we'll underline it twice. Who or what celebrates? The college does. It's the subject. We'll underline it once.)

The team members shared several boxes of chocolates. (Which word shows the action? Shared shows the action. Who or what shared? Members shared.)

Internet users crowd the popular services. (Which word shows the action? The verb is crowd. Who or what crowd? Users crowd.)

Often the verb doesn't show action but links the subject with a description of what the subject *is, was,* or *will be*. Learn to spot such linking verbs—*is, am, are, was, were, has been, seem, feel, appear, become, look* . . . . (For more information on linking verbs, see the discussion of sentence patterns on p. 133).

> Marshall is a neon artist. (First spot the verb is. Then ask who or what is? Marshall is.)

> The sandwiches in the cafeteria look stale. (First spot the verb look. Then ask who or what look? Sandwiches look.)

Sometimes the subject comes after the verb, especially when a word like *there* or *here* begins the sentence without being a real subject.

> In the audience were two reviewers from the *Times*. (Who or what were in the audience? Two reviewers from the *Times* were in the audience.)

> There was a fortune-teller at the carnival. (Who or what was there? A fortune-teller was there at the carnival.)

> There were name tags for all the participants. (Who or what were there? Name tags were there for all the participants.)

> Here are two examples. (Who or what are here? The examples are here.)

> **NOTE**—Remember that *there* and *here* (as used in the last three sentences) are not subjects. They simply point to something.

When a sentence is a command, it may appear to be missing a subject. However, an unwritten *you* is understood by the reader.

> Fill in all spaces on the form. (You fill in all spaces on the form.) Place flap A into slot B. (You place flap A into slot B.)

> Make an appointment for Tuesday. (You make an appointment for Tuesday.)

A sentence may have more than one subject.

> Toys and memorabilia from the 1950s–1990s are valuable collectibles.

Celebrity dolls, board games, and even cereal boxes from those decades sell for high prices online.

A sentence may also have more than one verb.

Water boils at a certain temperature and freezes at another.

The ice tray fell out of my hand, skidded across the floor, and landed under the table.

E X E R C I S E S

Identify the subjects and verbs in the following sentences. Remember to start by double-underlining the verb(s), then single-underlining the subject(s). When you finish each exercise, compare your markings carefully with the answers at the back of the book. Refer back to the explanations and examples whenever necessary.

Exercise 1

1. Morpheus is a new kind of robot.
2. His creators named him after the character in *The Matrix* and gave him Moe as a nickname.
3. Scientists at the University of Washington in Seattle developed Moe's hardware and software.
4. They designed Moe for a very useful purpose.
5. Some disabled people have limited movement and need physical help at times.
6. Only a person's thoughts control Moe's movements and tasks.
7. The thoughts reach Moe through sensors in a cap on the person's head.
8. Moe requires no physical contact.
9. Currently, Moe is still in his experimental stages.
10. The possibilities for thought-controlled robots are almost endless.

Source: Discover, May 2007

Exercise 2

1. All U.S. presidents give speeches as a part of their duties.
2. They deliver different styles of speeches, however.
3. In U.S. history, there are many famous presidential speakers.
4. Their unique voices, phrases, and mannerisms contribute to their fame.
5. *Presidential Voices* is a book about the speaking styles of the presidents.
6. John Adams included a 700-word sentence in his Inaugural Address.
7. The first speech of William Henry Harrison lasted for two hours and partially caused his death.
8. Harrison developed pneumonia from the cold, wet weather on his inaugural day.
9. Surprisingly, the book places Thomas Jefferson on the list of poor speakers.
10. At times, Jefferson avoided important speeches, even the State of the Union.

Source: Newsweek, July 26, 2004

Exercise 3

1. Ancient Egyptians worshipped cats of all sizes.
2. Archaeologists find many mummies of cats in Egyptian tombs.
3. Carvings in the tombs reveal a strong belief in the god-like powers of large cats.
4. Scientists always look for new evidence of ancient beliefs.
5. Archaeologists recently discovered the mummy of a lion in a tomb in Saqqara, Egypt.
6. It is the first discovery of a lion skeleton in an Egyptian tomb.
7. There were no bandages around the lion.
8. But there were other signs of mummification.
9. The lion rested in the tomb of King Tutankhamen's nurse.

10. Archaeologists now have real evidence of lion worship in Egypt.

Source: Science News, January 31, 2004

Exercise 4

1. I never knew much about curses and magic spells.
2. According to *Smithsonian* magazine, the ancient Greeks and Romans used them all the time.
3. There were magicians for hire back then.
4. These magicians made money through their knowledge of the art of cursing.
5. Some citizens took revenge on their enemies with special curses for failure.
6. Others wanted only love and placed spells on the objects of their desire.
7. The magicians wrote the commissioned curses or love spells on lead tablets.
8. Then they positioned these curse tablets near their intended victims.
9. Archaeologists found one 1,700-year-old curse tablet over the starting gate of an ancient race course.
10. It named the horses and drivers of specific chariots and itemized the specifics of the curse.

Source: Smithsonian, April 1996

Exercise 5

1. Human beings are creatures of habit.
2. They visit predictable places and do predictable things.
3. In their work, scientists study such behavior.
4. George Karev is a member of the Bulgarian Academy of Sciences.
5. Karev studied the habits of people in movie theaters.

6. Karev's results about moviegoers make a lot of sense.

7. Most people prefer seats on the right side of the theater and always sit there.

8. Therefore, their left eye sees most of the movie.

9. The left eye generally reports to the right hemisphere of the brain.

10. The right hemisphere connects people with their own feelings and with the emotions of others.

Source: Current Science, May 11, 2001

PARAGRAPH EXERCISE

Underline the subjects once and the verbs twice in the following student paragraph.

Al Levis invented the popular snack Slim Jims. Slim Jims are stick-shaped meat snacks. Levis was a high-school dropout but eventually made a fortune from his snack product. Slim Jims originally came in jars full of vinegar. In the 1940s and 50s, bar customers ate Slim Jims with their cocktails. Then Levis's company offered Slim Jims in individual packages. People ate them on camping trips and at sporting events. Levis sold his invention in the late 1960s but continued his good work. Before his death in March of 2001, Levis donated millions of dollars to worthy causes.

SENTENCE WRITING

Write ten sentences about any subject—your favorite color, for instance. Keeping your subject matter simple in these sentence-writing exercises will make it easier to find your sentence structures later. After you have written your sentences, go back and underline your subjects once and your verbs twice.

Locating Prepositional Phrases

Prepositional phrases are among the easiest structures in English to learn. Remember that a phrase is just a group of related words (at least two) without a subject and a verb. And don't let a term like *prepositional* scare you. If you look in the middle of that long word, you'll find a familiar one—*position*. In English, we tell the *positions* of people and things in sentences using prepositional phrases.

Look at the following sentence with its prepositional phrases in parentheses:

Our trip (to the desert) will begin (at 6:00) (in the morning) (on Friday).

One phrase tells *where* the trip will take us (*to the desert*), and three phrases tell *when* the trip will begin (*at 6:00, in the morning,* and *on Friday*). Most prepositional phrases show the position of someone or something in *space* or in *time*.

Here is a list of some prepositions that can show positions in *space*:

to	across	next to	against
at	through	inside	under
in	beyond	between	beneath
on	among	above	around
by	near	behind	past
over	with	from	below

Here are some prepositions that can show positions in *time* (note some repeats):

at	for	past	within
by	after	until	since
in	before	during	throughout

These lists include only individual words, *not phrases*. Remember, a preposition must be followed by a noun or pronoun object—a person, place, thing, or idea—to create *a prepositional phrase*. Notice that as the preposition changes in the prepositional phrases below, the balloon's position in relation to the object, *the clouds*, changes completely.

The hot-air balloon floated *above the clouds.*
below the clouds.
within the clouds.
between the clouds.
past the clouds.
near the clouds.

Now notice how these other prepositions similarly affect the time of its landing:

The balloon landed *before 3:30.*
at precisely 3:30.
after 3:30.
before the thunderstorm.
during the thunderstorm.
after the thunderstorm.

NOTE—A few words—*of, as,* and *like*—are prepositions that do not fit neatly into either the space or time category, yet they are very common prepositions (book *of essays,* note *of apology,* type *of bicycle;* act *as a substitute,* use *as an example,* testified *as an expert;* sounds *like a computer,* acts *like a sedative,* moves *like an athlete*).

By locating prepositional phrases, you will be able to find subjects and verbs more easily. For example, you might have difficulty finding the subject and verb in a long sentence like this:

During the rainy season, one of the windows in the attic leaked at all four of its corners.

But if you put parentheses around all the prepositional phrases like this

(During the rainy season), one (of the windows) (in the attic) leaked (at all four) (of its corners).

then you have only two words left—the subject and the verb. Even in short sentences like the following, you might pick the wrong word as the subject if you don't put parentheses around the prepositional phrases first.

A box (of books) arrived (with a return address) (from Italy).

The mood (around campus) is cheerful today.

NOTE—Don't mistake *to* plus a verb for a prepositional phrase. Special forms of verbals always start with *to,* but they are not prepositional phrases (see p. 122). For example, in the sentence "I like to take the train to school," *to take* is a verbal, not a prepositional phrase. However, *to school* is a prepositional phrase because it begins with a preposition (to), ends with a noun (school), and shows position in space.

E X E R C I S E S

Put parentheses around the prepositional phrases in the following sentences. Be sure to start with the preposition itself (*in, on, to, at, of* . . .) and include the word or words that go with it (*in the morning, on our sidewalk, to Hawaii* . . .). Then underline the sentences' subjects once and verbs twice. Remember that the subject and verb in a sentence are never inside prepositional phrases, so if you locate the prepositional phrases *first,* the subjects and verbs will be much easier to find. Check your answers for each exercise before continuing to the next.

Exercise 1

1. Viganella is a tiny village at the bottom of the Alps in Italy.

2. Due to its physical position between the mountains, the town of Viganella suffered from an unusual problem.

3. The sun's rays never reached the village from the middle of November to the first week in February.

4. The mountains kept the little town in shadow without any direct sunlight for several months each year.

5. Then Giacomo Bonzani found a high-tech solution to Viganella's dreary situation.

6. In 2006, engineers installed a huge mirror thousands of feet above Viganella on the side of one of the mountains around it.

7. A computer at the mirror's location keeps track of the sun's movements.

8. The computer's software rotates the mirror into the perfect position to reflect sunlight into the village square.

9. The mirror began its work in December of 2006.

10. Now the sun "shines" on the town of Viganella during all months of the year.

Source: International Herald Tribune, February 5, 2007

Exercise 2

1. The many cases of food poisoning in America each year alarm people.

2. Some food scientists point to food irradiation as one possible solution.

3. The irradiation of food kills bacteria through exposure to gamma rays.

4. With irradiation, farmers spray fewer pesticides on their crops.

5. And irradiated food lasts longer on the shelf or in the refrigerator.

6. However, many scientists and consumers worry about the risks of food irradiation.

7. Irradiation reduces vitamins and changes nutrients in the food.

8. The radioactive materials at the irradiation plants are also potentially dangerous.

9. Critics predict accidents in the transportation and use of these radioactive substances.

10. In the United States, the controversy about food irradiation continues.

Exercise 3

1. *Romeo and Juliet* is a famous play by William Shakespeare.

2. It remains one of the most popular love stories in the world.

3. Many movies use aspects of it in their plots.

4. One thing about Shakespeare's version of the story surprises people.

5. Both Romeo and Juliet have other love interests in the play.

6. Romeo has a crush on Rosaline before Juliet.

7. Juliet elopes with Romeo in secret.

8. Then Juliet accepts a marriage proposal from another man against her will.

9. Friar Lawrence helps Romeo and Juliet with a plan for their escape.

10. However, the complicated timing of his plan has tragic results on the lives of the famous couple.

Exercise 4

1. As a change of pace, I shopped for my Mother's Day gift at an antique mall.

2. I found old Bakelite jewelry in every shade of yellow, red, blue, and green.

3. There were even linens from the pioneer days.

4. One booth sold drinking glasses with advertising slogans and cartoon characters on them.

5. Another stocked old metal banks with elaborate mechanisms for children's pennies.

6. In the back corner of the mall, I found a light blue pitcher with a familiar dark blue design.

7. My mother had one like it in the early years of my childhood.

8. My sisters and I drank punch from it on hot days in the summer.

9. I checked the price on the tag underneath the pitcher's handle.

10. I reached for my credit card without hesitation.

Exercise 5

1. Over the weekend, I watched a hilarious old movie, *Genevieve,* on late-night television.

2. The story takes place in the countryside of England.

3. It is a black-and-white movie from the 1930s or 1940s.

4. The clothes and manners of the characters in *Genevieve* are very proper and old-fashioned.

5. Two young couples enter their cars in a road rally for fun.

6. They participate in the race strictly for adventure.

7. Genevieve is the name of the main couple's car.

8. During the road rally, the polite manners of the two couples disappear in the rush for the finish line.

9. Predictably, they fight with each other and sabotage each other's cars.

10. Like all good comedies, *Genevieve* has an ending with a surprise in it for everyone.

PARAGRAPH EXERCISE

Put parentheses around the prepositional phrases in the following excerpt from the book *Joey Green's Amazing Kitchen Cures: 1,150 Ways to Prevent and Cure Common Ailments with Brand-Name Products.* In this fun but challenging exercise, you'll find prepositional phrases ranging in length from two to eight words. Don't forget to look for one in the title!

HEARSAY ON Q-TIPS

In 1922, Leo Gerstenrang, an immigrant from Warsaw, Poland, who had served in the United States Army during World War I and worked with the fledgling Red Cross Organization, founded the Leo Gerstenrang Infant Novelty Co. with his wife, selling accessories used for baby care. After the birth of the couple's daughter, Gerstenrang noticed that his wife would wrap a wad of cotton around a toothpick for use during their baby's bath and decided to manufacture a ready-to-use cotton swab.

After several years, Gerstenrang developed a machine that would wrap cotton uniformly around each blunt end of a small stick of carefully selected and cured nonsplintering birch wood, package the swabs in a sliding tray-type box, sterilize the box, and seal it with an outer wrapping of glassine—later changed to cellophane. The phrase "untouched by human hands" became widely known in the production of cotton swabs. The *Q* in the name Q-Tips stands for *quality* and the word *tips* describes the cotton swab on the end of the stick.

SENTENCE WRITING

Write ten short sentences on different types of shampoo or toothpaste. Such simple descriptive topics will prompt you to write sentences with prepositional phrases: for example, "Many people use shampoos (with citrus scents)." When you finish your sentences, put parentheses around any prepositional phrases and underline your subjects once and your verbs twice.

Understanding Dependent Clauses

All clauses are groups of related words that contain a subject and a verb. However, there are two kinds of clauses: *independent* and *dependent*. Independent clauses have a subject and a verb and make complete statements by themselves. Dependent clauses also have a subject and a verb, but these clauses don't make complete statements because of the words that begin them. Here are some of the words (all types of conjunctions or pronouns) that can begin dependent clauses:

after	since	where
although	so that	whereas
as	than	wherever
as if	that	whether
because	though	which
before	unless	whichever
even if	until	while
even though	what	who
ever since	whatever	whom
how	when	whose
if	whenever	why

When a clause begins with one of these dependent words, it is usually a dependent clause. To see the difference between an independent and a dependent clause, look at this example of an independent clause:

We studied history together.

It has a subject (We) and a verb (studied), and it makes a complete statement. But as soon as we put one of the dependent words in front of it, the clause becomes *dependent* because it no longer makes a complete statement:

After we studied history together . . .

Although studied history together . . .

As we studied history together . . .

Before we studied history together . . .

Since we studied history together . . .

That we studied history together . . .

When we studied history together . . .

While we studied history together . . .

Each of these dependent clauses leaves the reader expecting something more. Each would depend on another clause—an independent clause—to make it a sentence. For the rest of this discussion, we'll place a dotted line beneath dependent clauses.

After we studied history together, we went to the evening seminar.

We went to the evening seminar *after* we studied history together.

The speaker didn't know *that* we studied history together.

While we studied history together, the library became crowded.

As you can see in these examples, *when a dependent clause comes before an independent clause, it is followed by a comma.* Often the comma prevents misreading, as in the following sentence:

When we returned, our library books were on the floor.

Without a comma after *returned,* the reader would read *When we returned our library books* before realizing that this was not what the writer meant. The comma prevents misreading. Sometimes if the dependent clause is short and there is no danger of misreading, the comma can be left off, but it's safer simply to follow the rule that a dependent clause coming before an independent clause is followed by a comma. You'll learn more about the punctuation of dependent clauses on page 171, but for now just remember to use a comma when a dependent clause comes before an independent clause.

Note that a few of the dependent words (*that, who, which, what*) can do "double duty" as both the dependent word and the subject of the dependent clause:

Thelma wrote a poetry book *that* sold a thousand copies.

The manager saw *what* happened.

Sometimes the dependent clause is in the middle of the independent clause:

The book *that* sold a thousand copies was Thelma's.

The events *that* followed the parade delighted everyone.

The dependent clause can even be the subject of the entire sentence:

What you do also affects me.

How your project looks counts for ten percent of the grade.

Also note that sometimes the *that* of a dependent clause is omitted:

I know that you feel strongly about this issue.

I know you feel strongly about this issue.

Everyone received the classes *that* they wanted.

Everyone received the classes they wanted.

Of course, the word *that* doesn't always introduce a dependent clause. It may be a pronoun and serve as the subject or object of the sentence:

That was a really long movie.

We knew *that* already.

That can also be an adjective, a descriptive word telling *which one:*

That movie always makes me laugh.

We took them to *that* park last week.

EXERCISES

Exercise 1

Each of the following sentences contains *one* independent and *one* dependent clause. Draw a dotted line beneath the dependent clause in each sentence. Start at the dependent word and include all the words that go with it. Remember that dependent clauses can show up in the beginning, middle, or end of a sentence.

Example: We study together whenever we meet in the library.

   1. Tina, my twin sister, got a job that requires late-night hours.

   2. The hours that I like the best are between six and eleven in the morning.

3. Now Tina sleeps until noon (because she works all night.)

4. (When she comes home from work) our whole family is asleep.

5. (Since Tina is at work all night) I rarely see her.

6. Our dad thinks (that Tina works too hard.)

7. Our mom believes (that Tina's new hours are a good challenge for her.)

8. Yesterday, Tina's boss asked me (if I want a job like Tina's.)

9. I am not sure (when I will find the right job for me.)

10. (Whenever I do find a good job) it will be during the day.

Exercises 2–5

Follow the same directions as in Exercise 1; however, this time draw your dotted lines far below the dependent clauses. Then go back to both the independent and dependent clauses and draw a double underline beneath the verbs and a single underline beneath their subjects.

Example: We study together whenever we meet in the library.

Exercise 2

1. Although it happened several years ago, one news story stays in my mind.

2. It was the story of a puppy that shot his owner in self-defense.

3. The man decided to kill the large litter of puppies because he could not find anyone to adopt them.

4. As he held this special little dog in his arms, the man fired a revolver at the other puppies.

5. The hero puppy pawed at the man's hand that held the gun.

6. The puppy fought and struggled so hard that the gun turned and fired a shot into the man's wrist.

7. After the incident, many people wanted to adopt the puppies that escaped.

8. I remember this story because it is so incredible.

9. The sad part of the story is that a few of the puppies died.

10. The man recovered from the shot that the hero puppy fired to save himself and several of his litter mates.

Source: msnbc.com, September 21, 2004

Exercise 3

These sentences may have more than one dependent clause.

1. People who need glasses often wear contact lenses.

2. Clear contact lenses maintain a person's appearance because they fit over the eye and have no frames.

3. But there are contact lenses that change a person's eye color.

4. Someone who has green eyes makes them blue or brown with colored contact lenses.

5. Now even people who don't need glasses change their eye color with contact lenses.

6. Colored lenses are fashion statements that are especially popular with young people.

7. Unless a doctor fits them, contact lenses that people buy or trade with friends invite injuries.

8. Ill-fitting lenses squeeze or scratch the eyes as they move around under the eyelids.

9. After a scratch occurs, germs easily infect the eyes' surface.

10. Such infections sometimes lead to damage that is permanent.

Source: Current Science, May 11, 2001

Exercise 4

These sentences may have more than one dependent clause or none at all.

1. I am not very talkative when I'm in school.

2. Whenever my teacher asks a question in class, I get nervous.

3. If I know the answer, I usually look straight ahead.

4. When I forget the answer, I check my shoes or a note in my notebook.

5. Usually, the teacher chooses someone else before I finish my fidgeting.

6. Obviously, when I take a speech class, I talk sometimes.

7. In my last speech class, we all demonstrated some sort of process that we knew.

8. The speech that I gave explained how I make crepes.

9. Since I work at a French restaurant, I borrowed a crepe pan for my demonstration.

10. The crepes cooked so quickly that the teacher and students passed the plates around before I said anything at all.

Exercise 5

1. Many people remember when microwave ovens first arrived in stores.

2. People worried about whether they were safe or not.

3. Before they had the microwave oven, people cooked all food with direct heat.

4. At first, microwave ovens seemed strange because they heated only the food.

5. And microwave ovens cooked food so much faster than ordinary ovens did.

6. Eventually, people welcomed the convenience that microwave ovens offered.

7. Since they are fast and cool, microwave ovens work well almost anywhere.

8. People who are on a budget bring lunch from home and heat it up at work or school.

9. Now that microwave ovens are here, people make a lot more popcorn.

10. As each new technology arrives, people wonder how they ever lived without it.

PARAGRAPH EXERCISE

Draw a dotted line beneath the dependent clauses in the following paragraphs about the value of friendship from Alain de Botton's book *The Consolations of*

Philosophy. We've added the word *that* in brackets to two of the clauses in which it was left out (as described on p. 71). See if you can find all thirteen dependent clauses in this challenging exercise.

We don't exist unless there is someone who can see us existing, what we say has no meaning until someone can understand, while to be surrounded by friends is constantly to have our identity confirmed; their knowledge and care for us have the power to pull us from our numbness. In small comments, many of them teasing, they reveal [that] they know our foibles and accept them and so, in turn, accept that we have a place in the world. We can ask them "Isn't he frightening?" or "Do you ever feel that . . . ?" and be understood, rather than encounter the puzzled "No, not particularly"—which can make us feel, even when in company, as lonely as polar explorers.

True friends do not evaluate us according to worldly criteria, it is the core self [that] they are interested in; like ideal parents, their love for us remains unaffected by our appearance or position in the social hierarchy, and so we have no qualms in dressing in old clothes and revealing that we have made little money this year. The desire for riches should perhaps not always be understood as a simple hunger for a luxurious life, a more important motive might be the wish to be appreciated and treated nicely. We may seek a fortune for no greater reason than to secure the respect and attention of people who would otherwise look straight through us. Epicurus, discerning our underlying need, recognized that a handful of true friends could deliver the love and respect that even a fortune may not.

SENTENCE WRITING

Write ten sentences about one of your weekend routines (sleeping late, eating a big breakfast, doing house or yard work, etc.). Try to write sentences that contain both independent and dependent clauses. Then draw a dotted line beneath your dependent clauses, underline your subjects, and double underline your verbs.

Correcting Fragments

Sometimes a group of words looks like a sentence—with a capital letter at the beginning and a period at the end—but it may be missing a subject, a verb, or both. Such incomplete sentence structures are called *fragments*. Here are a few examples:

Just raises his hand in class without thinking. (*Who* does? There is no subject.)

Pauline and her sister with the twins. (*Did* what? There is no verb.)

Plenty to do in the lab. (This fragment is missing a subject and a real verb. *To do* is a verbal, see p. 122.)

To change these fragments into sentences, we must make sure each has a subject and a real verb:

That <u>student</u> just <u>raises</u> his hand in class without thinking. (We added a subject.)

Pauline and her <u>sister</u> with the twins <u>volunteered</u>. (We added a verb.)

The <u>tutors</u> <u>had</u> plenty to do in the lab. (We added a subject and a real verb.)

Sometimes we can simply attach such a fragment to the previous sentence:

<u>I</u> <u>want</u> a fulfilling career. Teaching, for example. (fragment)

<u>I</u> <u>want</u> a fulfilling career—teaching, for example. (correction)

Or we can add a subject or a verb to the fragment and make it a complete sentence:

<u>I</u> <u>want</u> a fulfilling career. <u>Teaching</u> <u>is</u> one example. (correction)

PHRASE FRAGMENTS

By definition, phrases are word groups *without* subjects and verbs, so whenever a phrase is punctuated as a sentence, it is a fragment. Look at this example of a sentence followed by a phrase fragment beginning with *hoping* (see p. 122 for more about verbal phrases):

The <u>actors</u> <u>waited</u> outside the director's office. Hoping for a chance to audition.

We can correct this fragment by attaching it to the previous sentence:

The <u>actors</u> <u>waited</u> outside the director's office, hoping for a chance to audition.

Or we can change it to include a subject and a real verb:

> The <u>actors</u> <u>waited</u> outside the director's office. <u>They</u> <u>were hoping</u> for a chance to audition.

Here's another example of a sentence followed by a phrase fragment:

> Language <u>classes</u> <u>are</u> difficult. Especially when taken in summer school.

Here the two have been combined into one complete sentence:

> Language <u>classes</u> taken in summer school <u>are</u> especially difficult.

Or a better revision might be

> Language <u>classes</u> <u>are</u> especially difficult when taken in summer school.

Sometimes, prepositional phrases are also incorrectly punctuated as sentences. Here a series of prepositional phrases follows a sentence, but the word group is a fragment—it has no subject and verb of its own. Therefore, it needs to be corrected.

> <u>I</u> <u>live</u> a simple life. With my family on our farm in central California.

Omitting the period is one possible correction:

> <u>I</u> <u>live</u> a simple life with my family on our farm in central California.

Or it could be corrected this way:

> My <u>family</u> and <u>I</u> <u>live</u> a simple life on our farm in central California.

DEPENDENT CLAUSE FRAGMENTS

A dependent clause punctuated as a sentence is another kind of fragment. A sentence needs a subject, a verb, *and* a complete thought. As discussed in the previous section, a dependent clause has a subject and a verb, but it begins with a word that makes its meaning incomplete, such as *after, while, because, since, although, when, if, where, who, which,* and *that.* (See p. 69 for a longer list of these words.) To correct such fragments, we can either eliminate the word that makes the clause dependent *or* add an independent clause.

FRAGMENT

While <u>some</u> of us <u><u>wrote</u></u> in our journals.

CORRECTED

<u>Some</u> of us <u><u>wrote</u></u> in our journals.

or

While <u>some</u> of us <u><u>wrote</u></u> in our journals, the fire <u>alarm</u> <u><u>rang</u></u>.

FRAGMENT

Which <u><u>kept</u></u> me from finishing my journal entry.

CORRECTED

The fire <u>alarm</u> <u><u>kept</u></u> me from finishing my journal entry.

or

<u>I</u> <u><u>responded</u></u> to the fire alarm, *which* <u><u>kept</u></u> me from finishing my journal entry.

You might ask, are fragments ever permissible? Professional writers sometimes use fragments in books, articles, advertising, and other kinds of writing. But professional writers use these fragments intentionally, not in error. Until you're an experienced writer, it's best to write complete sentences. Especially in college writing, you should avoid using fragments.

EXERCISES

Some of the following word groups are sentences, and some are fragments. The sentences include subjects and verbs and make complete statements. Write the word "correct" next to each of the sentences. Then change the fragments into sentences by making sure that each has a subject, a real verb, and a complete thought.

Exercise 1

1. Soon we will wear clothes that clean themselves.

2. Improvements in fabric coatings making it possible.

3. Clothes treated with certain chemicals.

4. These chemicals kill bacteria and keep dirt from soaking into fabrics.

5. Already tested by the military for soldiers' uniforms.

6. U.S. soldiers wore self-cleaning T-shirts and underwear in one study.

7. The chemicals worked but eventually wore off.

8. Helped cure soldiers' skin problems, too.

9. Fabric that stays clean and dry is a great idea.

10. Also could be used for hospital bedding, kitchen linens, and sport-related clothing.

Source: Sunday Telegraph, December 30, 2006

Exercise 2

1. Duct tape has many uses.

2. Holds objects together firmly.

3. Patches holes in backpacks and tents.

4. People are very creative with duct tape.

5. Books written about the unique uses for it.

6. A yearly contest by the makers of Duck Brand duct tape.

7. High school prom couples make their outfits entirely from duct tape.

8. Strips of duct tape forming tuxedos, cummerbunds, gowns, hats, and corsages.

9. A $2,500 prize to the couple with the best use of duct tape and another $2,500 to their high school.

10. Hundreds of couples from across the country participate in this contest every year.

Source: http://www.ducktapeclub.com

Exercise 3

Each pair contains one sentence and one phrase fragment. Correct each phrase fragment by attaching the phrase to the complete sentence before or after it.

1. We shopped all day at the mall. Looking for the perfect suitcases.
2. We knew of a specialty store. Selling hard and soft luggage, large and small sizes, and lots of accessories.
3. Walking from store to store and getting tired. We gave up after a while and sat down.
4. Resting on a bench for a few minutes. We enjoyed ourselves by "people-watching."
5. Crowds of people filled the mall. In every shop and at the food court, too.
6. Crowding the walkways and window shopping. Our fellow consumers circulated in every direction.
7. Teenagers gathered in groups. Laughing at each other and ignoring the other shoppers.
8. Using the mall as an exercise facility. Pairs of older people walked briskly around the balconies.
9. We finally found the perfect luggage at a little store. Near the elevators at the end of the mall.
10. Because of all the interesting people and the final outcome. Our shopping trip was a complete success.

Exercise 4

Each pair contains one sentence and one dependent clause fragment. Correct each dependent clause fragment by eliminating its dependent word or by attaching the dependent clause to the independent clause before or after it.

1. Thrift stores, yard sales, and flea markets are popular places to shop. Because they sell items that aren't available anywhere else.
2. Since most thrift stores help charities. They are there to assist people in need.
3. Although the objects in thrift stores are often five to thirty years old. Many people prefer their vintage designs.
4. For instance, thrift stores sell old metal shelving units. Which are much better than modern ones made of cheap wood or plastic.
5. There are many famous stories of people becoming rich. Because they shopped at flea markets and yard sales.

6. When one man bought a framed picture for a few dollars at a flea market. He liked the frame but not the picture.

7. As he removed the picture from the frame. He found one of the original copies of the "Declaration of Independence."

8. At a yard sale, a woman bought a small table. That she later discovered was worth half a million dollars.

9. Of course, collectors always shop at these places. Where they hope to find historical treasures and other objects of value.

10. In a way, shopping at thrift stores, yard sales, and flea markets is a kind of recycling. Which is something that benefits everyone.

Exercise 5

All of the following word groups are individual fragments punctuated as sentences. Make the necessary changes to turn each fragment into a sentence that makes sense to you. Your corrections will most likely differ from the sample answers at the back of the book. But by comparing your answers to ours, you'll see that there are many ways to correct fragments.

1. As the players congratulated each other and walked off the field.

2. My favorite television show having been canceled.

3. The fact that cell phones are distracting when you drive.

4. Where the technology of cloning will be in ten years.

5. Because the government protects people's property with laws.

6. Since that car costs too much.

7. An understanding of math being a requirement for most students.

8. Voting in most elections but never feeling represented.

9. On the desk between my computer and my golfing trophy.

10. A dog's keen sense of smell making it the perfect detective.

PROOFREADING EXERCISE

Find and correct the five fragments in the following paragraph.

Shark attacks have been on the rise. We've all heard the heartbreaking news stories. Of people on their honeymoons or children playing in only a few feet of water being attacked by sharks. Movies like *Jaws* and *Open Water* make us wary and scared. When we watch them. But their effects fade over time, and we forget about the risks. Of entering the habitats of dangerous animals. Experts try to convince us. Saying that sharks and other powerful species are not targeting human beings on purpose. To a shark, a person is no different from a seal or a sea turtle. Facts such as these prompt many of us to think twice. Before we take a dip in the ocean.

SENTENCE WRITING

Write ten fragments (like the ones in Exercise 5) and then revise them so that they are all complete sentences. For even more good practice, exchange papers with another student and turn your classmate's ten fragments into sentences.

Correcting Run-on Sentences

A word group with a subject and a verb is a clause. As we have seen, the clause may be independent (making a complete statement and able to stand alone as a sentence), or it may be dependent (beginning with a dependent word and unable to stand alone as a sentence). When two *independent* clauses are written together without proper punctuation between them, the result is called a *run-on sentence*. Here are some examples.

World music offers a lot of variety I listen to it in my car.

I love the sound of drums therefore, bhangra is one of my favorite styles.

Run-on sentences can be corrected in one of six ways:

1. Separate the independent clauses into two sentences with a period.

World music offers a lot of variety. I listen to it in my car.

I love the sound of drums. Therefore, bhangra is one of my favorite styles.

2. Connect the two independent clauses with a semicolon alone.

World music offers a lot of variety; I listen to it in my car.

I love the sound of drums; therefore, bhangra is one of my favorite styles.

3. Connect the two independent clauses with a semicolon and a transition.

Look over the following list of connecting words (transitions):

also	however	otherwise
consequently	likewise	then
finally	moreover	therefore
furthermore	nevertheless	thus

When one of these words is used to join two independent clauses, a semicolon comes before the connecting word, and a comma usually comes after it.

Mobile devices are essential in our society; however, they are very expensive.

Earthquakes scare me; nevertheless, I live in Los Angeles.

Yasmin traveled to London; then she took the "Chunnel" to Paris.

The college recently built a large new library; thus we have more study areas.

> **NOTE**—The use of the comma after the connecting word depends on how long the connecting word is. If it is only a short word, like *then* or *thus,* the comma is not necessary.

4. **Connect the two independent clauses with a comma and one of the following seven words (the first letters of which create the word *fanboys,* an easy way to remember them): *for, and, nor, but, or, yet,* or *so.***

   Swans are beautiful birds, *and* they mate for life.

   Students may sign up for classes in person, *or* they may register online.

Each of the *fanboys* has its own meaning when used as a connecting word. For example, *so* means "as a result," and *for* means "because":

   World music offers a lot of variety, *so* I never get bored with it.

   Bhangra is one of my favorite styles, *for* I love the sound of drums.

   I applied for financial aid, *but* (or *yet*) I make too much money to receive it.

   My brother doesn't know how to drive, *nor* does he plan to learn.

Before you put a comma before a *fanboys,* be sure there are two independent clauses. Note that the first sentence that follows has two independent clauses. However, the second sentence contains just one clause with two verbs and therefore needs no comma.

   Registration begins next week, and it continues throughout the summer.

   Registration begins next week and continues throughout the summer.

5. **Add a dependent word—such as *when, since, after, while,* or *because*—to the clause used at the beginning of the sentence, and follow the dependent clause with a comma.**

   Because I enjoy acoustic guitar music, I listen to it in my car.

6. **Add a dependent word—such as *when, since, after, while,* or *because*—to the clause used at the end of the sentence (no comma necessary).**

   I listen to acoustic guitar music in my car *because* I enjoy it.

Learn these ways to join two clauses, and you'll avoid run-on sentences.

SIX WAYS TO CORRECT RUN-ON SENTENCES

Run-on: The movie had a dull plot many people left early.

1. The movie had a dull plot. Many people left early. (period)
2. The movie had a dull plot; many people left early. (semicolon)
3. The movie had a dull plot; therefore, many people left early.
    (semicolon + transition)
4. The movie had a dull plot, and many people left early.
    (comma + *fanboys*)
5. Because the movie had a dull plot, many people left early.
    (dependent clause at beginning + comma)
6. Many people left early because the movie had a dull plot.
    (dependent clause at end, no comma)

EXERCISES

Exercises 1 and 2

CORRECTING RUN-ONS WITH PUNCTUATION

Some of the following sentences are run-ons. If the sentence contains two independent clauses without proper punctuation, use one of the first four ways to correct the run-on (using punctuation only). All existing punctuation in the sentences is correct. When correcting punctuation, remember to capitalize after a period but not after a semicolon and to insert a comma only when the words *for, and, nor, but, or, yet,* or *so* are already used to join the two independent clauses.

Exercise 1

1. In early 2007, a mobile phone company sponsored a new kind of contest, it wanted to find the fastest text-messager in the United States.

2. To participate in the LG National Texting Championship, contestants had to be U.S. residents, and they had to be at least thirteen years old.

3. The West Coast participants competed in Hollywood, and the East Coast contestants battled in New York City.

4. Both the Hollywood and New York Regional Champions won $10,000, but the Hollywood winner also received a trip to New York to participate in the National Championship.

5. Eli Tirosh, a 21-year-old woman from Los Angeles, won the West Coast title Morgan Pozgar, a 13-year-old girl from Claysburg, Pennsylvania, won the East Coast title.

6. At the Roseland Ballroom in Manhattan, the two texting champions fought for the title of LG National Texting Champion and an additional $15,000.

7. The two contestants were shown phrases on a screen and they had to type the phrases on their tiny keypads quickly and perfectly.

8. Pozgar beat Tirosh by typing several lines of the lyrics to the song "Supercalifragilisticexpialidocious" Pozgar typed 151 characters in just 42 seconds.

9. Morgan Pozgar's fast thumbs and her ability to read and type accurately earned her $25,000 and the first-ever title of U.S. National Texting Champion.

10. The LG company increases prize money each year and it also sponsors an international texting competition.

Sources: lifewithlg.com, August 20, 2007, and *usatoday.com*, Jan. 14, 2010

Exercise 2

1. Nearly everyone yawns but few understand the dynamics of yawning.

2. One person's yawn often triggers another person's yawn.

3. Yawning clearly seems to be contagious.

4. Scientific studies of yawning verify this phenomenon and also explain the reasons for it.

5. Groups of people do similar things for they are acting somewhat like herds of animals.

6. During times of transition, such as getting up from or going to bed, members of a family or a dorm full of roommates synchronize their activities through yawning.

7. The yawning helps the group act as one so it minimizes conflict.

8. There are a few misconceptions about yawns one of them has to do with oxygen levels.

9. Some people explain yawning as the body's way to increase oxygen intake.

10. Surprisingly, studies show no changes in yawning patterns due to levels of oxygen in fact, research subjects inhaling pure oxygen yawned the same number of times as those breathing normally.

Source: Discover, June 2001

Exercises 3 and 4

CORRECTING RUN-ONS WITH DEPENDENT CLAUSES

Most of the following sentences are run-ons. Use one of the last two ways to correct run-ons, by making one or more of the clauses *dependent.* You may rephrase the sentences, but be sure to use dependent words (such as *since, when, as, after, while, because,* or the other words listed on p. 69) to begin dependent clauses and to add a comma only if the dependent clause comes first. Since various words can be used to form dependent clauses, your answers might differ from those suggested at the back of the book.

Exercise 3

1. On summer evenings, people around the world enjoy the sight of little lights they are flying around in the air.

2. Most people know the glowing insects as fireflies they are also called lightning bugs and glowworms.

3. Glowworms are unique they don't fly.

4. The term "fireflies" may be a little misleading they are not technically flies.

5. Lightning bugs are beetles they have special substances in their bodies.

6. These substances make them glow these substances are luciferin and luciferase.

7. The luciferin and luciferase combine with oxygen they produce a greenish light.

8. The light can be very intense people in some countries use caged fireflies as lamps.

9. In addition to their ability to light up, fireflies blink on and off.

10. Incredibly, groups of fireflies blink out of order at first they seem to coordinate their blinking within a few minutes.

Source: Current Science, May 11, 2001

Exercise 4

1. My family and I get a lot of annoying phone calls in the early evenings.
2. The calls are made by companies, their salespeople try to interest us in the newest calling plan or credit card offer.
3. They don't call during the day then nobody is home.
4. I feel sorry for some of the salespeople, they are just doing their job.
5. My father tells them to call during business hours they hang up right away.
6. Sometimes I pick up the receiver and hear a computerized voice trying to sell me a subscription to a magazine.
7. My mother answers, she is too polite, so they just keep talking.
8. We try to ignore the ringing, it drives us all crazy.
9. One time my brother pretended to be my father and almost ordered a new roof for the house.
10. We never buy anything over the phone, maybe these companies will all get the message and leave us alone.

Exercise 5

Correct the following run-on sentences using any of the six ways covered in this section. You can add punctuation or use dependent words to create dependent clauses. See the chart on p. 85 if you need to review the ways as you work through the exercise.

1. In 2001, American businessman Dennis Tito did something. No one had done it before.
2. Tito became the world's first tourist in space, he paid twenty million dollars for a ride to the International Space Station.
3. Tito wanted the United States to take him into space, but NASA said no.
4. NASA declined Tito's offer. However, Russian space officials accepted it gladly.
5. In early May 2001, Tito boarded a Russian Soyuz rocket, and he blasted off into outer space.
6. Tito could talk to the cosmonauts on board he studied Russian for six months before his trip.
7. Dennis Tito's first-of-its-kind vacation was just the beginning of civilian travel into outer space, more and more individuals will want to follow Tito's example.

8. Soon there will be travel agents they will specialize in space travel.

9. Other countries besides Russia will welcome the income from such trips for example, China may soon have the ability to take people into space.

10. In 2001, NASA chose not to let Tito on one of its space shuttles, In the future, NASA may welcome space tourists.

Source: USA Today, May 4, 2001

REVIEW OF FRAGMENTS AND RUN-ON SENTENCES

If you remember that all clauses include a subject and a verb, but only independent clauses can be punctuated as sentences (since only they can stand alone), then you will avoid fragments in your writing. And if you memorize these six ways to punctuate clauses, you will be able to avoid most punctuation errors.

PUNCTUATING CLAUSES	
I am a student. I am still learning.	(two sentences)
I am a student; I am still learning.	(two independent clauses)
I am a student; therefore, I am still learning.	(two independent clauses connected by a transition such as *also, consequently, finally, furthermore, however, likewise, moreover, nevertheless, otherwise, then, therefore, thus*)
I am a student, so I am still learning.	(two independent clauses connected by a *fanboys: for, and, nor, but, or, yet, so*)
I am a student *who* is still learning.	(dependent clause at end of sentence)
Because I am a student, I am still learning.	(dependent clause at beginning of sentence) Dependent words include *after, although, as, as if, because, before, even if, even though, ever since, how, if, since, so that, than, that, though, unless, until, what, whatever, when, whenever, where, whereas, wherever, whether, which, whichever, while, who, whom, whose*, and *why*.

It is essential that you learn the italicized words in the previous chart—which ones transition between independent clauses and which ones create dependent clauses.

PROOFREADING EXERCISE

Rewrite the following paragraph, making the necessary changes to eliminate fragments and run-on sentences.

In 2001, a writer named Terry Ryan published a book about her mother and it later became a movie. The title of the book *The Prize Winner of Defiance: How My Mother Raised 10 Kids on 25 Words or Less.* Ryan had already written two poetry books and was busy writing a comic strip for a San Francisco newspaper. When she decided to tell her mom's story. Terry's mother, Evelyn Ryan, was a remarkable woman she entered contest after contest in the 1950s and won most of them. In those days, companies sponsored competitions and they gave prizes to the writers of the best slogan, poem, or song about their product. Evelyn Ryan being such a naturally good writer that she won countless prizes, ranging from small appliances to large cash awards. All of them earned through skill and perseverance. Terry Ryan clearly described her mother's organizational skills and generosity. Evelyn Ryan, her daughter explained, was also motivated by her circumstances as the wife of an alcoholic. Evelyn did it all for her family winning such contests was her way of staying at home, supporting ten children, and keeping the family together.

SENTENCE WRITING

Write a sample sentence of your own to demonstrate each of the six ways to correct run-on sentences by punctuating two clauses properly. You may model your sentences on the examples used in the box on page 85 or the chart on page 89.

Identifying Verb Phrases

Sometimes a verb is one word, but often the verb includes two or more words. Verbs made of more than one word are called *verb phrases*. Look at that following list of forms of the verb *speak,* for example. Most of them are verb phrases, made up of the main verb (*speak*) and one or more helping verbs.

speak	is speaking	had been speaking
speaks	am speaking	will have been speaking
spoke	are speaking	is spoken
will speak	was speaking	was spoken
has spoken	were speaking	will be spoken
have spoken	will be speaking	can speak
had spoken	has been speaking	must speak
will have spoken	have been speaking	should have spoken

Note that words certain words are not verbs, but they may be near a verb or in the middle of a verb phrase. These words usually act as adverbs—but they are never verbs:

already	ever	not	really
also	finally	now	sometimes
always	just	often	usually
probably	never	only	possibly

Jason has *never* spoken to his instructor before. He *always* speaks with other students.

Two forms of *speak—speaking* and *to speak—*look like verbs, but neither form can ever be the only verb in a sentence. No *ing* word by itself or *to* _____ form of a verb can act as the main verb of a sentence.

Jeanine speaking French. (a fragment lacking a complete verb phrase)

Jeanine has been speaking French. (a sentence with a complete verb phrase)

And no verb with *to* in front of it can ever be the real verb in a sentence.

Ted to speak in front of groups. (a fragment without a real verb)

Ted <u><u>hates</u></u> to speak in front of groups. (a sentence with a real verb)

These two forms, *speaking* and *to speak,* may be used as subjects or other parts of a sentence.

adj

Speaking on stage <u>is</u> an art. *To speak* on stage <u>is</u> an art. Ted <u><u>had</u></u> a *speaking* part in that play.

E X E R C I S E S

Double-underline the verbs or verb phrases in the following sentences. For now, you do not need to mark subjects. The sentences may contain independent *and* dependent clauses, so there may be several verbs and verb phrases. (Remember that *ing* verbs alone and the *to* _____ forms of verbs are never real verbs in sentences.)

Exercise 1

1. Scientists of all kinds have been learning a lot lately.
2. Those who study traffic safety have recently discovered a puzzling truth.
3. People drive more safely when they encounter fewer traffic signs and traffic lights.
4. The reason behind the "Shared Space" theory is easy to explain.
5. Drivers will regulate their speed and pay closer attention to other drivers when they are not told to do so by signs and lights.
6. Traffic signs and signals give drivers a false sense of security that often leads to recklessness.
7. When no signs or signals exist, drivers think about their own safety and drive more cautiously.
8. Many towns in Europe and America have already taken steps to test the truth of this theory.
9. In some cases, all lights, signs, and barriers have been removed so that all drivers and pedestrians must negotiate with each other to proceed through the town.

10. These changes have usually resulted in lower speeds, fewer accidents, and shorter travel times.

Sources: Discover, May 2007, and *International Herald Tribune,* January 22, 2005

Exercise 2

1. Shopping for holiday items has changed in recent years.

2. Before one celebration has arrived, another holiday's decorations are on display in stores.

3. In early July, for instance, shoppers will not find banners to celebrate Independence Day.

4. Instead, they will see Halloween items for sale.

5. And by October, store owners will have placed turkeys and pilgrims in their windows.

6. Of course, Kwanzaa, Hanukah, and Christmas sales begin in September on their own special aisles.

7. What can people do about this trend?

8. Shoppers could protest and boycott early displays.

9. They could tell store managers about their concerns.

10. But they might miss the spring-fever sales in January.

Exercise 3

1. Felix Hoffmann, a chemist, was trying to ease his own father's pain when he discovered aspirin in 1897.

2. Although aspirin can cause side effects, each year people around the world give themselves fifty billion doses of the popular pain killer.

3. But different countries take this medicine in different ways.

4. The British dissolve aspirin powder in water.

5. The French have insisted that slow-release methods work best.

6. Italians prefer aspirin drinks with a little fizz.

7. And Americans have always chosen to take their aspirin in pill form.

8. However it is taken, aspirin surprises researchers with benefits to human health.

9. It has been a benefit to people with heart problems, colon cancer, and Alzheimer's disease.

10. Where would we be without aspirin?

Exercise 4

1. I have recently read about the life of Philo T. Farnsworth.

2. Thirteen-year-old Philo T. Farnsworth was plowing a field in 1922 when he visualized the concept that led to television as we know it.

3. Others were working on the idea of sending images through the air, but Farnsworth actually solved the problem in that open field.

4. He looked at the rows that the plow had made in the earth.

5. And he reasoned that images could be broken down into rows and sent line by line through the air and onto a screen.

6. Farnsworth's idea made television a reality, but historically he has not been fully recognized for this and his other accomplishments.

7. In 1957, he was featured as a guest on *I've Got a Secret,* a television show that presented mystery contestants.

8. The panelists on the show were supposed to guess the guest's secret, which the audience was shown so that everyone knew the answer except the people asking the questions.

9. They asked if he had invented something painful, and he replied that he had; the panelists never guessed that he was the inventor of television.

10. Farnsworth did receive a box of cigarettes and eighty dollars for being on the show.

Exercise 5

1. On December 16, 2000, the London stage production of Agatha Christie's play *The Mousetrap* marked a milestone.

2. On that night, actors were performing Christie's play for the twenty-thousandth time.

3. In fact, *The Mousetrap* broke the record as the world's longest running play.

4. The play opened in London on November 25, 1952, and had been running continually ever since.

5. More than ten million people had attended the London performances.

6. Here are some other interesting facts about this production.

7. Two pieces of the original set—the clock and the armchair—had survived on stage for half a century.

8. The cast, however, changed more often.

9. Some actors had remained in the show for years while others had played parts for a short time.

10. One actress understudied for over six thousand performances, but she was needed on stage only seventy-two times.

REVIEW EXERCISE

To practice finding all of the sentence structures we have studied so far, mark the following paragraphs from *Isaac Asimov's Guide to Earth and Space*. First, put parentheses around prepositional phrases; then underline verbs or verb phrases twice and their subjects once. Finally, put a broken line beneath dependent clauses. Begin by marking the first paragraph; then check your answers at the back of the book before marking the rest. (Remember that *ing* verbs alone and the *to* _____ forms of verbs are never real verbs in sentences. We will learn more about them on p. 122.)

Sometimes when the moon is a thin crescent, you can see the dim reddish structure of the rest of the moon filling out the circle. It *is* the rest of the moon, and not some other body, because the moon has certain visible markings on it, and the dim reddish structure has those same markings. People still call this effect "the old moon in the new moon's arms". . . .

When the moon is in a thin crescent stage, it is almost exactly between us and the sun so that we see only a little bit of its lighted surface along one edge. If you were on the moon at this time, however, you would see the sun shining over the moon's shoulder and lighting up the entire face of the Earth that happens to be pointed toward the moon. In short, when you see a new moon from Earth, you see a *full Earth* from the moon. . . .

The unlit side of the moon is therefore receiving the light of the full Earth. *Earthlight* is far feebler than sunlight is, but it is enough to light up the dark side of the moon measurably, and it allows us to see the moon's dark side very faintly at the time of the new moon. Galileo was the first to advance this explanation of the "old moon in the new moon's arms," and it made so much sense that few have doubted it since.

Using Standard English Verbs

The next two discussions are for those who need to practice using Standard English verbs. Many of us grew up doing more speaking than writing. But in college and in the business and professional worlds, knowledge of Standard Written English is essential.

The following charts show the forms of four verbs as they are used in Standard Written English. These forms might differ from the way you use these verbs when you speak. Memorize the Standard English forms of these important verbs. The first verb (*talk*) is one of the regular verbs (verbs that all end the same way according to a pattern); most verbs in English are regular. The other three verbs charted here (*have, be,* and *do*) are irregular and are important because they are used not only as main verbs but also as helping verbs in verb phrases.

Don't go on to the exercises until you have memorized the forms of these Standard English verbs.

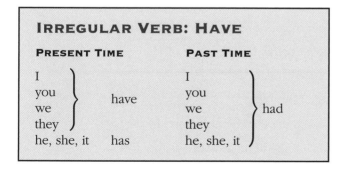

IRREGULAR VERB: BE

PRESENT TIME		PAST TIME	
I	am	I	was
you		you	
we	are	we	were
they		they	
he, she, it	is	he, she, it	was

IRREGULAR VERB: DO

PRESENT TIME		PAST TIME	
I		I	
you		you	
we	do	we	did
they		they	
he, she, it	does	he, she, it	

Sometimes you may have difficulty with the correct endings of verbs because you don't actually hear the words correctly. Note carefully the *s* sound and the *ed* sound at the end of certain words. Occasionally, the *ed* is not clearly pronounced, as in "They tri*ed* to finish their essays," but most of the time you can hear it if you listen.

Read the following sentences aloud, making sure that you exaggerate every sound.

1. He seems satisfied with his new job.

2. She likes saving money for the future.

3. It takes strength of character to control spending.

4. Todd brings salad to every party that he attends.

5. I used to know all of the state capitals.

6. They were supposed to sign both forms.

7. He recognized the suspect and excused himself from the jury.

8. The chess club sponsored Dorothy in the school's charity event.

Now read some other sentences aloud from this text, making sure that you say all the *s*'s and *ed*'s. Reading aloud and listening to others will help you use the correct verb endings automatically.

E X E R C I S E S

In these pairs of sentences, use the *present* form of the verb in the first sentence and the *past* form in the second. All the verbs follow the pattern of the regular verb *talk* except the irregular verbs *have, be,* and *do.* Keep referring to the charts if you're not sure which form to use. Check your answers in the back of the book after each set.

Exercise 1

1. (walk)   I often _____ around the block for exercise. I _____ around it twice yesterday.

2. (be)   Max _____ glad to be graduating. He _____ unsure about his future just two years ago.

3. (have)   The Clarks _____ an SUV now. They _____ a small car before.

4. (do)   I _____ my studying in the afternoons. I _____ my studying in the evenings in high school.

5. (need)   She _____ to wear bifocals now. She _____ only single lenses before.

6. (be)   Now I _____ a fully paid employee. I _____ a work-study student last year.

7. (have)   My class ring _____ a large green stone in its setting. It _____ other stones around it, but they fell out.

8. (be)   They _____ my first choice as roommates. They _____ not my parents' first choice.

9. (do)   My sister usually _____ my taxes. She _____ my taxes last year.

10. (work)   He _____ for two companies right now. He _____ for only one company before.

Exercise 2

1. (be)   She _____ a lawyer now. She _____ a law student last year.

2. (do)   They _____ their best work on the weekends. They _____ a great job last weekend.

3. (have) I _____ a new education plan. I originally _____ a plan that would have taken too long to complete.

4. (ask) She _____ for help when she needs it. She _____ her tutor for help with her latest essay.

5. (have) I always _____ the flu at this time of year. I _____ the flu last year right on schedule.

6. (learn) We _____ something about writing each week. Yesterday we _____ how to write a thesis.

7. (be) Most of us _____ right handed. Therefore, we _____ not comfortable drawing with our left hands.

8. (do) She _____ well on all of her assignments. She _____ very well on the term project.

9. (play) He _____ the piano now. He _____ the guitar as his first instrument.

10. (be) I _____ a natural comedian. However, last month I _____ too depressed to be funny.

Exercise 3

Circle the correct Standard English verb forms.

1. I (start, started) a new volunteer job last month, and so far I really (like, likes) it.

2. The organization (offer, offers) relief boxes to victims of crime or natural disasters around the world.

3. The other volunteers (is, are) all really nice, so we (has, have) a good work environment.

4. Yesterday, we (finish, finished) a project that (need, needed) lots of boxes.

5. The supervisors who (run, runs) the organization always (do, does) their best to explain the victims' situations to us.

6. And they (advise, advises) us to make sure that the boxes (comfort, comforts) the victims as much as possible.

7. I can tell that the supervisors (enjoy, enjoys) their work; they (is, are) always happy to see the relief on the victims' faces.

8. My fellow volunteers and I (complete, completed) our latest project in just one week even though the supervisor (expect, expected) it to take us two weeks.

9. We (has, have) our supervisors to thank for a smooth-running organization.

10. And I (thank, thanks) my coworkers for being my friends.

Exercise 4

Circle the correct Standard English verb forms.

1. My sister and I (do, does) our homework together every night so that we (don't, doesn't) fall behind.

2. I (is, am) better at math, and my sister Kate (is, am) better in English.

3. When I (need, needs) help with grammar, Kate (explain, explains) the rule to me.

4. And if she gets stuck on a math problem, I (help, helps) her understand it; then she (do, does) it herself.

5. This system (work, works) very well for us, and I (hope, hopes) we will always use it.

6. Before we (do, did) it this way, I (drop, dropped) an English class.

7. It (was, were) too hard for me, but now I (do, does) as well as the other students.

8. Kate and I both (work, works) hard, and we (check, checks) each other's progress.

9. When I (learn, learns) more English skills and Kate (learn, learns) more math skills, we will be equal.

10. Our parents (expect, expects) a lot from both of us, and we (don't, doesn't) want to let them down.

Exercise 5

Correct any of following sentences that do not use Standard English verb forms.

1. This year, the theater class is presenting a brand new musical.

2. We are all trying to be very responsible about rehearsals.

3. It take a lot of time and effort to produce a musical.

4. Fifty actors and musicians has to coordinate their schedules to practice.

5. The results is going to be worth the effort.

6. When our lead actress sing, the people in the theater goes completely quiet.

7. Our dance numbers is also impressing everyone who come to rehearsals.

8. The final song definitely have the best choreography in the show.

9. During that song, we dance on top of real cars on stage.

10. I can't wait to see the audience's reaction on opening night.

PROOFREADING EXERCISE

In the following paragraph, correct any sentences that do not use Standard English verb forms.

Every day as we drive though our neighborhoods on the way to school or to work, we see things that needs to be fixed. Many of them cause us only a little bit of trouble, so we forget them until we face them again. Every morning, drivers in my neighborhood has to deal with a truck that someone park right at the corner of our street. It block our view as we try to turn onto the main avenue. We need to move out past the truck into the oncoming lane of traffic just to make a left turn. One day last week, I turn too soon, and a car almost hit me. This truck do not need to be parked in such a dangerous place.

SENTENCE WRITING

Write ten sentences about a problem in your own neighborhood. Check your sentences to be sure that they use Standard English verb forms. Try exchanging papers with another student for more practice.

Using Regular and Irregular Verbs

All regular verbs end the same way in the past form and when used with helping verbs. Here is a chart showing all the forms of some *regular* verbs and the various helping verbs with which they are used.

REGULAR VERBS				
BASE FORM	**PRESENT**	**PAST**	**PAST PARTICIPLE**	*ING* **FORM**
(Use after *can, may, shall, will, could, might, should, would, must, do, does, did.)*			(Use after *have, has, had.* Some can be used after forms of *be.*)	(Use after forms of *be.*)
ask	ask *(s)*	asked	asked	asking
bake	bake *(s)*	baked	baked	baking
count	count *(s)*	counted	counted	counting
dance	dance *(s)*	danced	danced	dancing
decide	decide *(s)*	decided	decided	deciding
enjoy	enjoy *(s)*	enjoyed	enjoyed	enjoying
finish	finish *(es)*	finished	finished	finishing
happen	happen *(s)*	happened	happened	happening
learn	learn *(s)*	learned	learned	learning
like	like *(s)*	liked	liked	liking
look	look *(s)*	looked	looked	looking
mend	mend *(s)*	mended	mended	mending
need	need *(s)*	needed	needed	needing
open	open *(s)*	opened	opened	opening
start	start *(s)*	started	started	starting
suppose	suppose *(s)*	supposed	supposed	supposing
tap	tap *(s)*	tapped	tapped	tapping
walk	walk *(s)*	walked	walked	walking
want	want *(s)*	wanted	wanted	wanting

NOTE—When there are several helping verbs, the one closest to the verb determines which form of the main verb should be used: They *should* finish soon; they could *have* finished an hour ago.

When do you write *ask, finish, suppose, use?* And when do you write *asked, finished, supposed, used?* Here are some rules that will help you decide.

Write *ask, finish, suppose, use* (or their *s* forms) when writing about the present time, repeated actions, or facts:

He *asks* questions whenever he is confused.

They always *finish* their projects on time.

I *suppose* you want me to help you move.

Birds *use* leaves, twigs, and feathers to build their nests.

Write *asked, finished, supposed, used*

1. **When writing about the past:**

   He *asked* the teacher for another explanation.

   She *finished* her internship last year.

   They *supposed* that there were others bidding on that house.

   I *used* to study piano.

2. **When some form of *be* (other than the word *be* itself) comes before the word:**

   He was *asked* the most difficult questions.

   She is *finished* with her training now.

   They were *supposed* to sign at the bottom of the form.

   My essay was *used* as a sample of clear narration.

3. **When some form of *have* comes before the word:**

   The teacher has *asked* us that question before.

   She will have *finished* all of her exams by the end of May.

   I had *supposed* too much without any proof.

   We have *used* many models in my drawing class this semester.

All the verbs in the chart on page 103 are *regular*. That is, they're all formed in the same way—with an *ed* ending on the past form and on the past participle. But many verbs are irregular. Their past and past participle forms change spelling instead of just adding an *ed*. Here's a chart of some *irregular* verbs. Notice that the base, present, and *ing* forms end the same as regular verbs. Refer to this list when you aren't sure which verb form to use. Memorize all the forms you don't know.

IRREGULAR VERBS

BASE FORM	PRESENT	PAST	PAST PARTICIPLE	*ING* FORM
(Use after can, may, shall, will, could, might, should, would, must, do, does, did.)			*(Use after* have, has, had. *Some can be used after forms of* be.*)*	*(Use after forms of* be.*)*
be	is, am, are	was, were	been	being
become	become *(s)*	became	become	becoming
begin	begin *(s)*	began	begun	beginning
break	break *(s)*	broke	broken	breaking
bring	bring *(s)*	brought	brought	bringing
buy	buy *(s)*	bought	bought	buying
build	build *(s)*	built	built	building
catch	catch *(es)*	caught	caught	catching
choose	choose *(s)*	chose	chosen	choosing
come	come *(s)*	came	come	coming
do	do *(es)*	did	done	doing
draw	draw *(s)*	drew	drawn	drawing
drink	drink *(s)*	drank	drunk	drinking
drive	drive *(s)*	drove	driven	driving
eat	eat *(s)*	ate	eaten	eating
fall	fall *(s)*	fell	fallen	falling
feel	feel *(s)*	felt	felt	feeling
fight	fight *(s)*	fought	fought	fighting
find	find *(s)*	found	found	finding
forget	forget *(s)*	forgot	forgotten	forgetting
forgive	forgive *(s)*	forgave	forgiven	forgiving
freeze	freeze *(s)*	froze	frozen	freezing
get	get *(s)*	got	got *or* gotten	getting
give	give *(s)*	gave	given	giving
go	go *(es)*	went	gone	going
grow	grow *(s)*	grew	grown	growing
have	have *or* has	had	had	having
hear	hear *(s)*	heard	heard	hearing
hold	hold *(s)*	held	held	holding
keep	keep *(s)*	kept	kept	keeping
know	know *(s)*	knew	known	knowing
lay (to put)	lay *(s)*	laid	laid	laying

IRREGULAR VERBS (CONTINUED)

BASE FORM	PRESENT	PAST	PAST PARTICIPLE	*ING* FORM
lead (like "bead")	lead *(s)*	led	led	leading
leave	leave *(s)*	left	left	leaving
lie (to rest)	lie *(s)*	lay	lain	lying
lose	lose *(s)*	lost	lost	losing
make	make *(s)*	made	made	making
meet	meet *(s)*	met	met	meeting
pay	pay *(s)*	paid	paid	paying
read	read *(s)*	read	read	reading
(pron. "reed")		(pron. "red")	(pron. "red")	
ride	ride *(s)*	rode	ridden	riding
ring	ring *(s)*	rang	rung	ringing
rise	rise *(s)*	rose	risen	rising
run	run *(s)*	ran	run	running
say	say *(s)*	said	said	saying
see	see *(s)*	saw	seen	seeing
sell	sell *(s)*	sold	sold	selling
shake	shake *(s)*	shook	shaken	shaking
shine (give light)	shine *(s)*	shone	shone	shining
shine (polish)	shine *(s)*	shined	shined	shining
sing	sing *(s)*	sang	sung	singing
sleep	sleep *(s)*	slept	slept	sleeping
speak	speak *(s)*	spoke	spoken	speaking
spend	spend *(s)*	spent	spent	spending
stand	stand *(s)*	stood	stood	standing
steal	steal *(s)*	stole	stolen	stealing
strike	strike *(s)*	struck	struck	striking
swim	swim *(s)*	swam	swum	swimming
swing	swing *(s)*	swung	swung	swinging
take	take *(s)*	took	taken	taking
teach	teach *(es)*	taught	taught	teaching
tear	tear *(s)*	tore	torn	tearing
tell	tell *(s)*	told	told	telling
think	think *(s)*	thought	thought	thinking
throw	throw *(s)*	threw	thrown	throwing
wear	wear *(s)*	wore	worn	wearing
win	win *(s)*	won	won	winning
write	write *(s)*	wrote	written	writing

Sometimes verbs from the past participle column are used after some form of the verb *be* (or verbs that take the place of *be* like *appear, seem, look, feel, get, act, become*) to describe the subject or to say something in a passive, rather than an active, way.

She is contented.

You appear pleased. (You *are* pleased.)

He seems delighted. (He *is* delighted.)

She looked surprised. (She *was* surprised.)

I feel shaken. (I *am* shaken.)

They get bored easily. (They *are* bored easily.)

You acted concerned. (You *were* concerned.)

They were thrown out of the game. (Active: *The referee threw them out of the game.*)

We were disappointed by the news. (Active: *The news disappointed us.*)

Often these verb forms actually become adjectives (words that describe the subject); at other times they still act as part of the verb in the sentence. What you call them doesn't matter. More important is to be sure that you use the correct form from the past participle column.

EXERCISES

Write the correct form of the verbs in the blanks. Refer to the charts and explanations on the preceding pages if you aren't sure which form to use after a certain helping verb. Check your answers after each exercise.

Exercise 1

1. (look) Once again, I have _____ everywhere for my cell phone.

2. (look) I could _____ in a few more places, but I'm late.

3. (look) I feel so foolish while I am _____ for it.

4. (look) I know that if I _____ too hard I won't find it.

5. (look) Once I _____ for it for over two hours.

6. (look) I can _____ right past it if I am too frantic.

7. (look) I have _____ in places where it would never be.

8. (look)   My dad once caught me while I was _____ for it in the trash can.

9. (look)   In fact, my family now _____ at me with scorn whenever I ask, "Has anybody seen my phone?"

10. (look)   From now on I will _____ in the obvious places first and keep my problem to myself.

Exercise 2

1. (drive)   I always _____ my brother to school; in fact, I have _____ him to school for a whole year now.

2. (think)   The other day, I was _____ of new ways to get him there in the morning, but he _____ that they were all bad ideas.

3. (take)   He could _____ a school bus that stops nearby; instead he _____ me for granted.

4. (tell)   It all started when he _____ our mother that some of the other children were _____ him to stay out of their seats.

5. (write)   I _____ a note to the bus driver to see if she could help ease my brother's mind, but so far she hasn't _____ back.

6. (know)   When I was my brother's age, I _____ some tough kids at school, so I _____ how he must feel.

7. (teach)   But experiences like that _____ us how to get along with everyone; they sure _____ me.

8. (tear)   Now I am _____ between wanting to help him avoid the tough kids and _____ my hair out from having to take him to school every day.

9. (ride)   We have _____ together for so long that I might miss him if I _____ alone.

10. (make)   I have _____ up my mind. I will _____ the best of it while he still needs me. What else are big brothers for?

Exercise 3

1. (be, hear)

We _____ surprised when we _____ from our Aunt Shelby yesterday.

2. (see, begin)

We hadn't _____ her in over a year, and we had _____ to wonder if she would ever visit us again.

3. (fly, eat)

She had _____ in from France earlier in the day but hadn't _____ dinner yet.

4. (get, do)

We _____ back to her at her hotel and _____ our best to convince her to join us for dinner.

5. (take, eat)

It did not _____ much to convince her, and soon we were _____ dinner together.

6. (write, come, lose)

She said that she had _____ to tell us that she was _____, and she asked if we had _____ the letter.

7. (swear, feel)

We _____ that we never received it, and she _____ better.

8. (buy, pay)

Just to make sure there were no hard feelings, we _____ her dinner, and she _____ the tip.

9. (get, think)

It was _____ late, so she _____ that she should go back to her hotel to get some sleep.

10. (see, tell, lie)

When we _____ Shelby the next day, she _____ us that she was so tired the night before that as soon as she _____ down on the hotel pillow, she fell asleep.

Exercise 4

1. (use, suppose)

My brothers and I _____ to stay up all night in our room when we were _____ to be sleeping.

2. (catch, come, hear)

Our parents would _____ us sometimes when they _____ upstairs and _____ us talking.

3. (be, leave)   We _____ not very smart about it; sometimes we even _____ the light on.

4. (read, draw, build)   That way we could _____ or _____ or _____ our secret inventions.

5. (feel, draw)   Those nights _____ really special, and I _____ some of my best pictures then.

6. (do, sleep)   We _____ suffer from fatigue during the day as we _____ through our classes at school.

7. (know, spend)   We _____ that we had to fix the problem, so we _____ several nights withdrawing from our late-night schedule.

8. (go, be)   Gradually we _____ to bed earlier and earlier until we _____ back to a normal sleeping pattern.

9. (wake, stay)   We _____ up on time and _____ awake in our classes.

10. (forget, spend, be)   I will never _____ the quiet, creative, and carefree nights I _____ with my brothers when we _____ just kids.

Exercise 5

1. (lay, lie, feel)   I _____ my blanket down on the cool grass under a big tree and was _____ face-down on the blanket when I _____ a wasp land on the back of my ankle.

2. (know, be)   I _____ that special sensation of a wasp's legs on my skin because I have _____ stung by one before.

3. (break, have)   Last time, I _____ out in hives and _____ to go to the hospital to get an injection of antihistamine.

4. (become, think)   My eyes _____ swollen, and I _____ that I was going to die.

5. (be)   I _____ not going to let that happen again.

6. (read, frighten)   I had _____ that insects like wasps only sting when they're _____.

7. (keep, shake)   So this time I _____ calm and gently _____ my ankle to shoo away the wasp without angering it.

8. (work, rise, sneak) My plan _____, and as soon as the wasp _____ in the air to find a new spot to land, I _____ away.

9. (leave, go)   I _____ my blanket under the tree, and I didn't even _____ back to the park for it later.

10. (lose, sting)   Of course, I would rather _____ a blanket than be _____ by a wasp again.

PROGRESS TEST

This test covers everything you've studied so far. One sentence in each pair is correct. The other is incorrect. Read both sentences carefully before you decide. Then write the letter of the incorrect sentence in the blank. Try to name the error and correct it if you can.

1. _____ **A.** Textbooks can be purchased in bookstores or online.

   _____ **B.** Online, books can be less expensive however, they are often older editions.

2. _____ **A.** Although I don't like the taste of pineapple and coconut.

   _____ **B.** I do like shampoos that smell like pineapple and coconut.

3. _____ **A.** Our assignment requires a trip to the Museum of Science and Industry.

   _____ **B.** I don't no how to get there, but my friend does.

4. _____ **A.** Her research paper will probably be late.

   _____ **B.** She should of gone to the library last week.

5. _____ **A.** The last student to leave was suppose to lock the door after class.

   _____ **B.** I forgot and had to drive back to school.

6. _____ **A.** Alex and Zee have finished all of their schoolwork.

   _____ **B.** They're going away for spring break but I'm staying at home.

7. _____ **A.** The package did not have an official label, just a name and address in pencil.

   _____ **B.** We were surprise that it was delivered to us on time.

8. _____ **A.** In my math class, their have already been three quizzes.

   _____ **B.** There will be six more quizzes before the final exam.

9. _____ **A.** Thanks to the teacher's stopwatch, our speeches were all the same length.

   _____ **B.** However, Janets' speech was the clearest one of all.

10. _____ **A.** I was the last one to finish the midterm.

   _____ **B.** As soon as I wrote my final answer, the bell rung.

Maintaining Subject-Verb Agreement

As we have seen, the subject and verb in a sentence work together, so they must always agree. Different subjects need different forms of verbs. When the correct verb follows a subject, we call it subject-verb agreement.

The following sentences illustrate the rule that *s* verbs follow most singular subjects but not plural subjects.

One student studies.	Two students study.
The bell rings.	The bells ring.
A democracy listens to the people.	Democracies listen to the people.
One person writes the dialogue.	Many people write the dialogue.

The following sentences show how forms of the verb *be* (*is, am, are, was, were*) and helping verbs (*be, have,* and *do*) are made to agree with their subjects. We have labeled only the verbs that must agree with the subjects.

This puzzle is difficult.	These puzzles are difficult.
I am amazed.	You are amazed.
He was studying.	They were studying.
That class has been canceled.	Those classes have been canceled.
She does not want to participate.	You do not want to participate.

The following words are always singular and take an *s* verb or the irregular equivalent (*is, was, has, does*):

one	anybody	each
anyone	everybody	
everyone	nobody	
no one	somebody	
someone		

Someone feeds my dog in the morning.

Everybody was at the party.

Each does her own homework.

Remember that prepositional phrases often come between subjects and verbs. You should ignore these interrupting phrases, or you may mistake the wrong word for the subject and use a verb form that doesn't agree.

Someone from the apartments feeds my dog in the morning. (*Someone* is the subject, not *apartments.*)

Everybody on the list of celebrities was at the party. (*Everybody* is the subject, not *celebrities.*)

Each of the twins does her own homework. (*Each* is the subject, not *twins.*)

However, the words *some, any, all, none,* and *most* are exceptions to this rule of ignoring prepositional phrases. These words can be singular or plural, depending on the words that follow them in prepositional phrases. Again, we have labeled only the verbs that must agree with the subjects.

Some of the *information* is helpful.

Some of the *facts* are convincing.

Does any of the *furniture* come with the apartment?

Do any of the *chairs* and *tables* come with the apartment?

All of her *work* has been published.

All of her *poems* have been published.

None of the *jewelry* was missing.

None of the *jewels* were missing.

On July 4th, <u>most</u> of the *country* <u>celebrates</u> with a picnic or a party.

On July 4th, <u>most</u> of the *citizens* <u>celebrate</u> with a picnic or a party.

When a sentence has more than one subject joined by *and,* the subject is plural:

The <u>teacher</u> *and* the <u>tutors</u> <u>eat</u> lunch at noon.

A <u>doughnut</u> *and* a <u>bagel</u> <u>were</u> sitting on the plate.

However, when two subjects are joined by *or,* then the subject *closest* to the verb determines the verb form:

Either the <u>teacher</u> *or* the *<u>tutors</u>* <u>eat</u> lunch at noon.

Either the <u>tutors</u> *or* the *<u>teacher</u>* <u>eats</u> lunch at noon.

A <u>doughnut</u> *or* a *<u>bagel</u>* <u>was</u> sitting on the plate.

In most sentences, the subject comes before the verb. However, in some cases, the subject follows the verb, and subject-verb agreement needs special attention. Study the following examples:

Over the building <u>flies</u> a solitary <u>flag</u>. (flag flies)

Over the building <u>fly</u> several <u>flags</u>. (flags fly)

There <u>is</u> a good <u>reason</u> for that deadline. (reason is)

There <u>are</u> good <u>reasons</u> for that deadline. (reasons are)

E X E R C I S E S

Circle the correct verbs in parentheses to maintain subject-verb agreement in the following sentences. Remember to ignore prepositional phrases, unless the subjects are *some, any, all, none,* or *most*. Check your answers after the first exercise.

Exercise 1

1. Many people (is, are) trying to find ways to save fuel and lower the emissions from cars.

2. Robin Chase (has, have) created a carpooling Web site called GoLoco.org.

3. GoLoco.org's design and mission (is, are) simple.

4. Its design (is, are) the same as other social-networking sites.

5. Its mission (involve, involves) filling cars with passengers so that the gas, expenses, and emissions (is, are) not wasted on just one person.

6. Potential carpoolers (enter, enters) their information at the site.

7. Members' information (include, includes) such things as musical preferences, languages spoken, and even recordings of their voices.

8. Passengers (set, sets) up accounts, and drivers (receive, receives) payments through the site for each trip with members on board.

9. This carpooling method (has, have) become an especially popular way to travel to sporting events and concerts since all of the riders (has, have) the same interest in seeing the event and saving the planet.

10. Of course, one of the most popular benefits (is, are) the time saved by using carpool lanes.

Source: The Boston Globe, April 23, 2007

Exercise 2

1. Human beings (is, are) unpredictable in their reactions at times.

2. A recent study in England asked a thousand people what their top fears (is, are).

3. The number one fear (is, are) the fear of spiders.

4. Next on the list (come, comes) the fear of terrorists.

5. The fear of snakes (rank, ranks) third on the list.

6. People's responses (put, puts) a fear of heights in fourth place.

7. Strangely, the fear of death (is, are) fifth on the list of top worries.

8. Dentists and needles (is, are) the sixth and seventh most common fears, respectively.

9. Speaking in public (is, are) another big fear, coming in eighth overall.

10. And the fears of debt and flying (fill, fills) out the bottom of the list of the top-ten fears.

Source: CNN.com, October 13, 2004

Exercise 3

1. No one in my film class (has, have) ever seen *2001: A Space Odyssey* before, except me.

2. All of them (has, have) heard of it, but none of them (has, have) actually watched it.

3. Most of my friends outside of school (love, loves) old movies, especially science fiction ones like *Slaughterhouse Five* and *Fahrenheit 451*.

4. Each of these sci-fi movies (make, makes) its own point about the human situation.

5. But everybody I know (say, says) *2001: A Space Odyssey* makes the biggest point of all.

6. One of my roommates (think, thinks) that it is the greatest movie ever made.

7. I believe that either it or *Fahrenheit 451* (is, are) the best, but I (hasn't, haven't) decided which one yet.

8. Now George Orwell's famous year 1984 (has, have) passed.

9. And each of us (look, looks) back at the shocking events of the real year 2001.

10. No one really (know, knows) what surprises await us in the future.

Exercise 4

1. Some of the world's gems (has, have) been designated as birthstones.

2. Each of these stones (is, are) unique.

3. Either a zodiac sign or a month of the year (is, are) represented by a particular gem.

4. The stone for January (is, are) garnet, and February's (is, are) amethyst.

5. Aquamarine and diamond (is, are) March and April's birthstones.

6. Someone who is born in May (has, have) emerald as a birthstone.

7. The pearl, the ruby, and peridot (represent, represents) those with birthdays in June, July, and August, respectively.

8. And the remaining months—September, October, November, and December—(is, are) associated with sapphire, opal, topaz, and turquoise—in that order.

9. The custom of assigning birthstones to signs of the zodiac (come, comes) from the connection between gems and the stars.

10. Both gemstones and stars (shine, shines).

Source: Gemstones (Dorling Kindersley, 1994)

Exercise 5

1. One of the world's most popular places (is, are) Disneyland in Buena Park, California.

2. Some of Disneyland's little-known facts (surprise, surprises) people.

3. For instance, the buildings on Main Street itself (isn't, aren't) really as tall as they appear.

4. Each of the upper floors (is, are) built in smaller scale than the floor below to create the illusion of height.

5. In one of Main Street's Fire House windows (shine, shines) a light in honor of Walt Disney, the park's creator.

6. None of the characters roaming the park in full-body costumes ever (speak, speaks).

7. Only the "human" characters, such as Snow White, Cinderella, and Aladdin (talk, talks).

8. There (is, are) also a "kid switch" policy to help parents with small children go on the adult rides.

9. One parent stands in line and (enjoy, enjoys) the ride.

10. At the exit gate (waits, wait) the other parent to switch places once the ride has finished so that both of the adults have a good time without waiting in line twice.

PROOFREADING EXERCISE

Find and correct the ten subject-verb agreement errors in the following paragraph.

My teachers for this school year are really interesting. Each of their personalities are different. Some of them requires us to be on time every day and follow directions to the letter. Others treats students almost as casual friends. The expectations of my geography teacher is higher than I expected. Students in that class has to do just what the teacher says, or they risk failing. Most of my other professors takes a more lenient approach. But two of them has an odd grading technique; at least it seems odd to me. These two teachers wants us to turn in all of our papers over the Internet. We can't turn in any handwritten work. I guess there is good reasons behind their demands. My friends say that turning in work over the Internet makes the teachers' jobs easier because it eliminate the possibility of plagiarizing.

SENTENCE WRITING

Write ten sentences in which you describe the clothes you are wearing. Use verbs in the present time. Then go back over your sentences—underline your subjects once, underline your verbs twice, and be sure they agree. Exchange papers with another student and check each other's subject-verb agreement.

Avoiding Shifts in Time

People often worry about using different time frames in writing. Let common sense guide you. If you begin writing a paper in past time, don't shift back and forth to the present unnecessarily; and if you begin in the present, don't shift to the past without good reason. In the following paragraph, the writer starts in the present and then shifts to the past, then shifts again to the present:

> In the novel *To Kill a Mockingbird*, Jean Louise Finch is a little girl who lives in the South with her father, Atticus, and her brother, Jem. Everybody in town calls Jean Louise "Scout" as a nickname. When Atticus, a lawyer, defended a black man against the charges of a white woman, some of their neighbors turned against him. Scout protected her father by appealing to the humanity of one member of the angry mob. In this chapter, five-year-old Scout turns out to be stronger than a group of adult men.

All the verbs should be in the present:

> In the novel *To Kill a Mockingbird,* Jean Louise Finch is a little girl who lives in the South with her father, Atticus, and her brother, Jem. Everybody in town calls Jean Louise "Scout" as a nickname. When Atticus, a lawyer, defends a black man against the charges of a white woman, some of their neighbors turn against him. Scout protects her father by appealing to the humanity of one member of the angry mob. In this chapter, five-year-old Scout turns out to be stronger than a group of adult men.

This sample paragraph discusses only the events that happen within the novel's plot, so it needs to maintain one time frame—the present, which we use to write about literature and repeated actions.

However, sometimes you will write about the present, the past, and even the future together. Then it may be necessary to use these different time frames within the same paragraph, each for its own reason. For example, if you were to give biographical information about Harper Lee, author of *To Kill a Mockingbird,* within a discussion of the novel and its influence, you might need to use all three time frames:

> Harper Lee grew up in Alabama, and she based elements in the book on experiences from her childhood. Like the character Atticus, Lee's father was a lawyer. She wrote the novel in his law offices. *To Kill a Mockingbird* is Harper Lee's most famous work, and it received the Pulitzer Prize for fiction in 1961. Lee's book turned fifty years old in the year 2010. It deals with the effects of prejudice unforgivingly, and it will always remain one of the most moving and compassionate novels in American literature.

The previous paragraph uses past (*grew, based, was, wrote, received, turned*), present (*is, deals*), and future (*will remain*) in the same paragraph without committing the error of unnecessary shifting. A shift in time occurs when the writer changes time frames *inconsistently* or *for no reason,* confusing the reader (as in the first example given).

PROOFREADING EXERCISES

Which of the following student paragraphs shift *unnecessarily* back and forth between time frames? In those that do, change the verbs to maintain one time frame, thus making the entire paragraph read smoothly. One of the paragraphs is correct, even though it includes multiple time frames because those time frames make sense.

1. I am taking an art history class right now. Every day, we watched slide shows of great pieces of art throughout history. We memorized each piece of art, its time period, and the artist who created it. I enjoy these slide shows, but I had trouble remembering the facts about them. I always get swept away by the beautiful paintings, drawings, and sculptures and forgot to take notes that I could study from at home.

2. My high school Shakespeare teacher told us that in Shakespeare's day, all of the characters' parts were played by male actors. That information surprised me. The Elizabethans probably accepted all-male actors without question. However, now that we are so used to realistic action and special effects on stage, I have a hard time imagining a man playing Juliet convincingly. As a theater major, I know how much costume and voice really help to create a believable character. I was also glad to read that, more recently, there have been all-female casts of *Hamlet* and other plays around the country. These productions seem to balance the scales somehow, and I will try to see one as soon as possible.

3. I enjoyed traveling by plane to Texas. Even though I have to arrive three hours early at the airport, it didn't bother me. I watch all the people taking off their shoes for security. And once I am through to the boarding gates, I bought some food and relax until it was time to enter the plane. Before I board the plane, the passengers who were arriving walked off the ramp with all of their carry-on luggage. They look tired but happy to be at their destination. Both of my flights were comfortable, and the flight attendants are so nice and cheerful. I liked the way they said, "Y'all come back to Texas real soon."

Recognizing Verbal Phrases

You know from the discussion on p. 91 that a verb phrase is made up of a main verb and at least one helping verb. But some forms of verbs can be used not as real verbs but as some other part of speech in a sentence. Verbs put to other uses are called *verbals*.

A verbal can be a noun acting as a subject:

Skiing is my favorite sport. (*Skiing* is a noun. Here, it is the subject of the sentence, not the verb. The real verb in the sentence is *is*.)

A verbal can be a noun acting as an object:

I like *to ski* during the winter. (*To ski* is a noun object; it is *what I like*. I could similarly write, "I like *cocoa* during the winter." The real verb in both sentences is *like*, and the two objects are *to ski*, a verbal as a noun, and *cocoa*, a regular noun.)

A verbal can be an adjective:

My *bruised* ankle healed quickly. (*Bruised* is an adjective that describes the noun, ankle. The real verb in the sentence is *healed*.)

A verbal can also be an adverb:

My ankle swelled, *doubling* in size. (*Doubling* is an adverb, adding to the verb *swelled*.)

Verbals link up with other words to form *verbal phrases*. To see the difference between a real verb phrase and a verbal phrase, look at these two sentences:

I was bowling with my best friends. (*Bowling* is the main verb in a verb phrase. Along with the helping verb *was*, it shows the action of the sentence.)

I enjoyed *bowling* with my best friends. (Here the real verb is *enjoyed*. *Bowling* is not the verb; it is the object, and it links up with a prepositional phrase to form a verbal phrase—*bowling with my best friends*—which is the whole activity I enjoyed.)

THREE KINDS OF VERBALS

   1. *ing* verbs used without helping verbs (*running, thinking, baking* . . .)
   2. verbs that follow *to* ___ (*to walk, to eat, to cause* . . .)
   3. verb forms that often end in *ed, en,* or *t* (*tossed, spoken, burnt* . . .)

Look at the following sentences using the boxed examples in verbal phrases:

Running two miles a day <u><u>is</u></u> great exercise. (real verb = is)

She <u><u>spent</u></u> two hours *thinking of a title for her essay.* (real verb = spent)

We <u><u>had</u></u> such fun *baking those cherry vanilla cupcakes.* (real verb = had)

I <u><u>like</u></u> *to walk around the zoo by myself.* (real verb = like)

To eat exotic foods <u><u>takes</u></u> courage. (real verb = takes)

They actually <u><u>wanted</u></u> *to cause an argument.* (real verb = wanted)

Tossed in a salad, artichoke <u>hearts</u> <u><u>add</u></u> zesty flavor. (real verb = add)

Spoken in Spanish, the <u>dialogue</u> <u><u>sounds</u></u> even more beautiful.
(real verb = sounds)

Our peach <u>trees,</u> partially *burnt in the wild fire,* <u><u>recovered</u></u> quickly.
(real verb = recovered)

E X E R C I S E S

Each of the following sentences contains at least one verbal or verbal phrase. Double underline the real verbs or verb phrases and put brackets around the verbals and verbal phrases. Remember to locate the verbals first (*running, wounded, to sleep . . .*) and include any word(s) that go with them (*running a race, wounded in the fight, to sleep all night*). Real verbs will never be inside verbal phrases. Check your answers after the first set before going on to the next.

Exercise 1

1. Parents who like to go clubbing can now take their children along—well, sort of.

2. On weekend afternoons, nightclubs around the country childproof their facilities to allow children to dance the day away.

3. An organization called Baby Loves Disco orchestrates these events, offering real drinks for the parents and juice boxes and healthy snacks for the kids.

4. The nightclubs try to keep the club atmosphere realistic for the families while making sure that the volume of the music is not too loud for the children's ears.

5. They keep the music real, too, playing songs by the best-known bands of the 1970s and 80s.

6. Kids up to eight years old have fun dancing, dressing in disco styles, wearing fake tattoos, jumping around, and yelling with other kids and parents.

7. Baby Loves Disco provides special areas for parents to change their children's diapers or to treat themselves to a massage.

8. Baby Loves Disco has its own Web site, posting videos, news stories, and future events taking place in cities across the country.

9. To attract parents who don't like disco music, the BLD home page includes links to a kids' version of hip hop—called "Skip Hop"—and jazz for kids.

10. Videos and testimonials on the site show that kids love dancing at nightclubs as much as adults do.

Exercise 2

1. Many people dislike speaking in front of strangers.

2. That is why there is an almost universal fear of giving speeches.

3. Feeling exposed, people get dry mouths and sweaty hands.

4. Note cards become useless, rearranging themselves in the worst possible order.

5. To combat this problem, people try to memorize a speech, only to forget the whole thing as the audience stares back at them expectantly.

6. And when they do remember parts of it, the microphone decides to quit at the punch line of their best joke.

7. Embarrassed and humiliated, they struggle to regain their composure.

8. Then the audience usually begins to sympathize with and encourage the speaker.

9. Finally used to the spotlight, the speaker relaxes and finds the courage to finish.

10. No one expects giving a speech to get any easier.

Exercise 3

1. I have learned how to manage my time when I am not working.

2. I like to go to the movies on Friday nights.

3. Watching a good film takes me away from the stress of my job.

4. I especially enjoy eating buttery popcorn and drinking a cold soda.

5. It is the perfect way for me to begin the weekend.

6. I get to escape from the deadlines and pressure of work.

7. I indulge myself and try to give myself a break—nobody's perfect, and everybody has setbacks.

8. All day Saturday I enjoy lounging around the house in my weekend clothes.

9. I do a little gardening and try to relax my mind.

10. By Sunday evening, after resting for two days, I am ready to start my busy week all over again.

Exercise 4

1. Choosing a major is one of the most important decisions for students.

2. Many students take a long time to decide about their majors.

3. But they fear wasting time on the wrong major more than indecision.

4. They spend several semesters as undecided majors taking general education classes.

5. Distracted by class work, students can forget to pay attention to their interests.

6. Finally, a particular subject area will attract them to study it further.

7. One student might find happiness in doing a psychology experiment.

8. Writing a poem in an English class may be the assignment to make another decide.

9. Attracted by telescopes, a student might choose to major in astronomy.

10. Finding a major takes time and patience.

Exercise 5

1. What would cause a television to send out an SOS signal?

2. After moving into his own apartment, Chris van Rossman received a Toshiba television as a present from his parents.

3. Positioned safely in the living room, van Rossman's TV had a built-in VCR, DVD, and CD player.

4. Not subscribing to a cable service, however, van Rossman could watch only four broadcast channels.

5. On October 2, 2004, van Rossman's TV started to do something very unusual.

6. Sending out an SOS, the international distress signal, the television called for help.

7. An orbiting satellite designed to pick up such calls from downed planes or sunk boats heard the distress signal and alerted Air Force officials.

8. After receiving the information, local Civil Air Patrol authorities in van Rossman's town traced the signal to his apartment complex.

9. Van Rossman opened his door to a team of uniformed officers dispatched to rescue his television.

10. Surprised by the discovery of the source of the call for help, authorities told van Rossman to turn off the TV to avoid a $10,000 fine for emitting a false distress signal.

Source: Corvallis Gazette-Times, October 23, 2004

PARAGRAPH EXERCISE

Double underline the real verbs or verb phrases and put brackets around the verbals and verbal phrases in the following excerpt from the book *Owls: Whoo Are They?* by Kila Jarvis and Denver W. Holt.

Feather colors are not the only things that help camouflage owls. They have other neat tricks to conceal, or hide, themselves. Many stand tall and pull their feathers in tightly, making the owls skinnier and harder to see. When trying to conceal themselves, owls raise the whitish feathers surrounding the bill. Tufted owls also raise their tufts, and round-headed owls lift their facial and "eyebrow" feathers.

When an owl tries to hide itself by changing its shape, it is in concealment posture. In this posture, the owl's rounded outline is broken up and is less likely to be seen by humans or predators.

SENTENCE WRITING

Write ten sentences that contain verbal phrases. Use the ten verbals listed here to begin your verbal phrases: *speaking, typing, driving, reading, to eat, to go, to chat, to cook, impressed, taken*. The last two are particularly difficult to use as verbals. There are sample sentences listed in the Answers section at the back of the book. But first, try to write your own so that you can compare the two.

Correcting Misplaced or Dangling Modifiers

When you modify something, you change whatever it is, usually by adding to it. You might modify a car, for example, by adding special tires. In English, words, phrases, and clauses are *modifiers* when they add extra information to part of a sentence. To do its job properly, a modifier should be in the right spot—as close to the word it describes as possible. If you put new tires on the roof of the car instead of where they belong, they would be misplaced. In the following sentence, the modifier is too far away from the word it modifies to make sense. It is a misplaced modifier:

Swinging through the trees, Jonathan watched the monkeys at the zoo.

Was it *Jonathan* who was swinging through the trees? That's what the sentence says because the modifying phrase *Swinging through the trees* is next to *Jonathan*. It should be next to *monkeys* in order for the monkeys to be swinging through the trees.

At the zoo, Jonathan watched the monkeys, swinging through the trees.

The next example includes no word for the phrase *At the age of eight* to modify:

At the age of eight, my family finally bought a dog.

Obviously, the family was not eight when it bought a dog. Nor was the dog eight. The modifier *At the age of eight* is a dangling modifier with no word to attach itself to, no word for it to modify. You can get rid of a dangling modifier by turning it into a dependent clause with a clear subject and verb. (See p. 69 for a discussion of dependent clauses.)

When I was eight, my family finally bought a dog.

Now the meaning of the sentence is clear. Here's another dangling modifier:

After a two-hour nap, the train pulled into the station.

Can you identify the dangling modifier? You are correct if you think it is *After a two-hour nap*. Did the train take a two-hour nap? Who did? Here is a correction:

After a two-hour nap, I awoke just as the train pulled into the station.

E X E R C I S E S

Carefully rephrase any of the following sentences that contain misplaced or dangling modifiers. Note that many misplaced and dangling modifiers sound comical because of the confusion about what's happening in the sentence. Some sentences are correct.

Exercise 1

1. After watching TV for half an hour, the pasta was ready.
2. I found a dollar jogging around the block.
3. The children ate the cupcakes sitting in their chairs.
4. One year after becoming manager, the company closed the store.
5. That tutor works well with all of the instructors.
6. My mom's smiling face appeared with a bouquet of flowers for my birthday.
7. The usher slipped and fell on someone's program.
8. They gave directions to the driver through the window.
9. Trying to fix my clock, I broke it instead.
10. I bought a new shirt with silver buttons.

Exercise 2

1. Hanging from my rearview mirror, I proudly display my new parking pass.
2. The students went to the museum on a train.
3. After driving around the block three times, a parking space finally opened up right in front of the restaurant.
4. Denise wanted to ask her sister for a loan, but decided against it.
5. Stalled in the middle of the freeway, drivers swerved to avoid the old car.
6. She sent us a picture of her dog mounted in a gold frame.
7. Looking through my backpack, the police officer waited for me to find my driver's license.
8. They gave their mother a new television for her birthday.
9. After shouting, "Surprise!" the TV was presented to her in a huge wrapped box.
10. Without wearing sunglasses, the sun can do real damage to people's eyes.

Exercise 3

1. Five people stood behind the bench and waited for the bus.
2. The applicants listened to each of the employers taking careful notes.
3. I saw that movie with my sister three times.
4. Giving my order in a low voice, the waiter asked me to speak louder.
5. I went to a play with my theater class last week.
6. We received an invitation to their party in a pink envelope.
7. Filled with gas, we were able to drive our car all the way to San Francisco.
8. After setting the table, our guests started eating.
9. Taped to the door, I wrote a note that I would return shortly.
10. The student workers built a nice wall with gloves and safety goggles.

Exercise 4

1. Clamped down on my windshield, I saw a parking ticket.
2. Team leaders will have many responsibilities at the new camp.
3. Using red ink, mistakes can be marked more clearly.
4. They noticed a loophole reading their policy very carefully.
5. She kicked her friend in the arena by accident.
6. The teacher handed the tests back to the students with a frown.
7. Talking with the other students, class finally started.
8. We bought a cat for our friend with a fluffy tail.
9. The pre-schoolers planted seedlings dressed in farmer outfits.
10. At the age of sixteen, driving permits are easy to obtain.

Exercise 5

1. One day after turning forty, my new car broke down on the freeway.
2. Liking the rush of fresh air on his face, my brother lets his dog hang out the window of the car.

3. I ran through the park to try out my new shoes.

4. Studying in the writing lab, my comma problems disappeared.

5. Helping other people gives me great pleasure.

6. Chasing each other up and down a tree, we saw a pair of squirrels.

7. I like to watch television at night.

8. We are proud of our sister for graduating with honors.

9. Lifting the heavy television, her face turned red.

10. I enjoy collecting things from days gone by.

PROOFREADING EXERCISE

Find and correct any misplaced or dangling modifiers in the following paragraphs.

I love parades, so last year my family and I traveled to Pasadena, California, to see one of the biggest parades of all—the Tournament of Roses Parade on New Year's Day. It turned out to be even more wonderful than I expected.

Arriving one day early, the city was already crowded with people. Lots of families were setting up campsites on Colorado Boulevard. We didn't want to miss one float in the parade, so we found our own spot and made ourselves at home. When the parade began, I had as much fun watching the spectators as the parade itself. I saw children pointing at the breathtaking horses and floats sitting on their fathers' shoulders. Decorated completely with flowers or plant material, I couldn't believe how beautiful the floats were and how good they smelled.

The crowd was overwhelmed by the sights and sounds of the parade. Marching and playing their instruments with perfect precision, everyone especially enjoyed hearing the school bands. They must have practiced for the whole year to be that good.

My experience didn't end with the parade, however. After the last float had passed by, I found a twenty dollar bill walking down Colorado Boulevard. Now hanging on my wall at home, I framed it as a souvenir of my trip to the Rose Parade.

SENTENCE WRITING

Write five sentences that contain misplaced or dangling modifiers; then revise those sentences to put the modifiers where they belong. Use the examples in the explanations as models. For more practice, exchange sentences with another student and correct each other's misplaced or dangling modifiers.

Following Sentence Patterns

Sentences are built according to a few basic patterns. For proof, rearrange each of the following sets of words to form a complete statement (not a question):

> apples a ate raccoon the

> classes have many together taken we

> your in am partner I lab the

> school was to she walking

> in wonderful you look scrubs

There are only one or two possible combinations for each due to English sentence patterns. Either *A raccoon ate the apples,* or *The apples ate a raccoon,* and so on. But in each case, the verb or verb phrase makes its way to the middle of the statement, and the nouns and pronouns take their places as subjects and objects.

To understand sentence patterns, you need to know that every verb performs one of three jobs. Note that the focus is on the *double-underlined* verbs below.

The Three Jobs of Verbs

1. Verbs can show actions:

> A raccoon ate the apples.

> We have taken many classes together.

> She was walking to school.

2. Verbs can link subjects with nouns, pronouns, or adjectives that describe them:

> I am your partner in the lab.

> You look wonderful in scrubs.

3. Verbs can help other verbs form verb phrases:

> We have taken many classes together. (Without the help of *have,* the main verb would be *take* or *took.*)

> She was walking to school. (Without *was,* the main verb would be *walked.*)

Look at these sentences for more examples:

> Mel grabbed a scholarship application. (The verb *grabbed* shows Mel's action.)

His pen was empty. (The verb *was* links *pen* with its description as *empty*.)

Mel had been waiting for his grades. (The verbs *had* and *been* help the main verb *waiting* in a verb phrase.)

Knowing the three jobs a verb can perform will help you gain an understanding of the three basic sentence patterns:

SUBJECT + ACTION VERB + OBJECT PATTERN

Some action verbs must be followed by an object (a person, place, thing, or idea) that receives the action.

> S   AV   Obj
> Sylvia completed her degree. (*Sylvia completed* makes no sense unless it is followed by the object that she completed—*her degree*.)

SUBJECT + ACTION VERB (+ NO OBJECT) PATTERN

At other times, the action verb itself completes the meaning and needs no object after it.

> S   AV
> She celebrated at home with her family. (*She celebrated* makes sense alone. It does not need the two prepositional phrases—*at home* and *with her family*, which simply tell where and how she celebrated.)

SUBJECT + LINKING VERB + DESCRIPTION PATTERN

A special kind of verb that does *not* show an action is called a *linking verb*. The linking verb acts like an equal sign in a sentence: "I am student" means "I = a student" means "A student = I." These verbs link the subject with a word that describes the subject. The description can be a noun, a pronoun, or an adjective. Learn to recognize the most common linking verbs: *is, am, are, was, were, seem, feel, appear, become, look*—even *taste* and *smell* can be linking verbs at times.

> S   LV   Desc
> Sylvia is a natural writer. (*Sylvia* equals *a natural writer*.)

> S   LV   Desc
> Sylvia seems very happy. (*Very happy* describes *Sylvia*.)

NOTE—You learned on page 91 that a verb phrase includes a main verb and its helping verbs. Note that helping verbs can be used in any of the sentence patterns.

      S   AV

Sylvia is moving to Seattle. (Here the verb *is* does not link Sylvia with a description but helps the verb *moving*, which is an action verb with no object followed by a prepositional phrase—*to Seattle*.)

The following chart outlines the patterns using short sentences that you could memorize:

THREE BASIC SENTENCE PATTERNS

S   + AV + Obj

Students eat pizza.

S + AV + (no object)

They relax (with their friends).

S + LV + Desc

They are music majors.

They look creative.

These are the basic patterns for most of the clauses used in English sentences. Knowing them can help you control your sentences and improve your phrasing.

E X E R C I S E S

First, put parentheses around any prepositional phrases. Next, underline the verbs or verb phrases twice and their subjects once. Then mark the correct sentence pattern above the words: S + AV + Obj, S + AV, or S + LV + Desc. Remember that the patterns *never* mix or overlap. For example, you won't find "She took tall," which mixes an action verb (AV) with a description of the subject (Desc). But if there are two clauses, each one may have a different pattern. Check your answers after the first exercise.

Exercise 1

    1. I am a fan of televised golf.

    2. Golf eases my mind.

3. During a weekend tournament, I sit in my office at home and watch the action on a portable TV.

4. With the soft sound of the announcer's voice, I can relax and participate at the same time.

5. I use the ongoing competition as a distraction.

6. By the middle of the tournament, I have finished the bills and have started next month's budget.

7. Then I pay closer attention to the leaders.

8. Occasionally, the competition becomes really intense.

9. I especially love tied scores and extra rounds.

10. I will always be a golf fan.

Exercise 2

1. People often travel with their dogs, cats, or other pets.

2. Veterinarians offer some suggestions about traveling with pets.

3. First, a pet should be old enough to travel.

4. All pets should travel in special carriers with food and water dishes.

5. Ordinary water in a pet's dish spills easily.

6. But ice cubes in the water dish will melt slowly.

7. During long car rides, pets should have enough shade and fresh air.

8. Small pets can ride with passengers.

9. However, a loose pet could cause an accident.

10. Sedatives for pets are risky but sometimes necessary.

Exercise 3

1. We live in a world with photocopiers, scanners, and fax machines.

2. If we need copies of documents, these machines make them for us.

3. During the late 1800s, people still copied all documents by hand.

4. As a solution to this problem, Thomas Edison invented an electric pen.

5. Unlike ordinary pens, Edison's electric pen made stencils; the pen itself was inkless.

6. Its sharp tip poked holes in the paper, and later a roller spread ink over the holes.

7. The ink went though the holes onto another sheet of paper underneath.

8. And an exact copy was the result; in fact, one stencil produced many copies.

9. The first documents Edison reproduced with his electric pen were a speech from *Richard III* and the outline of a photograph of Edison's wife, Mary.

10. Although Edison sold many thousands of his electric pens at the time, only six of them have survived.

Source: Smithsonian, August 1998

Exercise 4

1. On November 4, 1922, archaeologist Howard Carter discovered the tomb of King Tutankhamen.

2. Carter had been excavating in Egypt for years without success.

3. Then he made his famous discovery.

4. With the help of his workers, Carter found the top step of a stone stairway.

5. They followed the staircase down a total of sixteen steps.

6. At the bottom, Carter and his team encountered a sealed door.

7. They had found a tomb undisturbed for thousands of years.

8. It held the personal belongings of a young Egyptian king.

9. Some of the objects were precious; others were just ordinary household effects.

10. The job of cataloging and removing the items took ten years.

Exercise 5

1. In 1993, Sears discontinued its famous catalog.

2. For 97 years, a person could buy almost anything through the Sears catalog.

3. People called it "The Big Book."

4. The final issue contained 1,500 pages of merchandise for sale.

5. In 1897, before the government regulated such things, even medicines with opium were available through the catalog.

6. In 1910, Sears manufactured its own motor car; the Sears catalog advertised the automobile for sale at a cost of just under four hundred dollars.

7. From the 1918 version of the catalog, people could purchase a kit that included building instructions and the materials for an entire house; the price was fifteen hundred dollars.

8. Sears sold more than 100,000 houses through its catalog.

9. Before 1992, all customers used mail order forms, not phone calls, to place their orders.

10. When the merchandise arrived at the catalog center, customers went and picked it up; for most of its history, the catalog offered no delivery service.

Source: Time, February 8, 1993

PARAGRAPH EXERCISE

Label the sentence patterns in the following paragraphs from *Weather,* a book by Paul E. Lehr, R. Will Burnett, and Herbert S. Zim. The sentences have been modified slightly to clarify their sentence patterns.

Put parentheses around prepositional phrases first to isolate them from the words that make up the sentence patterns. Then mark the subjects (S), the verbs (AV or LV), and any objects (Obj) after action verbs or any descriptive words (Desc) after linking verbs—*is, was, were, seem, appear.* . . . Compare your answers with those on page 292 after marking the first paragraph to check your progress. Then mark the second paragraph.

THE EARTH'S MOTIONS AND WEATHER

The earth has five motions in space. It rotates on its axis once each 24 hours, with a slow wobble like that of a top. It revolves around the sun at 18½ miles per second, making the circuit in 365¼ days. It speeds with the rest of our solar system at 12 miles per second toward the star Vega. Finally, our entire galaxy, with its billions of stars, rotates in space.

Only two of these motions affect the weather. But their effect is profound. Earth's annual trip around the sun gives us our seasons and their typical weather. Earth's daily rotation not only results in night and day; it produces the major wind belts of our earth, and each has its typical pattern of weather.

SENTENCE WRITING

Write ten sentences describing the weather today and your feelings about it. Keep your sentences short to allow clear sentence patterns to develop naturally. Then go back and label the sentence patterns you have used.

Avoiding Clichés, Awkward Phrasing, and Wordiness

CLICHÉS

A cliché is an expression that has been used so often it has lost its originality and effectiveness. Whoever first referred to the most important result of something as "the bottom line" had thought of an original way to express it, but today that expression is worn out. Most of us use an occasional cliché in speaking, but clichés have no place in writing. The good writer thinks up fresh new ways to express ideas.

Here are a few clichés. Add some more to the list.

too little too late

older but wiser

last but not least

in this day and age

different as night and day

out of this world

white as a ghost

sick as a dog

tried and true

at the top of their lungs

the thrill of victory

one in a million

busy as a bee

easier said than done

better late than never

Clichés lack freshness because the reader always knows what's coming next. Can you complete these expressions?

the agony of . . .

breathe a sigh of . . .

lend a helping . . .

odds and . . .

raining cats and . . .

as American as . . .

been there . . .

worth its weight . . .

Clichés are expressions that too many people use. Try to avoid them in your writing.

AWKWARD PHRASING

Another problem—awkward phrasing—comes from writing sentence structures that *no one* else would use because they break basic sentence patterns, omit necessary words, or use words incorrectly. Like clichés, awkward sentences might *sound* acceptable when spoken, but as polished writing, they are usually unacceptable.

AWKWARD

There should be great efforts in terms of the communication between teachers and their students.

CORRECTED

Teachers and their students must communicate.

AWKWARD

During the experiment, the use of key principles was essential to ensure the success of it.

CORRECTED

The experiment was a success. *or* We performed the experiment carefully.

AWKWARD

My favorite in the movie was when the guy with the ball ran the wrong way all the way across the field.

CORRECTED

In my favorite scene, the receiver ran across the field in the wrong direction.

WORDINESS

Good writing is concise writing. Don't use ten words if you can say it better in five. "In today's society" isn't as effective as "today," and it's a cliché. "At this point in time" could be "presently" or "now."

Another kind of wordiness comes from saying something twice. There's no need to write "in the month of August" or "9 a.m. in the morning" or "my personal opinion." August *is* a month, 9 a.m. *is* morning, and anyone's opinion *is* personal. All you need to write is "in August," "9 a.m.," and "my opinion."

Still another kind of wordiness comes from using expressions that add nothing to the meaning of the sentence. "The point is that we can't afford it" says no more than "We can't afford it."

Here is a sample wordy sentence:

The construction company actually worked on that particular building for a period of six months.

And here it is after eliminating wordiness:

The construction company worked on that building for six months.

WORDY WRITING	**CONCISE WRITING**
advance planning	planning
an unexpected surprise	a surprise
ask a question	ask
at a later date	later
basic fundamentals	fundamentals
green in color	green
but nevertheless	but (or nevertheless)
combine together	combine
completely empty	empty
down below	below
each and every	each (or every)
end result	result
fewer in number	fewer
free gift	gift
in order to	to
in spite of the fact that	although
just exactly	exactly
large in size	large
new innovation	innovation
on a regular basis	regularly
past history	history
rectangular in shape	rectangular
refer back	refer
repeat again	repeat
serious crisis	crisis
sufficient enough	sufficient (or enough)
there in person	there
two different kinds	two kinds
very unique	unique

PROOFREADING EXERCISES

The following student paragraphs contain examples of clichés, awkward phrasing, and wordiness. Revise the paragraphs so that they are concise examples of Standard Written English. When you're done, compare your revisions with the sample answers at the back of the book.

1. Technologies in this day and age are getting more and more advanced. All of the friends that I have have cell phones with cameras in them. Anyone who doesn't have one is just not up with the times. For instance, my friend was getting robbed, and he took a picture of the guy who robbed him and of his truck as he was driving away from the scene of the crime. And when the police got there, my friend showed them the picture on his phone screen, and they sent out a description of the truck and the man who robbed my friend. They arrested him in just a few hours. When it came to the trial, if my friend hadn't had his cell phone with the camera in it, it would have just been my friend's word against the man's.

2. My favorite movie ~~of all time~~ is *Back to the Future.* ~~Back to the Future is my favorite movie~~ because it is funny, ~~and it is based on a great idea.~~ The great idea that it is based on ~~is the idea of~~ traveling back to the past but trying not to change the way that things are going to turn out in the future. ~~I think that~~ Michael J. Fox and all of the other actors ~~in the movie~~ did a fantastic job, and ~~their performances will always~~ make it my all-time favorite film.

3. I've been trying to help my small son finish his first-grade homework every night, but that's easier said than done. Of course, I think that he is the smartest kid in the world, but getting him to show it takes a lot of hard work. When I do get him to sit down in front of his workbooks, he will work for a few minutes on them and then run off as soon as my back is turned. I try to tell him that when I was his age, I got in big trouble if I didn't do my homework. Unfortunately, my son's teacher just doesn't give him a sticker for that day if he doesn't do his. Stickers don't do the trick as motivators. I hope with all my heart that my son will learn the value of keeping up in school.

Correcting for Parallel Structure

Your writing will be clearer and more memorable if you use parallel structure. That is, when you write two pieces of information or any kind of list, put the items in similar form. Look at this sentence, for example:

My favorite movies are comedies, romantic, and sci-fi fantasies.

The sentence lacks parallel structure. The second item in the list, an adjective, doesn't match the other two, which are nouns. Now look at this sentence:

My favorite movies are comedies, love stories, and sci-fi fantasies.

Here the items are parallel; they are all nouns. Or you could write the following:

I like movies that make me laugh, that make me cry, and that take me away.

Again the sentence has parallel structure because all three items in the list are dependent clauses. Here are some more examples. Note how much easier it is to read the sentences with parallel structure.

WITHOUT PARALLEL STRUCTURE	WITH PARALLEL STRUCTURE
I like hiking, skiing, and to go for a sail.	I like hiking, skiing, and sailing. (all *"ing"* verbals)
The office has run out of pens, paper, ink cartridges, and we need more toner, too.	The office needs more pens, paper, ink cartridges, and toner. (all nouns)
They decided that they needed a change, that they could afford a new house, and wanted to move to Arizona.	They decided that they needed a change, that they could afford a new house, and that they wanted to move to Arizona. (all dependent clauses)

The parts of an outline should always be parallel. Following are two brief outlines about food irradiation. The parts of the outline on the *left* are not parallel. The first subtopic (I.) is a question; the other (II.) is just a noun. And the supporting points (A., B., C.) are written as nouns, verbs, and even clauses. The parts of the outline on the *right* are parallel. Both subtopics (I. and II.) are plural nouns, and all details (A., B., C.) are action verbs followed by objects.

NOT PARALLEL	PARALLEL
Food Irradiation	Food Irradiation
I. How is it good?	I. Benefits
A. Longer shelf life	A. Extends shelf life
B. Using fewer pesticides	B. Requires fewer pesticides
C. Kills bacteria	C. Kills bacteria
II. Concerns	II. Concerns
A. Nutritional value	A. Lowers nutritional value
B. Consumers are worried	B. Alarms consumers
C. Workers' safety	C. Endangers workers

Using parallel structure will make your writing more effective. Note the parallelism in these well-known quotations:

> A place for everything and everything in its place.
>
> *Isabella Mary Beeton*

> Ask not what your country can do for you; ask what you can do for your country.
>
> *John F. Kennedy*

> We hold these truths to be self-evident, that all men are created equal, that they are endowed by their creator with certain unalienable rights, that among these are Life, Liberty, and the pursuit of Happiness.
>
> *Thomas Jefferson*

EXERCISES

In the following exercises, rephrase any sentences that do not contain parallel structures.

Exercise 1

1. Taking driving lessons was exciting, but I also considered it nerve-wracking.

2. At first, I learned how to start the car, steer it, and eventually how to make the car stop smoothly.

3. Between driving lessons, I studied the manual, watched videos about driving, and I even practiced the hand signals that people use in emergencies.

4. My instructors taught me, tested me, and were encouraging to me.

5. Each one had a tip or two to share about driving.

6. Finally, my teachers decided that I had learned enough, and I was probably ready to take the test for my driver's license.

7. I arrived at the testing location, waited in the lobby for a few minutes, and then I heard someone call my name.

8. Throughout the test, I started, steered, and stopped like a professional driver.

9. The man who tested me said that I knew the rules and was saying that I must have had good teachers.

10. I sent a box of chocolates to my driving school to thank everyone for helping me become a good driver.

Exercise 2

1. If I had a choice to live in the country or if I could live in the city, I would choose the city.

2. I like being surrounded by people and to have privacy at the same time.

3. The country is too quiet for me, as well as it's too peaceful.

4. The country has dirt everywhere and flies flying in the sky.

5. The city has pollution, smog, and it's noisy, but it just feels like home.

6. Houses in the city can be different shapes, sizes, colors, and materials.

7. Most country houses seem to be small, and red or white are their main colors.

8. The country also has many animals that look the same, and they smell the same, too.

9. In the city, I enjoy visiting the zoo and get to see all sorts of exotic animals anytime I want.

10. For these reasons, choosing between country life and life in the city is easy for me.

Exercise 3

1. My brothers and I learned many important lessons from our parents.

2. They taught us the joy of reading and to get good grades in school.

3. They told us to work hard in school and that we should always think about the future.

4. Throughout our childhood, our parents were there, but mostly always working.

5. I remember my parents working all day and even at night to support our family.

6. Before I started school myself, my brothers would take me with them to the "open house" nights at their school.

7. I loved to see their work on the walls of their classrooms and reading their names on their desks.

8. The teachers seemed so friendly and like they cared about their students.

9. Since that time, I never saw school as a stressful place or wasting time.

10. By making us take care of each other and with encouragement from each other, our parents taught us the value of an education.

Exercise 4

1. I read an article in a recent issue of *Newsweek.*

2. The article is written for adults, but the subject of the article is children.

3. It explains that many kids have become frightened by information about global warming and also mentions other environmental concerns.

4. Children are watching the same scary news stories, and they see the same upsetting images that adults see.

5. One animated movie, the sequel to *Ice Age* called *The Meltdown,* even tells the story of flooding and destruction caused by melting ice.

6. Some children suffer very strong reactions of fear, and they feel helpless when they encounter such information.

7. Others ignore or they don't seem bothered by the same troubling information.

8. The *Newsweek* article makes an interesting point: as kids, some of today's parents were panicked by the idea of nuclear war; now their children worry about the changing of the climate.

9. All these issues pose serious concerns for the future, but children need help dealing with them.

10. Adults can take certain steps to help kids cope: point out the positive aspects of nature, limit exposure to frightening images or information, and adults should find ways to help these children to take positive action.

Exercise 5

Make the following discussion of handy cooking hints parallel:

1. I've been learning to cook lately, but making the same mistake is something I keep doing.

2. I always put in too much salt, or I sweeten a dish too much.

3. I've just read about a few ways to correct these cooking mistakes.

4. To correct the use of too much salt, I could add a little sugar.

5. For soups or in the case of stews, a slice of raw potato can absorb the excess salt.

6. If the salt is still too overpowering, double the dish's ingredients and don't add any new salt to the new batch.

7. Then, if there's too much food, put half in the freezer for later.

8. For sweetening with too much sugar when baking, one remedy is to add some salt.

9. For overly sweet vegetables or entrees, some vinegar could be added.

10. By following these cooking tips, I hope to make better dishes in the future.

PROOFREADING EXERCISE

Proofread the following paragraph about Carry Nation and revise it to correct any errors in parallel structure.

Carry A. Nation was an American woman who lived from 1846 to the year 1911. She is most famous for two things: her name, which helped inspire her to be an activist, and the habit that she had of wrecking any saloon or bar in sight. Carry Nation hated alcohol as well as any place that sold it. She was a powerful woman who was almost six feet tall. During her adult life, she went on a mission to destroy saloons across the country one at a time. Her crusade began in Wichita. She used a hatchet to smash saloon windows, chop up saloon furniture, she cracked saloon mirrors, and made especially sure to break as many of a saloon's liquor bottles as possible. Carry A. Nation repeated this offense from the east coast to California's coast. Whenever she landed in jail, this enterprising American sold toy replicas of her hatchet and speeches were given by her to raise money for her bail. Carry Nation took action based on her beliefs. She caused a lot of trouble for some people, but people were also helped by her. She donated funds to the poor and made sure that the wives of alcoholics were given shelter in a home that she founded.

Source: *Guess Who? A Cavalcade of Famous Americans* (Platt and Munk, 1969)

SENTENCE WRITING

Write ten sentences that use parallel structures in pairs or lists of objects, actions, locations, or ideas. You may choose your own subject or describe a dream or goal of your own and the steps you plan to take to achieve it.

Using Pronouns

Nouns name people, places, things, and ideas—such as *students, school, computers,* and *literacy*. Pronouns take the place of nouns to avoid repetition and to clarify meaning. The pronouns *they* or *them* could replace *students* and *computers*; the pronoun *it* could replace *school* and *literacy*. Personal pronouns that replace people's names or descriptions vary depending on gender and number.

Of the many kinds of pronouns, the personal pronouns cause the most difficulty because they often include two ways of identifying the same person (or people), but only one form is correct in a given situation:

SUBJECT GROUP	OBJECT GROUP
I	me
we	us
you	you
he	him
she	her
they	them
it	it

Use a pronoun from the Subject Group in two instances:

1. Before a verb as a subject:

He is my cousin. (*He* is the subject of the verb *is*.)

He is older than *I*. (Here the meaning is not written out in full. It means "*He* is older than *I* am." *I* is the subject of the verb *am*.)

Whenever you see *than* to compare two items in a sentence, ask yourself whether a verb has been left off the end of the sentence. Add the verb, and you'll automatically use the correct pronoun. In both speaking and writing, always add the verb. Instead of incorrectly saying, "She's taller than *me*," say, "She's taller than *I am*." Then you will use the correct pronoun.

2. After a linking verb (is, am, are, was, were) as a pronoun that renames the subject:

The ones who should apologize are *we*. (*We* are *the ones who should apologize*. Therefore, the pronoun from the Subject Group is used.)

The winner of the lottery was *she*. (*She* was *the winner of the lottery*. Therefore, the pronoun from the Subject Group is used.)

Modern usage allows some exceptions to this rule, however. For example, *It's me* or *It is her* (instead of the grammatically correct *It is I* and *It is she*) may be common in spoken English.

Use pronouns from the Object Group for all other purposes. In the following sentence, *me* is not the subject, nor does it rename the subject. It is the object of a preposition; therefore, it comes from the Object Group.

My boss went to lunch with Jenny and *me.*

A good way to tell whether to use a pronoun from the Subject Group or the Object Group is to leave out any extra name (and the word *and*). By leaving out *Jenny and,* you will say, *My boss went to lunch with me.* You would never say, *My boss went to lunch with I.*

My father and *I* play chess on Sundays. (*I* play chess on Sundays.)

She and her friends rented a movie. (*She* rented a movie.)

It is up to *us* students to find a solution. (It is up to *us* to find a solution.)

The coach asked Craig and *me* to carry the trophy. (Coach asked *me* to carry the trophy.)

PRONOUN AGREEMENT

Just as subjects and verbs must agree, pronouns should agree with the words they refer to. If the word referred to is singular, the pronoun should be singular. If the noun referred to is plural, the pronoun should be plural.

Each classroom has its own chalkboard.

The pronoun *its* refers to the singular noun *classroom* and therefore is singular.

Both classrooms have their own chalkboards.

The pronoun *their* refers to the plural noun *classrooms* and therefore is plural.

The same rules that we use to maintain the agreement of subjects and verbs also apply to pronoun agreement. For instance, ignore any prepositional phrases that come between the word and the pronoun that takes its place.

That *box* of supplies arrived with a huge dent in *its* side.

Boxes of supplies often arrive with huge dents in *their* sides.

The *player* with the best concentration usually beats *her* opponent.

Players with the best concentration usually beat *their* opponents.

When a pronoun refers to more than one word joined by *and,* the pronoun is plural:

> The *teacher* and the *tutors* eat *their* lunches at noon.
>
> *Joshua* and *Kendra* ate lunch in *their* usual spots at the table.

However, when a pronoun refers to more than one word joined by *or,* then the word closest to the pronoun determines its form:

> Either the teacher or the *tutors* eat *their* lunches in the classroom.
>
> Either the tutors or the *teacher* eats *his* lunch in the classroom.

It is tempting to avoid gender bias by using pairs of pronouns that include both singular forms—*he or she, his or her, him or her.* The results are often wordy and awkward:

> As an actor, *he or she* must share *his or her* emotions with an audience.
>
> If anybody calls, tell *him or her* that I'll be back soon.
>
> Somebody left *his or her* cell phone in the classroom.

Here are a few ways to eliminate gender bias and wordiness *without* using pairs of pronouns:

> As actors, *they* must share *their* emotions with an audience. (use plurals)
>
> Tell *anybody* who calls that I'll be back soon. (use general pronouns)
>
> Somebody left *a* cell phone in the classroom. (use articles—*a, an, the*)

E X E R C I S E S

Exercise 1

Circle the correct pronoun or pair of pronouns. Remember the trick of leaving out the extra name to help you decide which pronouns to use. (Note: The pairs of pronouns in this exercise refer to two *different* people, so both pronouns are necessary. However, the method of using plurals to avoid wordiness could be applied to your answers for practice. *She and I* went to the museum = *We* went to the museum.)

1. My friend Kate and (I, me) took our third field trip to a museum last week.

2. I usually enjoy these museum visits more than (she, her).

3. Last time, however, (she and I, me and her) both enjoyed it.

4. Since Kate is less of an art lover than (I, me), at first she didn't feel comfortable just standing and looking at a painting or a sculpture.

5. The first two times that (she and I, her and me) had gone museum-hopping, the gallery and choice of collection were made by (I, me).

6. The one who made the choices this time was (she, her).

7. Kate may not get into art as much as (I, me), but she sure picked a great place to visit—a beautiful new gallery on a nearby university campus.

8. Since no one else chose this gallery, Kate and (I, me) had the sun-filled rooms lined with paintings all to ourselves.

9. They were lovely in the natural light, and one huge painting even drew (she and I, her and me) to sit by it for a long time before moving on.

10. When Kate comes with (I, me) again, I will leave all decisions up to (she, her).

Exercise 2

Circle the correct pronoun or pair of pronouns. If the correct answer is *he or she, his or her,* or *him or her,* revise the sentence to avoid gender bias *and* wordiness (as explained on p. 152). Check your answers at the end of each exercise.

1. The graduation ceremony was not without (its, their) problems.

2. Each of the dogs knows (its, their) trainer's commands.

3. Many of the older students had not rehearsed (his or her, their) speeches.

4. All of the prescription drugs have (its, their) own side effects.

5. Either the property owner or the tenants will win (his or her, their) case.

6. We like to hear our canary sing (its, their) beautiful song.

7. Everyone on the men's basketball team is doing well in (his, their) classes.

8. Everyone in the class sold (his or her, their) books back to the bookstore.

9. All of the participants at the convention left (his or her, their) business cards on a tray in the lounge.

10. Either the employees or the employer gets (his or her, their) settlement notice after a dispute.

Exercise 3

Circle the correct pronoun or pair of pronouns. If the correct answer is *he or she*, *his or her*, or *him or her*, revise the sentence to avoid gender bias *and* wordiness (as explained on p. 152).

1. The judge gave my fellow jurors and (I, me) very specific instructions.

2. (He and she, Him and her) are alike in many ways.

3. I was surprised to learn that Marilyn Monroe was shorter than (I, me).

4. All of the children finished (his or her, their) projects before the open house.

5. Hotels and motels are not competitive in (its, their) pricing.

6. The one responsible for preparing the food was (I, me).

7. Each of the new teachers has (his or her, their) own set of books.

8. The mixed-doubles tennis teams will continue (his or her, their) tournament.

9. Everyone at the polling place had (his or her, their) own opinion and expressed it with (his or her, their) vote.

10. When it comes to plants, no one knows more than (he, him).

Exercise 4

Circle the correct pronoun or pair of pronouns. If the correct answer is *he or she*, *his or her*, or *him or her*, revise the sentence to avoid gender bias *and* wordiness (as explained on p. 152).

1. Robert asked, "Are you taking as many classes as (I, me)?"

2. I like my real estate agent; it was (she, her) who called about the property.

3. Each student needs to buy (his or her, their) textbooks before classes begin.

4. At work, I always speak on the phone correctly by saying, "This is (she, her)."

5. All of the petals had fallen off (its, their) flowers.

6. Either the informant or the police officers will give (his or her, their) testimony.

7. My parents and (I, me) were counting the money from our garage sale.

8. When we get home, our dog Digit always jumps up on my brother or (I, me).

9. I bought the TV with advanced features listed in (its, *the* their) description.

10. Everybody chose a lottery ticket and scratched off (its, their *the*) results.

Exercise 5

Circle the correct pronoun or pair of pronouns. Again, if the correct answer is *he or she*, *his or her*, or *him or her*, revise the sentence to avoid gender bias *and* wordiness (as explained on p. 152).

1. The Hascoms or their neighbor on the right will need to relocate (his or her, their) driveway.

2. We sent him an arrangement of flowers with a card in (its, *the* their) foliage.

3. The credit card slips can be signed by my daughter or (I, me).

4. The students in that group got a lot of (its, their) work done.

5. He took the lenses out of the frame and checked (its, *they* their) prescription.

6. The winners of the contest were (they, them).

7. Few people have a larger collection of stamps than (he, him).

8. The judge sent the lawyers and (we, us) jurors a message.

9. Every person has to use (his or her, their) own password to access the computers in the lab.

10. The rejected applicants asked the committee to reconsider (its, their) decision.

PROOFREADING EXERCISE

The following paragraph contains several incorrect pronouns. Find and correct the errors.

I gave my friend James some advice at work the other day. The boss assigned James and I to different supervisors, and I advised James to ask his supervisor for a raise. Right before I gave him the advice, I said, "You and me have been friends for a long time, and you're not going to blame me if my advice doesn't work, right?" He assured me that the only person whose advice he would follow was me. I made the mistake of believing him. Later I noticed that him and his supervisor were talking in the lounge. James was following my advice, and I knew that the one that would be responsible for the outcome was me. Unfortunately, my advice backfired when James followed it. As a result, James and me are still coworkers, but we are no longer friends.

SENTENCE WRITING

Write ten sentences in which you compare yourself to someone else in terms of athletic ability or creativity. Then check that your pronouns are grammatically correct and that they agree with the words they replace.

Avoiding Shifts in Person

To understand what "person" means when using pronouns, imagine a conversation between three people. The *first* person would speak using "I." That person would call the *second* person "you." And when those two talked of a *third* person, they would use "he, she, or they." Here are more personal pronouns arranged by person:

First person—*I, me, my, we, us, our, mine*

Second person—*you, your, yours*

Third person—*he, him, his, she, her, they, them, their, one, anyone, it, its*

Although it is possible (and at times necessary) to use all three groups of pronouns in a paper, most writers try not to shift from one group to another without a good reason. Such errors are called shifts in person.

The following paragraph includes unnecessary shifts in person:

Few people know how to manage *their* time. *We* don't need to be efficiency experts to realize that *everyone* could get a lot more done by budgeting *his* or *her* time more wisely. Nor do *you* need to work very hard to become more organized.

To correct the shifts in person, you could use only *first-person* pronouns:

Few of *us* know how to manage *our* time. *We* don't need to be efficiency experts to realize that *we* could get a lot more done by budgeting *our* time more wisely. Nor do *we* need to work very hard to become more organized.

Or you could address the reader directly and use only *second-person* pronouns:

You are not alone if you don't know how to manage *your* time. *You* don't need to be an efficiency expert to realize that *you* could get a lot more done by budgeting *your* time more wisely. Nor do *you* need to work very hard to become more organized.

Finally, you could correct the shifts by using only *third-person* pronouns:

Few people know how to manage *their* time. *One* does not need to be an efficiency expert to realize that *everyone* could get a lot more done by budgeting *his* or *her* time more wisely. Nor does *anyone* need to work very hard to become more organized. (Note that "*his* or *her*" could then be deleted to avoid using this wordy pair of pronouns. See p. 152.)

PROOFREADING EXERCISES

Which of the following student paragraphs shift *unnecessarily* between first, second, and third person? In those that do, revise the sentences to eliminate such shifting. One of the paragraphs is already correct.

1. We have all seen images of astronauts floating in their space capsules, eating food from little silver freeze-dried cube-shaped pouches, and sipping Tang out of special straws made to function in the weightlessness of space. Now you can buy that same food and eat it yourself on earth. NASA has gone online with a site called thespacestore.com, and all one has to do is point and click and get these space munchies delivered to your door. If people want NASA souvenirs or clothing, they can purchase them at the same site.

2. People who drive need to be more aware of pedestrians. We can't always gauge what someone walking down the street will do. You might think that all pedestrians will keep walking forward in a crosswalk, but one might decide to turn back if he or she forgot something. You could run into him or her if that happens. A person's life could be affected in an instant. We all should slow down and be more considerate of others.

3. Scientists and others are working on several inventions that have not been perfected yet. Some of these developments seem like complete science fiction, but they're not. Each of them is in the process of becoming a real new technology. It's hard to imagine eating meat grown on plants or in petri dishes. Scientists will feed the plants artificially made "blood." Researchers are also working to produce animals (perhaps even humans) grown in artificial wombs. The most interesting development is selective amnesia (memory loss). Patients will be able to ask their doctors to erase painful memories as a mental-health tool. And, of course, computers will gain more and more personality traits to become more like human beings.

Source: The Futurist, August–September 1998, and Current Science, April 6, 2007

REVIEW OF SENTENCE STRUCTURE ERRORS

One sentence in each pair contains an error. Read both sentences carefully before you decide. Then write the letter of the *incorrect* sentence in the blank. Try to name the error and correct it if you can. You may find any of these errors:

awk	awkward phrasing
cliché	overused expression
dm	dangling modifier
frag	fragment
mm	misplaced modifier
pro	incorrect pronoun
pro agr	pronoun agreement
ro	run-on sentence
shift	shift in time or person
s-v agr	subject-verb agreement error
verb	incorrect verb form
wordy	wordiness
//	not parallel

1. _____ **A.** Family cruises have become a very popular way of taking a vacation.

   _____ **B.** They're suppose to be relaxing for parents and exciting for children.

2. _____ **A.** My speech professor is much luckier than me.

   _____ **B.** She has won two big prizes in the lottery.

3. _____ **A.** Community colleges offer day, night, and weekend classes.

   _____ **B.** I have taken day and night classes but never give up my weekends.

4. _____ **A.** As the teacher entered the classroom, he removed his Bluetooth headset and his backpack.

   _____ **B.** He put them on the podium and he immediately started lecturing.

5. _____ **A.** We always lock the door to the language lab.

   _____ **B.** Because too many people wander in if we don't.

6. _____ **A.** In today's society, people usually mind their own business.

   _____ **B.** If I see someone who really needs help, I will get involved.

7. _____ **A.** The library renewed the books that my friend and me had checked out.

   _____ **B.** Now we have enough time to finish our research papers.

8. _____ **A.** The store was offering a free gift of a coffee maker.

   _____ **B.** My uncle gave the coffee maker as a gift for his son's wedding.

9. _____ **A.** My essay is full of interesting details and had a strong thesis.

   _____ **B.** I don't understand why I have to revise it.

10. _____ **A.** The band members arrived in a stretch limo and took their guitars out of the trunk.

   _____ **B.** Everyone at the party had a shocked look on their faces.

11. _____ **A.** Some of the new furniture have scratches on it already.

   _____ **B.** The delivery company should have been more careful.

12. _____ **A.** Water bottles come in all sizes now.

   _____ **B.** From the size of a baby bottle to the size of a magnum of champagne.

13. _____ **A.** We walked around the park before dinner last night.

   _____ **B.** Hanging from the top of a tree, we saw a beautiful metallic kite.

14. _____ **A.** Shawn and Sharon are twin cousins of mine; they are both talented musicians.

   _____ **B.** However, there is one big difference between them Shawn is not as ambitious as Sharon is.

15. _____ **A.** Whenever I plan a whole meal around a single specific ingredient, the different dishes themselves don't always taste good.

   _____ **B.** For example, I like the flavor of curry with chicken but not with vegetables.

PROOFREADING EXERCISE

Find and correct the sentence structure errors in the following essay.

Let's Get Technical

In my child development classes, I'm learning about ways to keep girls interested in technology. Studies shows that girls and boys begin their school years equally interested in technology. After elementary school is the time that computers are less of an interest for girls. Because boys keep up with computers and other technology throughout their educations more than girls, they get ahead in these fields. Experts have come up with some suggestions for teachers and parents of girls to help them.

Girls need opportunities to experiment with computers. Girls spend time on computers, but they usually just do their assignments then they log off. Since computer games and programs are often aimed at boys. Parents and teachers need to buy computer products that will challenge girls not only in literature and art, but also in math, science, and business is important.

Another suggestion is to put computers in places where girls can socialize. One reason many boys stay interested in technology is that it is something he can do on his own. Girls tend to be more interested in working with others and to share activities. When computer terminals are placed close to one another, girls work at them for much longer periods of time.

Finally, parents and teachers need to be aware that nothing beats positive role models. Teach them about successful women in the fields of business, scientific, and technology. And the earlier we start interesting girls in these fields, the better.

Punctuation and Capital Letters

Period, Question Mark, Exclamation Point, Semicolon, Colon, Dash

Every mark of punctuation should help the reader. Here are the rules for six marks of punctuation. The first three (. ? !) you have known for a long time and probably have no trouble with. The rule about semicolons you learned when you studied independent clauses and the ways to correct run-on sentences (pp. 83–85). The rules about the colon and the dash may be less familiar.

Put a period (.) at the end of a sentence that makes a statement and after most abbreviations.

> The heavy rain caused many traffic delays. (statement)
>
> Oct.   Tues.   in.   pgs.   ft.   Ave.   est.   inc. (abbreviations)

Put a question mark (?) after a direct question but not after an indirect one.

> Do you know if we can use our notes during the test? (direct question)
>
> I wonder if we can use our notes during the test. (indirect question)

In sentences with quotation marks, put the question mark *outside* the quote marks if the sentence itself is a question but *inside* if the quotation or title is a question.

> Did you actually say, "I quit"? (sentence is a question)
>
> I asked my boss, "Do you want me to quit?" (quotation is a question)
>
> She always sings "Do You Know the Way to San Jose?" (title is a question)

Put an exclamation point (!) after an expression to emphasize it or to show loud sounds or strong emotions. This mark is used mostly in dialogue and informal correspondence. The same rule about using quotation marks with question marks applies to using them with exclamation points.

Let's go to a movie later. I need to escape from reality!

We finally memorized Robert Frost's poem " The Road Not Taken"!

Someone in the hallway yelled, "I can't believe I got an A!"

Put a semicolon (;) between two independent clauses in a sentence unless they are joined by one of the connecting words called *fanboys* (*for, and, nor, but, or, yet, so*).

My mother cosigned for a loan; now I have my own car.

Teaching is not a glamorous job; however, people will always need teachers.

To be sure that you are using a semicolon correctly, see if a period and capital letter can be used in its place. If they can, you are putting the semicolon in the right spot.

My mother cosigned for a loan. Now I have my own car.

Teaching is not a glamorous job. However, people will always need teachers.

Put a colon (:) after a complete statement that introduces one of the following elements: a name, a list, a quotation, or an explanation.

The company announced its Employee-of-the-Month: Lee Jones. (The complete statement before the colon introduces the name that follows it.)

That truck comes in the following colors: red, black, blue, and silver. (The complete statement before the colon introduces the list that follows it.)

That truck comes in red, black, blue, and silver. (*The truck comes in* is not a complete statement, so the sentence should not include a colon.)

Thoreau had this to say about time: "Time is but the stream I go a-fishing in." (The complete statement before the colon introduces the quotation that follows it.)

Thoreau said, "Time is but the stream I go a-fishing in." (The signal phrase *Thoreau said* leads directly into the quotation; therefore, no colon—just a comma—comes between them. See p. 226 for more about signal phrases.)

Use dashes (—) to isolate inserted information, to signal an abrupt change of thought, or to emphasize what follows. Dashes are always optional, and they can be used to replace commas, semicolons, and colons.

Lee Jones—the Employee-of-the-Month—gets his own special parking space.

I found out today—or was it yesterday?—that I have inherited a fortune.

We have exciting news for you—we're moving!

E X E R C I S E S

Exercises 1 and 2

Add to these sentences the necessary end punctuation (periods, question marks, and exclamation points). The semicolons, colons, dashes, and commas used within the sentences are correct and do not need to be changed. Pay close attention to them, however, to help with Exercises 3–5.

Exercise 1

1. My friend Kristine and I arrived early for work yesterday; it was a very important day

2. We had worked late the night before, perfecting our presentation

3. The boss had given us an opportunity to train our colleagues in the use of a new computer program

4. I wondered how the other workers would react when they heard that we had been chosen to teach them

5. Would they be pleased or annoyed

6. Kristine and I worked hard on the visual aid to accompany our workshop: a slideshow of sample screens from the program

7. Kristine thought our workshop should end with a test; however, I didn't think that was a good idea

8. I knew that our fellow employees—at least *some* of them—would not want us to test them

9. By the time we ended our presentation, we both realized that I had been right

10. Now our co-workers see us as a couple of experts—not a couple of know-it-alls

Exercise 2

1. People in Australia have been asking themselves a question: why are some dolphins carrying big sponges around on their heads

2. First, it was just one dolphin; now many dolphins are doing it

3. Marine biologists all over the world have been trying to understand this unusual sponge-carrying behavior

4. They wonder about whether the sponges decrease the dolphins' ability to maneuver under water

5. If they do, then why would the dolphins sacrifice this ability

6. The dolphins might be using the sponges for a very important reason: to help them find food

7. Some scientists think that the sponges may protect the dolphins' beaks in some way

8. The sponges might indicate position in the social order; that's another explanation

9. Or the dolphins could be imitating each other—a kind of dolphin "fad," in other words

10. Only one group of experts knows whether these sponges are hunting tools or just fashion statements; that is the dolphins themselves

Source: Discover, March 1998 and January 2006

Exercises 3 and 4

Add any necessary semicolons, colons, and dashes to these sentences. The commas and end punctuation do not need to be changed. Some sentences are correct.

Exercise 3

1. Ralph Waldo Emerson gave us this famous bit of advice "Build a better mousetrap, and the world will beat a path to your door."

2. People have not stopped inventing mousetraps in fact, there are more U.S. patents for mousetraps than for any other device.

3. Some are simple some are complicated, and some are just weird.

4. Nearly fifty new patents for machines to kill mice are awarded every year perhaps thanks to Mr Emerson's advice.

5. The most enduring mousetrap was designed by John Mast it is the one most of us picture when we think of a mousetrap a piece of wood with a spring-loaded bar that snaps down on the mouse just as it takes the bait.

6. John Mast's creation received Patent #744,379 in 1903 since then no other patented mousetrap has done a better job.

7. There is a long list of technologies that other inventions have used to trap mice electricity, sonar, lasers, super glues, etc.

8. One patented mousetrap was built in the shape of a multilevel house with several stairways however, its elaborate design made it impractical and expensive.

9. In 1878, one person invented a mousetrap for travelers it was a box that was supposed to hold men's removable collars and at night catch mice, but it was not a success.

10. Who would want to put an article of clothing back into a box used to trap a mouse?

Source: American Heritage, October 1996

Exercise 4

1. Have you ever heard of Vinnie Ream?

2. This young woman a very controversial figure in Washington, D.C. began her career as a sculptor in 1863 at the age of sixteen.

3. Miss Ream was a student of the famous sculptor Clark Mills he is perhaps best-known for his statue of Andrew Jackson located across from the White House.

4. Vinnie Ream started to work with Mills in his studio in the basement of the Capitol building soon members of Congress were volunteering to sit for Miss Ream, and she sculpted busts of them.

5. Her fame and reputation grew in the late 1860s that's when she was awarded a ten-thousand-dollar commission to create a life-size statue of Abraham Lincoln.

6. Vinnie Ream had known Lincoln in fact, before his assassination, President Lincoln would allow Miss Ream to sit in his office within the White House and work on a bust of him as he carried out the business of running the country.

7. Ream's intimate observation of Lincoln at work affected her design of Lincoln's posture and facial expression for her statue of him.

8. Vinnie Ream's relationships and the works she produced were not accepted by everyone Ream's youth and physical beauty led to much of this harsh criticism.

9. Some people questioned her motives others even questioned her abilities.

10. Ream prospered in spite of the jealous accusations of others and often demonstrated her sculpting abilities in public to prove that she did her own work.

Source: Smithsonian, August 2000

Exercise 5

Add the necessary periods, question marks, exclamation points, semicolons, colons, and dashes. Any commas in the sentences are correct and should not be changed.

1. I just read an article that connected two things that I would never have thought went together the Old West, with its miners and saloon life, and Shakespeare, with his poetry and politics

2. People who had traveled out West on the Oregon Trail brought their Shakespeare books and shared them with a willing audience the unruly population of the mining camps and tiny towns of the West

3. Mountain men like Jim Bridger paid others who could read to act out Shakespeare's plays then he memorized the speeches and performed them for others

4. Theaters staged productions of the tragedies of *Hamlet, Othello,* and *Romeo and Juliet* to the delight of the Western crowds however, if they weren't pleased with an actor, theatergoers threw vegetables as large as pumpkins at times to get the actor off the stage

5. Crowds likewise rewarded good acting, which was lively and not overly refined spectators in gold mining camps threw nuggets and bags of gold on stage if they liked a performance

6. Oral storytelling had always been popular in the West therefore, people of the time embraced Shakespeare's language without thinking of it as intellectual or sophisticated

7. In the mid-1800s, people across the country had strong opinions about how Shakespeare should be performed there was a riot at one New York City theater concerning a particularly snobby performance of *Macbeth*

8. The fight moved from the theater into the streets more than twenty people were killed, and a hundred were injured

9. The casting of characters in Western performances included everything from all-male casts in the mining camps to a female Juliet performing without a real Romeo a stuffed dummy played his part

10. There was even a little girl named Anna Maria Quinn just six years old who played Hamlet at the Metropolitan Theatre in San Francisco in 1854

Source: Smithsonian, August 1998

PROOFREADING EXERCISE

Find and correct the punctuation errors in the following paragraph. All of the errors involve periods, question marks, exclamation points, semicolons, colons, and dashes. Any commas used within the sentences are correct and should not be changed.

Who hasn't seen one of those inflatable jumping rooms at a park or in the front yard of a house hosting a child's birthday party. These jumpers are popular for several reasons; children can have fun playing with their friends—adults can keep an eye on many children at once, and everyone gets a lot of exercise. In 2007, a freak accident occurred on a beach in Hawaii it involved an inflated castle-shaped bouncer, a few brave adults, and several lucky children. As the kids bounced around as usual, a strong gust of wind—a whirlwind, according to one witness; lifted the castle straight up into the air and knocked all but two of the children out instantly. Then the castle bounced on the sand once before flying fifty yards out into the ocean. As the castle flew, another child dropped out of it luckily, he was unhurt. Many adults both lifeguards and others jumped in to save the two-year-old girl who remained inside the castle. One man was able to reach her incredibly, she was not seriously injured.

Source: The Honolulu Advertiser, June 10, 2007

SENTENCE WRITING

Write ten sentences of your own that use periods, question marks, exclamation points, semicolons, colons, and dashes correctly. Imitate the sentences used in the explanations or in Exercise 1.

Comma Rules 1, 2, and 3

Commas and other punctuation marks guide the reader through your sentence structures in the same way that signs guide drivers on the highway. Imagine what effects misplaced or incorrect road signs would have. From now on, try not to use any comma without a good reason for it.

Among all of the uses of commas, six are most important. If you learn these six rules, your writing will improve. You have already read about the first rule on pages 84–85.

1. **Put a comma before** *for, and, nor, but, or, yet, so* **(remember these seven words as the** *fanboys***) when they connect two independent clauses.**

   We all brought our essays to class, and the teacher congratulated us.

   My math book will be very expensive, so I'll look for a good deal online.

If you use a comma without a *fanboys* between two independent clauses, the result is an error called a **comma splice.**

   Dogs are people's best friends, people are cats' best friends. (comma splice)

   Dogs are people's best friends, *and* people are cats' best friends. (corrected)

Before using a comma, be sure one of the *fanboys* actually connects two independent clauses and not just two words or phrases. The following sentence contains only one independent clause with two verbs. Since no subject follows the *fanboys*, the sentence does not require a comma:

   My <u>dog</u> <u><u>curled</u></u> up under my chair and <u><u>waited</u></u> for me to finish my essay.

Now compare the previous sentence with this one that does require a comma:

   My <u>cat</u> <u><u>was</u></u> hungry, and <u>she</u> <u><u>meowed</u></u> for me to finish my essay.

2. **Use a comma to separate items in a series, date, or address.**

   Students in literature classes read short stories, poems, and plays.

   Today I walked to school, biked to work, and took a train to the movies.

Occasionally, writers leave out the comma before the *and* connecting the last two items in a series, but it is needed to separate all of the items equally.

   If a date or address is used in a sentence, put a comma after every item, including the last.

   My father was born on August 19, 1961, in Mesa, Arizona, and grew up there.

   Shelby lived in Lima, Peru, for two years.

When only the month and year are used in a date, no commas are needed.

> My aunt graduated from Yale in May 2009.

3. **Put a comma after an introductory word, phrase, or dependent clause that begins a sentence and before a tag question or comment that ends it.**

> Finally, he was able to get through to his insurance company. (introductory word)
>
> During her last performance, the actress fell and broke her leg. (introductory phrase)
>
> Whenever I finish my homework, I feel satisfied. (introductory dependent clause)
>
> The new chairs aren't very comfortable, are they? (tag question)
>
> My professor said he needed to ruminate, whatever that means. (tag comment)

EXERCISES

Add commas to the following sentences according to the Comma Rules 1, 2, and 3. Any other punctuation already in the sentences is correct. Check your answers after the first set.

Exercise 1

Add commas according to Comma Rule 1. Put a comma before a *fanboys* when it connects two independent clauses. Some sentences may be correct.

1. Scientists have been studying the human face, and they have been able to identify five thousand distinct facial expressions.

2. Researchers at the University of California in San Francisco have identified and numbered every action of the human face.

3. Winking is action number forty-six and we do it with the facial muscle that surrounds the eye.

4. People around the world make the same basic facial expressions.

5. These facial expressions are universally understood, but different societies have different rules about showing their emotions.

6. The smile is one of the most powerful expressions, and it can change the way we feel.

7. A real smile is someone's way of showing genuine happiness ,and our brains react by producing a feeling of pleasure.

8. In contrast, people give us polite imitation smiles all day, and our brains show no change.

9. Even babies have been shown to smile one way for strangers and another way for their mothers.

10. A smile also wins the long-distance record ,for facial expressions for it can be seen from as far away as several hundred feet.

Source: Psychology Today, October 1998

Exercise 2

Add commas according to Comma Rule 2. Use a comma to separate three or more items in a series. If a date or address is used, put a comma after each item, including the last. Some sentences may not need any commas.

1. An eleven-year-old boy from Kansas City Missouri recently took an unplanned 200-mile trip in the family car.

2. His only previous experience with driving had been running a tractor and pulling the car out of the garage for his parents.

3. On October 5 2004 he got in the family's 1995 Chevrolet and took off.

4. He started in Kansas City drove to Bethany continued through Macon County and ended up in Callao.

5. The boy's adventures along the way included driving 85 miles-an-hour running out of gas getting help from a group of construction workers and finally locking himself out of his car.

6. He found a post office nearby and went in to ask for help.

7. The boy's family had meanwhile noticed that their son their car and their keys were missing.

8. His parents called the police and waited.

9. They didn't have to wait for long.

10. Soon the police called to say that the boy had been located that he was unharmed and that the parents could pick him up in Callao.

Source: CNN.com, October 9, 2004

Exercise 3

Add commas according to Comma Rule 3. Put a comma after introductory words, phrases, or dependent clauses, and before tag questions or comments at the end.

1. Whenever I ask my friend Wendy a computer-related question, I end up regretting it.

2. Once she gets started, Wendy is unable to stop talking about computers.

3. When I needed her help, the last time my printer wasn't working.

4. Instead of just solving the problem, Wendy went on and on about print settings and font choices that I could be using.

5. When she gets like this, her face lights up, and I feel bad for not wanting to hear the latest news on software upgrades, e-mail programs, and hardware improvements.

6. Even though I feel guilty, I know that I am the normal one.

7. I even pointed her problem out to her by asking, "You can't control yourself can you?"

8. With a grin, she just kept trying to fix my printer.

9. Since Wendy always solves my problem, I should be grateful.

10. When I ask for Wendy's help in the future, I plan to listen and try to learn something.

Exercise 4

Add commas according to the first three comma rules.

1. I've been reading Helen Keller's autobiography and I have learned a lot more about her.

2. I originally thought that Keller was born deaf and blind, but I was wrong.

3. When she was about two years old Keller developed a terrible fever.

4. The family doctor believed that Keller was dying and prepared her family for the worst.

5. Not long after the doctor shared his fears with her family Keller recovered from her fever.

6. Unfortunately the high fever left Keller without the ability to see to hear or to speak.

7. The only tools that Keller had left were her sense of touch her active mind and her intense curiosity.

8. With her teacher Anne Sullivan's constant assistance Keller eventually learned to read to write and to speak several languages.

9. Keller was lucky to have so many people who loved and cared for her.

10. Helen Keller never stopped learning, and her story inspires me to do my best.

Exercise 5

Add commas according to the first three comma rules.

1. Gold is amazing isn't it?

2. Unlike metals that change their appearance after contact with water oil and other substances gold maintains its shine and brilliant color under almost any circumstances.

3. When a miner named James Marshall found gold in the dark soil of California in 1848 the gold rush began.

4. The piece of gold that Marshall discovered was only about the size of a child's fingernail but it meant that there was more to be found.

5. Before the gold rush San Francisco was a small town called Yerba Buena.

6. The town underwent a name change and gained thousands of citizens in search of gold.

7. Gold is actually present all over the world but the biggest nugget to be found so far came from a location on the Potomac River.

8. This chunk of gold is as big as a yam and it is on display at the National Museum of Natural History.

9. Some people have become rich directly because of gold and some have become rich indirectly because of gold.

10. For example if it had not been for California's gold rush Levi Strauss would not have had any customers and the world would not have blue jeans.

Source: Smithsonian, July 1998

PROOFREADING EXERCISE

Add commas to the following paragraph according to the first three comma rules:

Like other people who surf the Web regularly I like to keep up with important and interesting world events. In April 2010 an online friend told me about a contest that was going on in Europe. It's a yearly song contest called Eurovision and countries from across Europe participate in it. It began in 1956 as a way for European nations to come together share their songs and celebrate their unique cultures. To participate in the Eurovision contest countries pick a song and a singer to represent them. Then they make song videos to show to the other countries. All participating countries can vote during the competition but they can't vote for their own country's song. That seems fair doesn't it? On May 29 2010 the Eurovision Song Contest Final was held in Oslo Norway and the winning country was Germany with its song called "Satellite" sung by 19-year-old Lena Meyer-Landrut. Because Germany won in 2010 it will host the Eurovision Song Contest in 2011. People who don't live in Europe can watch the competition and learn more about the Eurovision Song Contest on www.eurovision.tv.

SENTENCE WRITING

Combine the following sets of sentences in different ways using all of the first three comma rules. You may need to reorder the details and change the phrasing. Compare your answers with those at the back of the book.

I drive to school alone every day.

I would consider carpooling.

My car alarm goes off.

I don't even look out the window anymore.

Melanie and Kurt are currently software developers.

They used to be dancers.

Now they both want to get back in shape.

My birthday is on the twenty-fifth of May.

My anniversary is on the twenty-fifth of May.

I have a special fondness for the twenty-fifth of May.

I graduated from high school on the twenty-fifth of May.

Comma Rules 4, 5, and 6

The next three comma rules all involve using pairs of commas to enclose what you might call "scoopable" elements. Scoopable elements are extra words, phrases, and clauses that can be scooped out of the middle of a sentence because they are not necessary to understand its meaning. Notice that the comma **(,)** is shaped somewhat like the tip of an ice cream scoop. Let this similarity help you remember to use commas to enclose *scoopable* elements. Two commas are used as they are here, one before and one after, to show where scoopable elements begin and end.

4. Put commas around the name of a person spoken to.

> Did you know, Danielle, that you left your backpack at the library?

> We regret to inform you, Mr. Davis, that your policy has been canceled.

5. Put commas around expressions that interrupt the flow of the sentence (such as *however, moreover, therefore, of course, by the way, on the other hand, I believe,* or *I think*).

> I know, of course, that I have missed the deadline.

> They will try, therefore, to use the rest of their time wisely.

> Today's exam, I think, was only a practice test.

Read the previous examples *aloud,* and you'll hear how these expressions surrounded by commas interrupt the flow of the sentence. Sometimes such expressions flow smoothly into the sentence and don't need commas around them.

> Of course he checked to see if there were any rooms available.

> We therefore decided to stay out of it.

> I think you made the right decision.

Remember that, when a word like *however* comes between two independent clauses, you should put a semicolon before it. (See p. 83.) It should also have a comma after it, following Comma Rule 3, to show that *however* introduces the second independent clause. (See p. 171.)

> The bus was late; *however,* we still made it to the museum before it closed.

> I am improving my study habits; *furthermore,* I am getting better grades.

> She was interested in journalism; *therefore,* she took a job at a local newspaper.

> I spent hours studying for the test; *finally,* I felt prepared.

Thus, you've seen a word like *however* used in three ways:

1. as a "scoopable" word that interrupts the flow of the sentence (needs commas around it)

2. as a word that flows smoothly within the sentence (needs no punctuation)

3. as a connecting word between two independent clauses (needs a semicolon before and a comma after it)

6. Put commas around additional information that is not needed in a sentence.

Certain additional information is "scoopable" and should be surrounded by commas. Look at the following sentence that includes additional information about its subject:

Maxine Taylor, who organized the fund-raiser, will introduce the candidates.

The clause *who organized the fund-raiser* is extra information in the sentence. Without it, we still know exactly who the sentence is about and what she is going to do: "Maxine Taylor will introduce the candidates." Therefore, the additional information is surrounded by commas to show that it is scoopable. Now read the following sentence:

The person who organized the fund-raiser will introduce the candidates.

The clause *who organized the fund-raiser* is not extra but necessary in this sentence. Without it, the subject would be unclear: "The person will introduce the candidates." The reader would not know *which person*. The clause *who organized the fund-raiser* is not scoopable, so there are no commas around it. Here's another example:

Avatar, James Cameron's film, was nominated for Best Picture.

The additional information *James Cameron's film* is scoopable. It could be left out without making the subject unclear: "Avatar was nominated for Best Picture." Therefore, two commas surround the scoopable information to show that it could be taken out. But here is the same sentence with the information reversed:

James Cameron's film Avatar was nominated for Best Picture.

In this sentence, the title of the movie is not additional, but necessary. Without it, the sentence would read, "James Cameron's film was nominated for Best Picture." The reader would not know which of Cameron's many films was nominated for Best Picture. Therefore, Avatar is not scoopable, and commas should not be used around it.

E X E R C I S E S

Surround any "scoopable" elements with commas according to Comma Rules 4, 5, and 6. Any commas already in the sentences follow Comma Rules 1, 2, and 3. Some sentences may be correct. Check your answers after the first set.

Exercise 1

1. People who own cats know that these pets often bring their owners unwelcome surprises.

2. Cats bring dead mice or birds to their owners and expect them to be pleased.

3. Cats become confused when their owners react angrily, not happily, to these "presents."

4. Desmond Morris, a renowned animal expert, explains this misunderstood behavior in his book, Catwatching.

5. Morris explains that, the cats that most frequently bring prey to their owners are female cats without kittens.

6. These cats have a strong instinct to teach their kittens how to hunt for food.

7. In the absence of kittens, these cats treat their owners as the next best thing, kitten replacements.

8. The first step in the process of teaching "kittens" how to hunt the one cat owners hate most is sharing the results of the hunt with them.

9. The owners' reaction, which usually involves yelling and disappointment, should include praise and lots of petting.

10. Cat owners who do understand their pets will be flattered next time they see what the cat dragged in.

Exercise 2

1. Paula who left at intermission missed the best part of the play.

2. Anyone who left at intermission missed the best part of the play.

3. Our teacher posted the results of the test that we took last week.

4. Our teacher posted the results of the midterm which we took last week.

5. The math teacher Mr. Simon looks a lot like the English teacher Mr. Simon.

6. Mr. Simon the math teacher looks a lot like Mr. Simon the English teacher.

7. My clothes dryer which has an automatic shut-off switch is safer than yours which doesn't.

8. An appliance that has an automatic shut-off switch is safer to use than one that doesn't.

9. Students who ask a lot of questions usually do well on their exams.

10. John and Brenda who ask a lot of questions usually do well on their exams.

Exercise 3

1. This year's photo directory I believe turned out a little better than last year's.

2. I believe this year's photo directory turned out a little better than last year's.

3. There were I think still a few problems.

4. I think there were still a few problems.

5. The employee whose picture is at the top of our page is my supervisor, but he's not listed at the bottom.

6. My supervisor whose picture is at the top of our page is wearing his name tag, but he's not listed at the bottom.

7. Ms. Tracy the photographer who took the pictures needed to help people with their poses.

8. The photographer who took the pictures needed to help people with their poses.

9. And no one it seems had time to look in a mirror.

10. And it seems that no one had time to look in a mirror.

Exercise 4

1. We hope of course that people will continue to vote in elections.
2. Of course we hope that people will continue to vote in elections.
3. The people who usually volunteer their house as a polling place may have to install new equipment.
4. The Fosters who usually volunteer their house as a polling place may have to install new equipment.
5. They may therefore decide not to participate in upcoming elections.
6. Therefore they may decide not to participate in upcoming elections.
7. The voting booth a small cubicle where each person casts a vote will probably become more high-tech.
8. The small cubicle where each person casts a vote will probably become more high-tech.
9. We trust that no one will attempt to influence our thoughts there.
10. No one we trust will attempt to influence our thoughts there.

Exercise 5

1. Jim Henson, creator of the Muppets, began his television career in the mid-1950s.
2. He was, it seems, eager to be on TV, and there was an opening for someone who worked with puppets.
3. Henson and a buddy of his quickly fabricated a few puppets including one called Pierre the French Rat, and they got the job.
4. Henson's next project, Sam and Friends, also starred puppets.
5. Sam and Friends was a live broadcast lasting only five minutes; however, it was on two times a day and ran for six years.
6. Kermit the Frog, the character which we now associate with *Sesame Street*, was part of the cast of *Sam and Friends*.
7. Henson provided the voice and animated the movements of Kermit and a few others from the beginning, and he worked with Frank Oz, who helped round out the cast of Muppet characters.

8. In 1969, the Muppets moved to *Sesame Street;* however, they graduated to their own prime-time program, *The Muppet Show*, in the late 1970s.

9. At the high point of its popularity worldwide, more than 200 million people adults and children tuned in to a single broadcast of *The Muppet Show*.

10. Jim Henson continued as a highly creative force in television until his death from a sudden and severe case of pneumonia in 1990.

Source: Time, June 8, 1998

PROOFREADING EXERCISE

Read the following paragraph; then go back and surround any "scoopable" elements with commas according to Comma Rules 4, 5, and 6. Any commas already in the paragraph correctly follow Comma Rules 1, 2, and 3 and should not be changed.

Two types of punctuation internal punctuation and end punctuation can be used in writing. Internal punctuation is used within the sentence, and end punctuation is used at the end of a sentence. Commas the most important pieces of internal punctuation are used to separate or enclose information within sentences. Semicolons the next most important also have two main functions. Their primary function separating two independent clauses is also the most widely known. A lesser-known need for semicolons to separate items in a list already containing commas occurs rarely in college writing. Colons and dashes likewise have special uses within sentences. And of the three pieces of end punctuation—periods, question marks, and exclamation points—the period which signals the end of the majority of English sentences is obviously the most common.

SENTENCE WRITING

Combine the following sets of sentences in different ways according to Comma Rules 4, 5, and 6. Try to combine each set in a way that needs commas and in a way that doesn't need commas. In other words, try to make an element "scoopable" in one sentence and not "scoopable" in another. You may reorder the details and change the phrasing as you wish. Sample responses are provided in the Answers section.

The 5,000 Fingers of Dr. T. is a great old movie written by Dr. Seuss.

It is a live-action film with outrageous sets and costumes from the 1950s.

I believe.

The songs in *Dr. T.* are better than in any other musical I have seen.

Dr. Terwilliker is a crazy piano teacher.

He wants to rule the world.

His plan involves forcing 500 little boys to play an enormous piano with 5,000 keys.

REVIEW OF THE COMMA

SIX COMMA RULES

1. Put a comma before a *fanboys (for, and, nor, but, or, yet, so)* when it connects two independent clauses.
2. Put a comma between three or more items in a series.
3. Put a comma after an introductory expression or before a tag comment or question at the end.
4. Put commas around the name of a person spoken to.
5. Put commas around words like *however* or *therefore* when they interrupt a sentence.
6. Put commas around unnecessary, additional ("scoopable") information.

COMMA REVIEW EXERCISE

Add the missing commas, and identify which one of the six comma rules applies in the brackets at the *end* of each sentence. Each of the six sentences illustrates a different rule.

I am writing you this note Michael to ask you to do me a favor. [ ] Before you leave for work today would you take the turkey out of the freezer? [ ] I plan to get started on the stuffing potatoes and desserts as soon as I wake up. [ ] I will be so busy however that I might forget to thaw out the turkey. [ ] It's the first time I've cooked all the food for Thanksgiving by myself and I want everything to be perfect. [ ] The big enamel roasting pan the one that is in the cupboard above the refrigerator will be the best place to keep the turkey as it thaws. [ ]

Thanks for your help.

SENTENCE WRITING

Write at least one sentence of your own to demonstrate each of the six comma rules. You could write the six sentences in the form of a note to a friend, like the one in the Comma Review Exercise. Be sure to think of a new situation that the note could explain. Exchange notes with a classmate and check each other's commas.

Quotation Marks and Underlining/*Italics*

Put quotation marks around any direct quotation (the exact words of a speaker or writer) but not around a paraphrase or an indirect quotation. For a full discussion of the methods for "Choosing and Using Quotations," see pages 224–229.

In his first speech as president, Franklin D. Roosevelt said the famous words, "the only thing we have to fear is fear itself." (a direct quotation)

In his first speech as president, Franklin D. Roosevelt reassured the nation and told people not to be afraid (a paraphrase)

The officer said, "Please show me your driver's license." (a direct quotation)

The officer asked to see my driver's license. (an indirect quotation)

If the writer or speaker says more than one sentence, quotation marks are used before and after the whole quotation.

She said, "One of your brake lights is out. You need to take care of the problem right away."

If the quotation begins the sentence, the words telling who is speaking (called the signal phrase) are set off with a comma unless the quotation ends with a question mark or an exclamation point. See page 226 for more about signal phrases.

"I didn't even know it was broken," I said.

"Do you have any questions?" she asked.

"You mean I can go!" I happily shouted.

"Yes, consider this just a warning," she said.

Notice that each of the previous quotations begins with a capital letter. But when a quotation is interrupted by the signal phrase, the second part doesn't begin with a capital letter unless the second part is a new sentence.

"If you knew how much time I spent on the essay," the student explained, "you would give me an A."

"An artist might work on a painting for years," the teacher replied. "That doesn't mean that the result will be a masterpiece."

Put quotation marks around the titles of essays, articles, poems, songs, short stories, TV episodes, and other short works.

We read George Orwell's essay "A Hanging" in my speech class.

I couldn't sleep after I read "The Lottery," a short story by Shirley Jackson.

My favorite Woodie Guthrie song is "This Land Is Your Land."

Jerry Seinfeld's troubles in "The Puffy Shirt" episode are some of the funniest moments in TV history.

Underline titles of longer works: books, newspapers, magazines, plays, albums or CDs, Web sites, movies, and TV or radio series.

The Host is a novel by Stephanie Meyer, author of the Twilight series.

I read about the latest discovery of dinosaur footprints on CNN.com.

Many people found the series finale of Lost to be very satisfying.

My mother listens to The Writer's Almanac radio program every morning.

You may choose to *italicize* instead of underlining when you have access to a computer. Just be consistent throughout any paper in which you use underlining or italics.

The Host is a novel by Stephanie Meyer, author of the *Twilight* series.

I read about the latest discovery of dinosaur footprints on *CNN.com*.

Many people found the series finale of *Lost* to be very satisfying.

My mother listens to *The Writer's Almanac* radio program every morning.

E X E R C I S E S

Correctly punctuate quotations and titles in the following sentences by adding quotation marks or underlining/*italics*.

Exercise 1

1. After all these years, Friends is still a popular TV series.

2. It is better to deserve honors and not have them, said Mark Twain, than to have them and not deserve them.

3. Twain continued, When people do not respect us, we are sharply offended, yet in his private heart no man much respects himself.

4. My roommate left an ominous note on the front door; all it said was, Fix plumbing.

5. In his book Crying: The Natural & Cultural History of Tears, Tom Lutz explains that Weeping is a human universal.

6. Whenever I see a new copy of People magazine, I buy it.

7. In Shakespeare's play Henry V, the French ambassador brings Henry a gift; when the king asks what it is, the ambassador replies, Tennis balls, my liege.

8. The bus driver shouted Hold on! right before we hit the curb.

9. The movie version of The Da Vinci Code was not as popular as the book.

10. Every issue of Smithsonian magazine has amazing pictures in it.

Exercise 2

1. The Raven is a poem by Edgar Allan Poe.

2. Once you complete your test, the teacher said, please bring it up to my desk.

3. I have a subscription to several magazines, including The New Yorker.

4. Pablo Picasso perceived, Everything exists in limited quantities, even happiness.

5. How many times, she asked, are you going to mention the price we paid for dinner?

6. After Babe Ruth's death, his wife remarked, I don't even have an autographed ball. You don't ask your husband for an autographed ball. He'd probably think you were nuts.

7. Sophocles, the Greek playwright, wrote the tragedy Oedipus Rex in the fifth century BCE.

8. Edward Hopper remarked, When you go by on a train, everything looks beautiful. But if you stop, it becomes drab.

9. A famous Mexican proverb says, Whoever sells land sells his mother.

10. When Fiorello La Guardia, who was just over five feet tall, was asked what it felt like to be short, he answered, Like a dime among pennies.

Exercise 3

1. In his book Catwatching, Desmond Morris has this to say about their preferences: Cats hate doors.

2. Phil Hartman was the voice of Troy McClure and many other memorable characters on the animated TV series The Simpsons.

3. Langston Hughes wrote about his childhood in a short essay called Salvation.

4. Langston Hughes' essay is part of his full-length autobiography The Big Sea.

5. Joan Didion describes her relationship with migraine headaches in her essay In Bed.

6. Where can I buy some poster board? the student asked.

7. There is a school-supply store around the corner, his friend replied, but I don't think that it's open this late.

8. Sylvia asked the other students if they had seen the Alfred Hitchcock movie called The Birds.

9. I don't remember, James answered.

10. It's not something you could ever forget! she yelled.

Exercise 4

1. Kurt Vonnegut begins his futuristic short story Harrison Bergeron by stating, The year was 2081, and everybody was finally equal.

2. Now he belongs to the ages! cried Edwin M. Stanton after Abraham Lincoln's assassination.

3. In her book The Mysterious Affair at Styles, Agatha Christie wisely observes that Every murderer is probably somebody's old friend.

4. Swear not by the moon, says Juliet to Romeo.

5. John F. Kennedy told the U.S. Congress, The human mind is our fundamental resource.

6. Abraham Lincoln stated that Public opinion in this country is everything.

7. Writers are always selling somebody out, Joan Didion observed.

8. The expression All animals are equal, but some animals are more equal than others can be found in George Orwell's novel Animal Farm.

9. A Swahili proverb warns When a person seizes two things, one always slips from his grasp!

10. Groucho Marx once remarked, I wouldn't want to belong to any club that would accept me as a member.

Exercise 5

1. Ovid reminded us that We can learn even from our enemies.

2. We know what a person thinks not when he tells us what he thinks, said Isaac Bashevis Singer, but by his actions.

3. The Spanish proverb El pez muere por la boca translated means The fish dies because it opens its mouth.

4. Ask yourself whether you are happy, and you cease to be so, John Stuart Mill wrote.

5. A Russian proverb states, Without a shepherd, sheep are not a flock.

6. William Faulkner felt that Some things you must always be unable to bear.

7. St. Jerome had the following insight: The friendship that can cease has never been real.

8. Oscar Wilde observed that In this world there are only two tragedies. One is not getting what one wants, and the other is getting it.

9. Henry Ford warned, You can't build a reputation on what you're going to do.

10. Choose a job you love, Confucius suggested, and you will never have to work a day in your life.

PARAGRAPH EXERCISE

Correctly punctuate quotations and titles in the following paragraph by adding quotation marks or underlining/*italics*. Some quotations have been shortened with the use of ellipses (. . .).

I admire the way that Helen Keller describes her feelings in her autobiography, The Story of My Life. Being totally blind and deaf, Keller tries to explain how she can experience something like moonlight. She writes, I cannot, it is true, see the moon climb up the sky behind the pines and steal softly across the heavens. Then she continues, But I know she is there, and . . . I feel the shimmer of her garments as she passes. Keller feels light rather than sees it. She explains that a certain combination of air and light makes her feel loved, or as she puts it, A luminous warmth seems to enfold me. . . . It is like the kiss of warm lips on my face. I really like Keller's writing style. When I read her descriptions, I feel very calm.

SENTENCE WRITING

Write ten sentences that list and discuss your favorite songs, TV shows, characters' expressions, movies, books, and so on. Be sure to punctuate quotations and titles correctly. Refer to the rules at the beginning of this section if necessary.

Capital Letters

1. **Capitalize the first word of every sentence.**

   Peaches and nectarines taste best when they are cold.

   Every piece of fruit is an amazing object.

2. **Capitalize the first word of a sentence-length quotation.**

   The college president asked, "What can we do for students today?"

   "The labs tools are a little dangerous," Zoe said, "but I am always careful." (The *but* is not capitalized because it does not begin a new sentence.)

   "I love my art classes," she added. "Maybe I'll change my major." (*Maybe* is capitalized because it begins a new sentence within the quoted material.)

3. **Capitalize the first, last, and main words in a title. Don't capitalize prepositions (*in, of, at, with, about...*), *fanboys* (*for, and, nor, but, or, yet, so*), or articles (*a, an,* or *the*). See p. 243 for more about titles.**

   I found a copy of Darwin's book *The Origin of Species* at a yard sale.

   Our class read the essay "How to Write a Rotten Poem with Almost No Effort."

   Shakespeare in Love is a film based on the life and work of William Shakespeare.

4. **Capitalize specific names of people, places, languages, and nationalities.**

English	Shah Rukh Khan	Cesar Chavez
Ireland	Spanish	Hindi
Ryan White	Philadelphia	Shanghai

5. **Capitalize names of months, days of the week, and special days, but not the seasons.**

March	Fourth of July	spring
Monday	Valentine's Day	summer
Earth Day	Labor Day	fall

6. **Capitalize a title of relationship if it takes the place of the person's name. If *my* (or *your, her, his, our, their*) is in front of the word, a capital is not used.**

I think Mom wrote to him.	*but*	I think my mom wrote to him.
We visited Aunt Sophie.	*but*	We visited our aunt.
They spoke with Grandpa.	*but*	They spoke with their grandpa.

7. **Capitalize names of particular people or things, but not general terms.**

I admire Professor Washborne.	*but*	I admire my professor.
We saw the famous Potomac River.	*but*	We saw the famous river.
Are you from the South?	*but*	Is your house south of the mountains?
I will take Philosophy 4 and English 100.	*but*	I will take philosophy and English.
She graduated from Sutter High School.	*but*	She graduated from high school.
They live at 119 Forest St.	*but*	They live on a beautiful street.
We enjoyed the Monterey Bay Aquarium.	*but*	We enjoyed the aquarium.

E X E R C I S E S

Add all of the necessary capital letters to the sentences that follow.

Exercise 1

1. many consider *the diary of anne frank* to be one of the most important books of the twentieth century.

2. anne frank wrote her famous diary during the nazi occupation of holland in world war ii.

3. the building in amsterdam where the frank family and several others hid during the two years before their capture is now a museum and has been recently renovated.

4. visitors to the anne frank house can stand before her desk and see pictures of movie stars like greta garbo on her wall.

5. they can climb the stairs hidden behind a bookcase that led to the annex where anne lived with her mother, edith; her father, otto; and her sister, margot.

6. one of the others hiding with the franks was peter van pels, who was roughly the same age as anne.

7. anne writes of her relationship with peter in her diary.

8. visitors to the museum can enter the room where peter gave anne her first kiss just a few months before the nazis discovered their hiding place in 1944.

9. anne's family and peter's were both sent to concentration camps in germany.

10. only anne's father lived to see the anne frank house open as a museum for the first time on may 3, 1960.

Source: Smithsonian, October 2001

Exercise 2

1. dad and i have both decided to take college classes next fall.

2. fortunately, in los angeles we live near several colleges and universities.

3. classes at the community colleges usually begin in late august or early september.

4. within twenty minutes, we could drive to los angeles valley college, los angeles city college, glendale community college, or pasadena city college.

5. i want to take credit classes, and my dad wants to sign up for community education classes.

6. for instance, i will enroll in the academic courses necessary to transfer to a university.

7. these include english, math, science, and history classes.

8. my father, on the other hand, wants to take noncredit classes with titles like "learn to play keyboards," "web pages made easy," and "be your own real estate agent."

9. dad already has a great job, so he can take classes just for fun.

10. i know that if i want to go to one of the university of california campuses later, i will have to be serious from the start.

Exercise 3

1. i grew up watching *the wizard of oz* once a year on tv before video stores like blockbuster rented movies to watch at home.

2. i especially remember enjoying it with my brother and sisters when we lived on topeka drive.

3. mom would remind us early in the day to get all of our homework done.

4. "if your homework isn't finished," she'd say, "you can't see the munchkins!"

5. my favorite part has always been when dorothy's house drops on one of the wicked witches, and her feet shrivel up under the house.

6. the wicked witch of the west wants revenge after that, but dorothy and toto get help from glinda, the good witch of the north.

7. glinda tells dorothy about the emerald city and the wizard of oz.

8. on their way, toto and dorothy meet the scarecrow, the tin man, and the cowardly lion.

9. together they conquer the witch and meet professor marvel the real man who has been pretending to be a wizard.

10. The ruby slippers give dorothy the power to get back to kansas and to her aunt em and uncle henry.

Exercise 4

1. oscar wilde was an irish-born writer who lived and wrote in england for much of his life during the late 1800s.

2. he was famous for his refined ideas about art and literature.

3. while still a young man, wilde traveled to america.

4. contrary to what many people expected, he was well received in rough mining towns such as leadville, colorado.

5. he gave one particularly long speech to the miners who lived in leadville.

6. wilde spoke on the following topic: "the practical application of the aesthetic theory to exterior and interior house decoration, with observations on dress and personal ornament."

7. during his stay in leadville, wilde had gained the miners' respect by visiting them down in the mines and by proving that he could drink as much whiskey as they could without getting drunk.

8. wilde wrote about one incident that took place in leadville.

9. before giving a lecture he called *the ethics of art,* wilde was told that two criminals accused of murder had been found in town.

10. earlier that evening on the same stage where wilde was about to give his speech, the two men were convicted and executed by leadville officials.

Source: Saloons of the Old West (Knopf, 1979)

Exercise 5

1. the southern writer known as flannery o'connor was born with the name mary flannery o'connor.

2. o'connor lived much of her life in milledgeville, georgia.

3. she attended peabody high school, georgia state college for women (currently georgia college), and the state university of iowa (currently the university of iowa).

4. while at college in georgia, o'connor edited the campus newspaper, *the colonnade,* and its literary magazine, *the corinthian.*

5. when she began publishing her writing, o'connor left off her first name, mary.

6. students in literature classes study o'connor's short stories, including "revelation," "good country people," "a good man is hard to find," and "the life you save may be your own."

7. o'connor's stories received the o. henry award many times.

8. organizations such as the ford foundation and the national institute of arts and letters awarded o'connor with grants to support her writing.

9. she also wrote the novels *wise blood* and *the violent bear it away*.

10. in 1962, notre dame's st. mary's college made flannery o'connor an honorary doctor of letters.

Source: Flannery O'Connor: Her Life, Library and Book Reviews (Edwin Mellen, 1980)

REVIEW OF PUNCTUATION AND CAPITAL LETTERS

Punctuate these sentences. They include all the rules for punctuation and capitalization you have learned throughout the book. Compare your answers carefully with those at the back of the book. Sentences may require several punctuation marks or capital letters.

1. the empire state building is one of the most famous locations in new york city

2. have you ever read gary sotos narrative essay the pie

3. we traveled to many european cities with our high school band it was an experience that well never forget

4. how much would someone pay for an autographed script from the original star wars movie

5. we received your résumé ms clark and will contact you if we have any openings

6. the participant who guessed the correct number of golfballs won an ipad.

7. prof mitchell teaches the beginning french class

8. whenever i go there i leave something behind then i have to drive back and get it

9. we brought the food but we forgot the plates forks and plastic cups

10. roy scheider came up with the famous line in the movie jaws we're gonna need a bigger boat

11. i love solving sudoku puzzles in the newspaper its my favorite thing to do on sundays

12. packing for a short trip should be easy however its not

13. our english instructor taught us the following rhyme about commas when in doubt leave them out

14. i wonder if i needed to bring my math book with me today

15. the simpsons is the only tv series that my whole family still thinks is funny

COMPREHENSIVE TEST

In these sentences, you'll find all the errors that have been discussed in the entire text. Try to name the error in the blank before each sentence, and then correct the error if you can. You may find any of the following errors:

adj	incorrect adjective
adv	incorrect adverb
apos	apostrophe
awk	awkward phrasing
c	comma needed
cap	capitalization
cliché	overused expression
cs	comma splice
dm	dangling modifier
frag	fragment
mm	misplaced modifier
p	punctuation
pro	incorrect pronoun
pro agr	pronoun agreement
ro	run-on sentence
shift	shift in time or person
sp	misspelled word
s-v agr	subject-verb agreement
verb	incorrect verb form
wordy	wordiness
ww	wrong word
//	not parallel

A perfect—or almost perfect—score will mean you've mastered the first part of the text.

1. _____ The tennis players put their gear away and grabbed a towel then they met with reporters.

2. _____ I felt badly about turning my paper in late.

3. _____ Each of the tutors have a different area of expertise.

4. _____ On the final day of my art class, we critiqued all of are projects.

5. _____ Students are suppose to use filtered water in the biology lab.

6. _____ Their going to visit London, Paris, and Rome this summer.

7. _____ Why are mens' locker rooms always bigger than womens' locker rooms?

8. _____ A thunderstorm was on its way, we decided to stay at school until it passed.

9. _____ Our hands were as cold as ice when we left the hockey game.

10. _____ Whenever I give a party the guests always stay later than I expect.

11. _____ The trunk of her car was totally empty when she looked inside of it.

12. _____ At the charity fundraiser, the adults washed the cars and the kids dried them.

13. _____ I wonder how some people save so much money for their vacations?

14. _____ The president of the college presented a special certificate to my friend and I.

15. _____ "In and of ourselves we Trust" is the title of an essay by Andy Rooney.

16. _____ Increasing gas prices causing people to take fewer car trips.

17. _____ They missed a real important quiz when they were absent.

18. _____ To see the actual animals at the zoo, we drove to the parking lot, rode a bus to the front gate, and had to take a tram to get to the animal viewing area.

19. _____ We ordered soup and salad, and you couldn't believe how small the portions were.

20. _____ Everyone was allowed to drop their lowest grade.

PART 4

Writing

What Is the Least You Should Know about Writing?

"Unlike medicine or the other sciences," William Zinsser points out, "writing has no new discoveries to spring on us. We're in no danger of reading in our morning newspaper that a breakthrough has been made in how to write [clearly]. . . . We may be given new technologies . . . to ease the burdens of composition, but on the whole we know what we need to know."

One thing is certain: people learn to write by *writing*—not by reading long discussions about writing. Therefore, the explanatory sections in Part 4 are as brief as they can be, and they include samples by both professional and student writers.

Understanding the basic structures and learning the essential skills covered in these sections will help you become a better writer.

BASIC STRUCTURES

  I. The Paragraph

 II. The Essay

WRITING SKILLS

  III. Writing in Your Own Voice

  IV. Finding a Topic

  V. Organizing Ideas

  VI. Supporting with Details

 VII. Choosing and Using Quotations

VIII. Writing an Argument

  IX. Writing Summaries

  X. Revising, Proofreading, and Presenting Your Work

Writing as Structure

Aside from the basics of word choice, spelling, sentence structure, and punctuation, what else do you need to understand to write better? Just as sentences are built according to accepted patterns, so are the larger "structures" in writing—paragraphs and essays, for example.

Think of writing as a system of structures, beginning small with words that connect to form phrases, clauses, and sentences. Then sentences connect to form paragraphs and essays. Each level has its own set of "blueprints." To communicate clearly in writing, words must be chosen and spelled correctly. Sentences must have a subject, a verb, and a complete thought. Paragraphs must be indented and should contain a main idea supported with sufficient detail. Essays should explore a valuable topic in several coherent paragraphs, usually including an introduction, a body, and a conclusion.

Not everyone approaches writing as structure, however. It is possible to write better without thinking about structure at all. A good place to start might be to write what you care about and to care about what you write. You can make an amazing amount of progress by simply being *genuine,* being who you are naturally. No one has to tell you to be yourself when you speak, but you might need encouragement to be yourself in your writing.

First-Person and Third-Person Approaches

You may have identified—and your professors may have pointed out—two main approaches to writing: the first-person approach (using *I, me, we, us*) and the third-person approach (using *one, he, she, it, they, them*). Note that the second-person pronoun—*you*—serves a special purpose, not commonly required in college papers. Writers use *you* to guide the reader through a process or to teach the reader how to do something, just as we use *you* in this book to teach "the least you should know about English." Unless you are writing a "how-to" paper of some kind, it's best to avoid using *you.* Let's focus, then, on first person vs. third person.

What are the benefits of the first-person approach? First-person pronouns allow you to express yourself directly ("I agree with Isaac Asimov.") and to connect with readers by including them in your observations. Here is an example from an excerpt about "Workaholism" on page 207: "Our culture celebrates the idea of the workaholic." The first-person approach establishes a direct connection between the writer, the information, and the reader.

How does the third-person approach compare? The third-person point of view presents information about people and ideas more objectively. For example, you'll find this sentence in an excerpt about traffic on page 208: "So much time is spent in cars in the United States, studies show, that drivers (particularly men) have higher rates of skin cancer on their left sides. . . ." The third-person approach creates a comfortable distance between the writer, the information, and the reader.

Most writers don't consciously restrict themselves to one approach, but in some cases they do. Lillian Woodward's excerpt on pages 212 and Patricia Fara's excerpt on page 233 adhere to the first-person and third-person approaches, respectively.

It is possible to use more than one approach when necessary. Professional writers often successfully blend first and third person (sometimes even first, second, and third person). See the excerpts about "Workaholism" on page 207 and about high school on page 229 for examples using a mixed point of view. Being aware of your options will help you grow as a writer.

Learning to write well is important, and confidence is the key. The Writing sections will help you build confidence, whether you are expressing your own ideas or presenting and responding to the ideas of others. Like the Sentence Structure sections, the Writing sections are best taken in order. However, each one discusses an aspect of writing that you can review on its own at any time.

Basic Structures

I. The Paragraph

A paragraph is unlike any other structure in English. It has its own visual profile: the first line is indented about five spaces, and sentences continue to fill the space between both margins until the paragraph ends (which may be in the middle of the line):

_____

_____

_____

_____

_____

_____.

As a beginning writer, you may forget to indent your paragraphs, or you may break off in the middle of a line within a paragraph, especially when writing in class. You must remember to indent whenever you begin a new paragraph and fill the space between the margins until it ends. (Note: In business writing, paragraphs are not indented but double-spaced in between.)

Defining a Paragraph

A typical paragraph develops one idea, usually phrased in a topic sentence from which all the other sentences in the paragraph radiate. The topic sentence does not need to begin the paragraph, but it most often does, and the other sentences support it with specific details. (For more on topic sentences and organizing paragraphs, see p. 219.) Paragraphs usually contain several sentences, though no set number is required. A paragraph can stand alone, but more commonly paragraphs are part of a larger composition, an essay. There are different kinds of paragraphs, based on the jobs they do.

Types of Paragraphs

SAMPLE PARAGRAPHS IN AN ESSAY

Introductory paragraphs begin essays. They provide background information about the essay's topic and usually include the thesis statement or main idea of the essay. (See pp. 216–218 for information on how to write a thesis statement.) Here is the introductory paragraph of a student essay entitled "A Cure for My Premature Old Age":

> Most people would love to live in a quiet neighborhood. I have heard that some people even camp out in front of a house they are planning to buy just to see if the block is as quiet as they have been told. Maybe I am unusual, but not long ago I felt that my community was too quiet. It was a problem for me, but I didn't get much sympathy when I told people about it. I learned that, from the problems in our lives, we become who we are.

In this opening paragraph, the student leads up to the main idea that "we become who we are" as a result of the challenges in our lives with background information about the "problem" of living in a quiet neighborhood.

Body paragraphs are those in the middle of essays. Each body paragraph contains a topic sentence and presents detailed information about one subtopic or idea that relates directly to the essay's thesis. (See p. 219 for more information on organizing body paragraphs.) Here are the body paragraphs of the same essay:

> The silence of my neighborhood affected me. Every day I woke up to an alarm clock of quiet. There were no birds chirping, no cars passing by, nothing noisy around to comfort me. I lived then (and still do) in a cul-de-sac next to a home for senior citizens. Even the ambulances that came to transport the old folks never used their sirens. I often felt lonely and spent time looking out the window at the bushes and the badly painted fence. I too was becoming old, but I was only nineteen. I found myself actually whispering at times.
>
> There was no easy solution to my problem. My grandmother hated loud sounds, and she would never consider moving. We didn't even watch television because the blaring commercials upset her. I wanted to get out of the house with friends and visit noisy places, but my grandmother needed me to help her while my parents were at work. I didn't mind spending time with her, and she did teach me to make an incredible spaghetti sauce.
>
> One day, I finally discovered a remedy for my problem. I took my grandmother to visit her friend Irene at the nursing home next door, and—no, I didn't leave her there. I started reading out loud to both of them. At first I read from the newspaper, but then someone suggested that I read a short story instead. As I read them the story, I realized that I had been silent for so long that I loved to hear my own voice, to act out the characters' personalities, and to live through the actions of the characters. Grandma and Irene loved it, too.

Notice that each of the three body paragraphs discusses a single aspect of the student's response to the problem—the ways it affected him, the lack of a simple solution, and finally the "cure."

Concluding paragraphs are the final paragraphs in essays. They bring the discussion to a close and share the writer's final thoughts on the subject. (See p. 218 for more about concluding paragraphs.) Here is the conclusion of the sample essay:

> Now I am in my first year of college, and I've chosen English as a major. My grandmother spends three days a week visiting Irene next door. After school, I read them the essays I write for my classes, and they give me advice on how to make them better. I also work on campus, making recordings of books for visually impaired students. And I will be playing the part of Mercutio in our theater department's production of *Romeo and Juliet*. I never imagined that the solution to my problem would turn out to be the beginning of my adult life.

In this concluding paragraph, the student describes his transformation from depressed "aging" teen to promising student and aspiring actor—all as a result of living in a quiet cul-de-sac and caring for his grandmother.

SAMPLE OF A SINGLE-PARAGRAPH ASSIGNMENT

Single-paragraph writing assignments may be given in class or as homework. They test your understanding of the unique structure of a paragraph. They may ask you to react to a reading or to provide details about a limited topic. Here is a sample paragraph-length reaction following the class's reading of an essay called "What Is Intelligence, Anyway?" by Isaac Asimov. In his essay, Asimov explains that there are other kinds of intelligence besides just knowledge of theories and facts. This student shares Asimov's ideas about intelligence and uses personal experiences to support her reaction:

> I agree with Isaac Asimov. Intelligence doesn't only belong to Nobel Prize winners. I define "intelligence" as being able to value that special skill a person has been born with. Not everyone is a math genius or a brain surgeon. For example, ask a brain surgeon to rotate the engine in a car. It isn't going to happen. To be able to take a certain skill that someone has inherited and push it to its farthest limits I would call "intelligence." Isaac Asimov's definition is similar to mine. He believes that academic questions are only correctly answered by academicians. He gives the example of a farmer. Questions on a farming test would only be correctly answered by a farmer. Not everyone has the same talent; we are all different. When I attend my math classes, I must always pay attention. If I don't, I end up struggling with what I missed. On the other hand, when I'm in my music classes, I really don't have to work hard because reading music, playing the piano, and singing all come easily to me. I see other students struggling with music the way I do with math. This is just another example of how skills and talents differ. Some people are athletic; others are brainy. Some people can sing; others can cook. It really doesn't matter what the skill might be. If it's a talent, to me that's a form of intelligence.

These shorter writing assignments help students practice presenting information within the limited structure of a paragraph. If this had been an essay-length reaction, the writer would have included more details about her own and other people's types of intelligence. And she may have wanted to quote from Asimov's essay and discuss his most important points at length.

II. THE ESSAY

Like the paragraph, an essay has its own profile, usually including a title and several paragraphs.

Title

_____

_____

_____

_____

_____.

_____

_____

_____

_____.

_____

_____

_____

_____.

_____

_____

_____

_____.

_____

_____

_____.

While the paragraph is the single building block of text used in almost all forms of writing (in essays, magazine articles, letters, novels, newspaper stories, e-mails, and so on), an essay is a larger, more complex structure.

The Five-Paragraph Essay and Beyond

The student essay analyzed on pages 203–204 illustrates the different kinds of paragraphs within essays. Many people like to include five paragraphs in an essay: an introductory paragraph, three body paragraphs, and a concluding paragraph. However, an essay can include any number of paragraphs. Three is a comfortable number of body paragraphs to start with—it is not two, which makes an essay seem like a comparison even when it isn't; and it is not four, which may be too many subtopics for the beginning writer to organize clearly.

An essay should be long enough to explore and support its topic without leaving unanswered questions in the reader's mind. As you become more comfortable with the flow of your ideas and gain confidence in your ability to express yourself, you can write longer essays. As with many skills, learning about writing begins with basic structures and then expands to include all possibilities.

Defining an Essay

There is no such thing as a typical essay. Essays may be serious or humorous, but the best of them present thought-provoking information or opinions. Try looking up the word *essay* in a dictionary right now. Some words used to define an essay might need to be explained themselves:

An essay is *prose* (meaning it is written in the ordinary language of sentences and paragraphs).

An essay is *nonfiction* (meaning it deals with real people, factual information, actual opinions and events).

An essay is a *composition* (meaning it is created in parts that make up the whole, several paragraphs that explore a single topic or issue).

An essay is *personal* (meaning it shares the writer's unique perspective, even if only in the choice of topic, method of analysis, and details).

An essay is *analytical* and *instructive* (meaning it examines the workings of a subject and shares the results with the reader).

An essay may be *argumentative* (meaning it tries to convince the reader to accept an opinion or take action).

A Sample Essay

For an example of a brief piece of writing that fits the above definition of an essay (but is *not* a typical "five-paragraph essay") read the following excerpt from the book *Rework* by Jason Fried and David Heinemeier Hansson:

Workaholism

Our culture celebrates the idea of the workaholic. We hear about people burning the midnight oil. They pull all-nighters and sleep at the office. It's considered a badge of honor to kill yourself over a project. No amount of work is too much work.

Not only is this workaholism unnecessary, it's stupid. Working more doesn't mean you care more or get more done. It just means you work more.

Workaholics wind up creating more problems than they solve. First off, working like that just isn't sustainable over time. When the burnout crash comes—and it will—it'll hit that much harder.

Wokaholics miss the point, too. They try to fix problems by throwing sheer hours at them. They try to make up for intellectual laziness with brute force. This results in inelegant solutions.

They even create crises. They don't look for ways to be more efficient because they actually *like* working overtime. They enjoy feeling like heroes. They create problems (often unwittingly) just so they can get off on working more.

Workaholics make the people who don't stay late feel inadequate for "merely" working reasonable hours. That leads to guilt and poor morale all around. Plus, it leads to an ass-in-seat mentality—people stay late out of obligation, even if they aren't really being productive.

If all you do is work, you're unlikely to have sound judgments. Your values and decision making wind up being skewed. You stop being able to decide what's worth extra effort and what's not. And you wind up just plain tired. No one makes sharp decisions when tired.

In the end, workaholics don't actually accomplish more than nonworkaholics. They may claim to be perfectionists, but that just means they're wasting time fixating on inconsequential details instead of moving on to the next task.

Workaholics aren't heroes. They don't save the day, they just use it up. The real hero is already home because she figured out a faster way to get things done.

Now that you have learned more about the basic structures of the paragraph and the essay, you are ready to practice the skills necessary to write them.

Writing Skills

III. Writing in Your Own Voice

All writing speaks on paper. And the person listening is the reader. Some beginning writers forget that writing and reading are two-way methods of communication, just like spoken conversations between two people. When you write, your reader hears you; when you read, you also listen.

When speaking, you express a personality in your choice of phrases, your movements, your tone of voice. Family and friends probably recognize your voice mail messages without your having to identify yourself. Would they also be able to recognize your writing? They would if you extended your *voice* into your writing.

Writing should not sound like talking, necessarily, but it should have a personality that comes from the way you decide to approach a topic, to develop it with details, to say it *your* way.

The beginning of this book discusses the difference between spoken English, which follows the looser patterns of speaking, and Standard Written English, which follows accepted patterns of writing. Don't think that the only way to add voice to your writing is to use the patterns of spoken English. Remember that Standard Written English does not have to be dull or sound academic. Look at this example of Standard Written English that has a distinct voice, part of the book *Traffic: Why We Drive the Way We Do (and What It Says about Us)* by Tom Vanderbilt:

> Traffic has even shaped the food we eat. "One-handed convenience" is the mantra, with forkless foods like Taco Bell's hexagonal Crunchwrap Supreme, designed "to handle well in the car." I spent one afternoon in Los Angeles with an advertising executive who had, at the behest of that same restaurant chain, conducted a test, in actual traffic, of which foods were easiest to eat while driving. The main barometer of success or failure was the number of napkins used. But if the food does spill, one can simply reach for Tide to Go, a penlike device for "portable stain removal," which can be purchased at one of the more than twelve hundred (and growing) CVS drugstores that feature a drive-through window. . . . Car commuting is so entrenched in daily life that National Public Radio refers to its most popular segments as "driveway moments," meaning that listeners are so riveted to a story they cannot leave their cars. . . . So much time is spent in cars in the United States, studies show, that drivers (particularly men)

have higher rates of skin cancer on their left sides—look for the opposite effect in countries where people drive on the left.

Vanderbilt's examination of traffic's effect on us illustrates Standard Written English at its liveliest—from its sentence structures to its precise use of words. But more importantly, Vanderbilt's clear voice speaks to us and involves us in his fascination with traffic. You can involve your reader, too, by writing in your own voice. Here is an example of a student response to a brief assignment that asked her to describe a person who had recently made an impression on her. Coincidentally, she chose to describe an encounter with a real-life "workaholic" like the ones described in the sample essay on page 207.

Sitting at the kids' play area of my local mall one afternoon last week, I glanced over at another parent paying closer attention to his Blackberry than to his son. Enclosed in an oval-shaped ring with cushioned benches lining the edges, shoppers' kids ran around and played as their parents caught their breaths. In the middle of the play area lay an array of toys: boats, turtles, and small mounds of plastic for kids to crawl on and cylinders for them to crawl through. The workaholic looked up occasionally, making sure his son was still there. His thick brimmed glasses sat loosely on the bridge of his nose. His straight, jet-black hair was about a month overdue for a cut. In his late thirties, he was obviously concentrating more on his career and business than on his family in its youth. As I watched my own daughter run and play, I looked over to see the workaholic diligently typing away. I wasn't sure if he was checking e-mail, responding to e-mail, or updating his calendar, but his small brown eyes squinted, and this gave a pained look to his face; half deep in thought, the other half confused and stressed. Alternately leaning forward and slouching back, he caused his khaki pants to wrinkle and crease. His plaid shirt, unevenly tucked in, was held in place by an old and fading brown belt. His professional successes hadn't translated into any sense of style. Even on what might have been a rare day off, he couldn't escape the electronic leash that dominated his life. While his son grew up right in front of his eyes, his vision seemed way out of focus.

Notice that both professional and student writers can engage readers by telling stories (narration) and painting pictures with words (description). Narration and description require practice, but once you master them, you will strengthen and clarify your voice and increase interest in your writing.

Narration

Narrative writing tells the reader a story from the writer's personal experience, and since most of us like to tell stories, it is a good place to begin writing in your own voice. An effective narration allows readers to experience an event with the writer. Since we all see the world differently and feel unique emotions, the purpose of narration is to take readers with us through an experience. As a result, the writer gains a better understanding of what happened, and readers get to live other lives momentarily.

A Sample Essay

Listen to the written *voice* of this student, telling the story of an important lesson that he learned while he was young enough to make a change:

That Damn Wire

I can still remember it vividly, the sound of the car tires stopping right in front of the wire. That damn wire started it all. My reaction to its discovery was that of a thief who turns to see that he's been found out. At that moment, I wondered how a thin piece of wire made the police stop.

My story began on a dead-end street known as Whitmore. We lived there for thirteen years. I was a hyperactive child who loved to get into trouble. The kids on the block would get together and cause some kind of havoc. There were John and Jesse, two of my cousins who loved to roam the streets. The other pair was my brother Raul and I. Raul was four years older, but he still had a little spark.

Now when the four of us got together, we did whatever we wanted. Sometimes we sounded like auctioneers with ideas that we would shout out. I would say, "Let's throw water balloons at cars." John would up the bid, "Let's throw rocks." Jesse, the oldest of the group and a future police officer, always had the best solutions. As we discussed our options, we came up with the wire-across-the-street idea. A wire would be placed across the street, each end tied to aluminum cans. The wire would be lifted upon sight of a vehicle and would act like a trip-wire used in combat movies. After a successful catch of the tires, the cans would be dragged. The sound of clanking aluminum made all of our planning and careful timing worth it. Sometimes people would pull over and check to see what the noise was. Could it be their car or something else? Reactions were always different. We had some close calls.

As we set up one evening for our normal routine, we made one mistake. Instead of putting the wire across the street that led out of Whitmore, we put it where it faced the dead-end. We were sitting ducks. I saw a car approach from my position behind a bush. I had a view of everything. Only this time, the driver didn't head into the wire. He stopped and got out of the car. The officer had his flashlight in hand and was wearing a green jacket with power-indicating letters "SHERIFF" on the back. The first of us that he spotted was John, jumping out of his position. The cop yelled, "Hey, stop!" He shined his light and made John turn around. It was all over. The officer located the wire and followed it with his eyes both ways across the street. At the two ends, he saw Jesse and Raul holding cans.

The officer asked us all to stand on the sidewalk; it looked like he thought John was drunk or on drugs. The smell of candy indicated that he was okay. The reaction of the police officer surprised me. We got lucky. I'll never forget the look on his face when he told us, "I remember when I was a kid. Just don't get my car with that damn wire."

I couldn't believe he let us go. The officer's reaction changed how I view people. Instead of getting mad and lashing out, he kept his cool and realized that he was just like us at one point. He remembered what it was like to be a kid. After this experience, we changed our bad habits and started playing like normal kids. We stayed out of trouble and started playing sports and video games. We all grew up and stayed out of trouble, but I still have "that damn wire" to help me remember who I was.

Description

Descriptive writing paints pictures with words that appeal to the reader's five senses—sight, sound, touch, taste, and smell. The writer of description often uses comparisons (figures of speech) to help readers picture one thing by imagining something else. For example, the writer of "That Damn Wire" compares his prank to "a trip-wire used in combat movies," and Vanderbilt describes the stain-remover Tide to Go as a "penlike device" in his excerpt about traffic on page 208 to help the reader *picture* the object.

Here is another example of clear description, from the book *Lillian Woodward's Moss Landing,* in which Woodward describes the effects of a winter sunset on her boatyard at Moss Landing, California. As you read her description, you can feel the cold, hear the buzzer, enjoy the birds, and watch the sun make its way to the top of the masts.

> Freezing mornings, bright days, and cold evenings is the pattern of this New Year's week. Every time the buzzer rings on the dock, we say, "Who could want anything when it's so cold?" But we are glad they do. It takes us out of the warm office into the brisk beauty of the outdoors to see, around the crescent of the bay, deep blue mountains standing clearly against a paler blue sky.
>
> Cold days don't hinder flights of seagulls and pelicans, propelled by strong northwest winds. They swoop and climb and dive as effortlessly as they do in mid-summer. We shiver inwardly as they land in the chilly water, but they look contented with their lot.
>
> In the second week of winter I stood on the dock at closing time. It seemed that already I noticed a minute more of daylight. That particular evening the sun wrought a miracle to the masts and poles of the fishing boats tied side by side. It turned them to gold. The encroaching darkness crept up the hulls and cabins and top spires until only the masts and poles stood briefly in that golden light.
>
> Darkness came and the whole scene turned gray. It was a lovely, almost eerie, scene witnessed before but always just a bit different. Whoever declares Moss Landing an ugly place, and there are some, has not been present at such moments of beauty.

You may have noticed that all of the examples in this section use both narration and description. In fact, most effective writing—even a good résumé or biology lab report—calls for clear storytelling and vivid word pictures to engage the reader.

Writing Exercises

The following two exercises will help you develop your voice as a writer. For now, don't worry about topic sentences or thesis statements or any of the skills we'll teach you in the sections to come. Narration and description have their own logical structures. A narrated experience is a story with a beginning, a middle, and an end. And we describe things from top to bottom, side to side, and so on. You will find more Writing Exercises throughout this section.

Writing Exercise 1

NARRATION: FAMOUS SAYINGS

The following is a list of well-known expressions. No doubt you have had an experience that proves at least one of these to be true. Write a short essay that tells a story from your own life and that relates to one of these sayings. (See if you can tell which of the sayings fits the experience narrated in the student essay "That Damn Wire" on p. 210.) You might want to identify the expression you have chosen in your introductory paragraph. Then tell the beginning, middle, and end of the story. Be sure to use vivid details to bring the story to life. Finish with a brief concluding paragraph in which you share your final thoughts on the experience.

> Truth is stranger than fiction.
>
> The grass is always greener on the other side of the fence.
>
> If at first you don't succeed . . . try, try again.
>
> Money can't buy happiness.
>
> We learn the best lessons from our mistakes.

Writing Exercise 2

DESCRIPTION: A PICTURE WORTH 250 WORDS?

Describe a picture that you respond to in a powerful way—one that you are drawn to, one that you *like*. It could be an advertisement, a well-known historical image, a famous drawing or painting, or a moment from a popular movie. Print a copy of the picture and observe it carefully. Your goal is to help the reader *visualize* the picture and convey the impression it makes. Try to use details and comparisons that appeal to the reader's senses in some way. Look back at the examples for inspiration. Be sure to attach the copy of your picture to your description so that the reader can see exactly what you're describing.

IV. FINDING A TOPIC

You will most often be given a topic to write about; however, when the assignment asks you to choose your own topic without any further assistance, try to go immediately to your interests.

Look to Your Interests

If the topic of your paper is something you know about and—more important— something you *care* about, then the whole process of writing will be smoother and more enjoyable for you. If you collect coins, if you can draw, or even if you just enjoy going to the movies, bring that knowledge and enthusiasm into your papers.

Take a moment to think about and jot down a few of your interests now (no matter how unrelated to school they may seem), and then save the list for use later when deciding what to write about. One student's list of interests might look like this:

buying and selling on eBay

playing poker on weekends

skiing in the mountains in winter

collecting baseball cards

Another student's list might be very different:

playing the piano

going to concerts

watching "Bollywood" movies

drawing pictures of my friends

Still another student might list the following interests:

bowling in a league

participating in my book club

traveling in the summer

buying lottery tickets

These students have listed several worthy topics for papers. And because they are personal interests, the students have the details needed to support them. With a general topic to start with, you can use several ways to gather the details you will need to support it in a paragraph or an essay.

Focused Free Writing (or Brainstorming)

Free writing is a good way to begin. When you are assigned a paper, try writing for ten minutes, putting down all your thoughts on one subject—"drawing pictures of my friends," for example. Don't stop to think about organization, sentence structures, capitalization, or spelling—just let details flow onto the page. Free writing will help you see what material you have and will help you figure out what aspects of the subject to write about.

Here is an example:

I like to draw pictures of my friends but sometimes they dont like it when I draw them. The nose is to big they think or the hair isn't just right. Once in awhile I got it perfect, but not that often. I like to style my drawings like cartoons kind of. Its almost like you'll see little baloons like in a cartoon strip with little sayings in them. I'm not a big talker myself, so I can express myself with my friends thru my drawings of them. Again, some of them like it and some of them don't.

Now the result of this free writing session is certainly not ready to be typed and turned in as a paragraph. But what does become clear in it is that the student can probably compare the two types of friends—those who like to be drawn and those who don't.

Clustering

Clustering is another way of putting ideas on paper before you begin to write an actual draft. A cluster is more visual than free writing. You could cluster the topic of "book club," for instance, by putting it in a circle in the center of a piece of paper and then drawing lines to new circles as ideas or details occur to you. The idea is to free your mind from the limits of sentences and paragraphs to generate pure details and ideas. When you are finished clustering, you can see where you want to go with a topic.

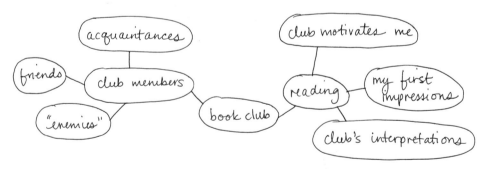

This cluster shows that the student has found two aspects of her book club that she could write about. This cluster might lead to another where the student chooses one subcategory—club members, for instance—and thinks of more details about them.

Talking with Other Students

It may help to talk to others when deciding on a topic. Many teachers divide their students into groups at the beginning of an assignment. Talking with other students helps you realize that you see things just a little differently. *Value* the difference—it will help your written voice that we discussed earlier emerge.

Writing Exercise 3

LIST YOUR INTERESTS

Make a list of four or five of your own interests. Be sure that they are as specific as the examples listed on p. 214. Keep the list for later assignments.

Writing Exercise 4

DO SOME FREE WRITING

Choose one of your interests, and do some focused free writing about it. Write for ten minutes with that topic in mind but without stopping. Don't worry about anything such as spelling or sentence structures while you are free writing. The results are meant to help you find out what you have to say about the topic *before* you start to write a paper about it. Save the results for a later assignment.

Writing Exercise 5

TRY CLUSTERING IDEAS

Choose another of your interests. Put it in the center of a piece of paper, and draw a cluster of details and ideas relating to it following the sample on page 215. Take the cluster as far as it will go. Then choose one aspect to cluster again on its own. This way you will arrive at specific, interesting details and ideas—not just the first ones that come to mind. Save the results of all your efforts.

V. ORGANIZING IDEAS

Most important to keep in mind, no matter what you are writing, is the idea you want to get across to the reader. Whether you are writing a paragraph or an essay, you must have in mind a single idea that you want to express. In a paragraph, such an idea is called a *topic sentence;* in an essay it's called a *thesis statement,* but they mean the same thing—an idea you want to get across. We will begin with a discussion of thesis statements.

Thesis Statements

Let's choose one of the student interests listed on page 214. "Buying and selling on eBay" is just a general topic; it doesn't make a point. What about eBay? Why do you like it? What does it do for you or for others? What point about eBay would you like to present to your reader? You might write a sentence like this:

Buying and selling on eBay is fun and educational.

This sentence is a start, but it's not focused enough to develop. You might move into more specific territory and write one of the following sentences:

I've learned a lot about business and geography by buying and selling on eBay.

or

Buyers and sellers learn a lot about business and geography through their transactions on eBay.

Now you have said something specific in two different ways. The first sentence uses the first-person pronoun *I*. The second sentence discusses "buyers" and "sellers" in general and uses *their*, a third-person pronoun, to refer to them. Some writing instructors may ask you to avoid writing in the first-person, and others may encourage you to use it. (See page 201 for more discussion of these approaches.) Whichever approach you use, when you write in one sentence the point you want to present to your reader, you have begun writing a thesis statement.

You may have a general idea in mind when you begin to write, but the support for it will evolve as you write. You can develop your thesis in various ways, but behind whatever you write will be your ruling thought, your reason for writing a particular essay, your thesis.

For any writing assignment, after you have done some free writing or clustering to explore your topic, the next step is to write a thesis statement. As you write your thesis statement, keep two rules in mind:

1. A thesis statement must be a sentence *with a subject and a verb* (not merely a topic).

2. A thesis statement must be *an idea that you can explain or defend* (not simply a statement of fact).

Writing Exercise 6

TOPIC, FACT, OR THESIS?

Which of the following are merely topics or facts, and which are statements that you could explain or defend in an essay? In front of each one that is just a topic or a fact, write TOPIC or FACT. In front of each one that could be a thesis statement, write THESIS. Check your answers with those at the back of the book.

1. _____ Scholarships can change students' lives in unexpected ways.

2. _____ Organic meats, fruits, and vegetables.

3. _____ Even though it's dangerous, people still use their cell phones while driving.

4. _____ *Democracy* means "government by the people."

5. _____ Some packaged, frozen, and canned foods can be as nutritious as fresh foods.

6. _____ Many young people don't take elections seriously, but they should.

7. _____ The lyrics to "America the Beautiful" were written by Katharine Lee Bates in 1893.

8. _____ Mother's Day and Father's Day are interesting holidays to compare.

9. _____ The parking problem at most colleges and universities.

10. _____ Our school's parking problem could be solved if we made a few sacrifices.

Writing Exercise 7

WRITE A THESIS STATEMENT

Use your free-writing or clustering results from Writing Exercises 4 and 5 (p. 216) and write at least one thesis statement based on your interests. Be sure that the thesis you write is phrased as a complete thought that can be defended or explained in an essay.

Organizing an Essay

Once you have written a good thesis and explored your topic through discussion with others or by free writing and clustering, you are ready to organize your essay.

First, you need an introductory paragraph. It should catch your reader's interest, provide necessary background information, and either include or suggest your thesis statement. (See p. 203 and p. 210 for two examples of student writers' introductory paragraphs.) In your introductory paragraph, you may also list supporting points, but a more effective way is to let them unfold paragraph by paragraph rather than to give them all away in the beginning of the essay. Even if your supporting points don't appear in your introduction, your reader will easily spot them later if your paper is clearly organized.

Your second paragraph will present your *first* supporting point—everything about it and nothing more.

Your next paragraph will be about your *second* supporting point—all about it and nothing more.

Each additional paragraph will develop *another* supporting point.

Finally, you'll need a concluding paragraph. In a short paper, it isn't necessary to restate your points. Your conclusion may be brief; even a single sentence to round out the paper may do the job. Remember that the main purpose of a concluding paragraph is to bring the paper to a close by sharing your final thoughts on the subject. (See p. 204 and p. 211 for two examples of successful concluding paragraphs.)

Learning to write a brief organized essay of this kind will help you to distinguish between the parts of an essay. Then when you're ready to write a longer paper, you'll be able to organize it clearly and be more creative in its design and content.

Topic Sentences

A topic sentence does for a paragraph what a thesis statement does for an essay—it states the main idea. Like thesis statements, topic sentences must be phrased as complete thoughts to be proven or developed through the presentation of details. But the topic sentence introduces an idea or subtopic that is the right size to cover in a paragraph. The topic sentence doesn't have to be the first sentence in a paragraph. It may come at the end or even in the middle, but putting it first is most common.

Each body paragraph should contain only one main idea, and no detail or example should be in a paragraph if it doesn't support the topic sentence or help to transition from one paragraph to another. (See p. 203 and pp. 210–211 for more examples of effective body paragraphs within essays and of paragraphs alone.)

Organizing Body Paragraphs (or Single Paragraphs)

A single paragraph or a body paragraph within an essay is organized in the same way as an entire essay, only on a smaller scale. Here's the way you learned to organize an essay:

Thesis: stated or suggested in introductory paragraph

First supporting paragraph

Second supporting paragraph

Additional supporting paragraphs

Concluding paragraph

And here's the way to organize a paragraph:

Topic sentence

First supporting detail or example

Second supporting detail or example

Additional supporting details or examples

Concluding or transitional sentence

You should have several details to support each topic sentence. If you find that you have little to say after writing the topic sentence, ask yourself what details or examples will make your reader believe that the topic sentence is true for you.

Transitional Expressions

Transitional expressions within a paragraph and between paragraphs help the reader move from one detail or supporting point in an essay to the next. When first learning to organize an essay, beginning writers may start each body paragraph and every new example with a transitional expression (*first, for example, next*). These common transitions are useful and clear, but they can sound mechanical. To improve the flow of your ideas and the strength of your written voice, try to replace some of these transitions with specific phrases (*at the start of the meeting* or *in many people's minds*) or with dependent clauses (*when drivers use cell phones* or *as I approached the intersection*).

Here are some transitions that show sequence:

Previously	Next	One (example, point. . .)
Later	Then	Another (example, point. . .)
Eventually	Finally	

Here are a few to show addition:

Also	First
Furthermore	Second
In addition	Third . . .

Here are several that show comparison or contrast:

Similarly	In the same way	In comparison
However	On the other hand	In contrast

Here are those that show consequence:

Therefore	Consequently	In conclusion
As a result	In other words	

Writing Exercise 8

ADDING TRANSITIONAL EXPRESSIONS

Place appropriate expressions from the lists above into the blanks in the following paragraph to make the transitions clear. Then try to replace one or two with specific transitional phrases or clauses to improve the flow of ideas and to add interest. Compare your answers with the ones suggested in the back of the book.

When I moved into my own apartment for the first time last month, I discovered the many hidden expenses of entering "the real world." _____, I had no idea that utility companies needed a security deposit from anyone who hasn't rented before. Each utility required a thirty-dollar to fifty-dollar deposit. _____ , my start-up costs just for gas, electricity, and phone used up all the money I had saved for furnishings. _____, I found out how expensive it was to supply a kitchen with the basic staples of food and cleaning supplies. My initial trip to the grocery store cost $225, and I hadn't even bought my curtains at that point. _____, I was able to budget my money and keep a little aside for any other unexpected expenses of living on my own.

Writing Exercise 9
HOW DO YOU GET READY TO WRITE?

To practice using transitions, write a paragraph about the steps you take to get ready to sit down and write a paper. Where do you go? What materials do you gather? How do you get in the right frame of mind to write? Report the steps in order, one by one, using transitional expressions from the list on page 220 wherever you see fit. Sometimes it's helpful to add humor to a process-based paragraph or essay to liven up the steps involved in an ordinary process and connect with the reader.

VI. Supporting with Details

Now you're ready to support your main idea with subtopics and specific details. That is, you'll think of ways to prove that your thesis is true. How could you convince your reader that buying and selling on eBay can teach valuable lessons about business and geography? Try adding the word "because" to the end of your thesis to generate at least three more specific statements. You might come up with something like the following:

> I've learned a lot about business and geography by buying and selling on eBay. (because)

or

> Buyers and sellers learn a lot about business and geography through their transactions on eBay. (because)

1. Honesty and fairness are very important when dealing with others on eBay.

2. Active eBay members must keep accurate records and be very organized.

3. Buyers and sellers learn about shipping methods and policies around the world.

NOTE—Imagining the word *because* at the end of your thesis will help you find subtopics that are clear and parallel in their level and presentation of ideas.

Types of Support

The subtopics developing a thesis and the details presented in a paragraph are not always *reasons* (like the ones outlined in the **analysis** of buying and selling on eBay, for instance). Supporting points may take many forms based on the purpose of the essay or paragraph. Other kinds of support include the following:

> *examples* (in an **illustration**)
>
> *meanings* (in a **definition**)
>
> *steps* or *stages* (in a "how-to" paper or **process analysis**)
>
> *types* or *kinds* (in a **classification**)
>
> *personal experiences* (in any kind of writing)
>
> *facts, statistics,* and *expert opinions* (in an **argument**)
>
> *causes* and/or *effects* (in a **causal analysis**)
>
> *similarities* and/or *differences* (in a **comparison-contrast**)

Whatever form they take, supporting points should develop the main idea expressed in the thesis statement of the essay or the topic sentence of the paragraph and help prove it to be true.

A Sample Final Draft

Here is the final draft of a first-person student essay about a challenging assignment for college students. Notice how the body paragraphs map out one student's personal experience as she struggles through the process of learning to draw a self-portrait. This essay could also have presented the same stages from a third-person point of view, using "they" to "them" to refer to "art students." The result would focus more on the process of drawing a self-portrait than on one student's unique experience with the assignment.

Drawing a Blank

On the day my drawing class started to learn about self-portraits last year, each of us had to bring a mirror to class. In backpacks and purses were make-up mirrors, dressing table mirrors—large and small mirrors of every shape and kind. I was nervous about drawing a self-portrait, so I brought only a tiny plastic pocket mirror. That way if I didn't do a good job, it would be my mirror's fault. I discovered that drawing a self-portrait involves observing myself from the outside and the inside.

I had never done well on human figure drawing. First our teacher, Ms. Newman, demonstrated the proportion of a human figure; she explained that a human body measures about seven times a human head. She used a tiny piece of chalk to draw on the board while she was talking. Then she showed how to sketch the face, from eyebrows to eyes, nose, mouth, and ears. After her lecture, she told us to begin drawing our self-portraits.

We all set up our mirrors. The ceiling danced with the reflections they made as we got to work. I looked down at my little square of scratched-up plastic and started to draw gingerly on my paper. I tried to put the eyes, nose, and mouth I had seen on the paper. When I finished, I wondered, "Who the heck is this?" The drawing didn't look anything like me. I was frustrated and sank down in my chair. After a minute, I told myself, "Try again." I drew another one, and it was a little better. But I could not really call it a self-portrait because it didn't look exactly like me.

I asked Ms. Newman for help. She glanced at my previous attempts and said, "A good self-portrait doesn't just look like you, it also shows your personality and your feeling." She did not see either of these in my other drawings. So I tried again. I borrowed my friend's

big glass mirror and stared into it; I was not only
looking at my face, but also deep inside my face. This
time, I freely sketched the shape of my face. Then I
roughly placed my eyebrows, eyes, nose, mouth, and ears.
I looked into the mirror again and drew the expression I
saw there.

When my portrait was finished, I wondered at the
amazing work I had done. Even though it did not perfectly
look like me, it really showed my personality and
emotions through the contrast of light and dark. When Ms.
Newman saw it, she applauded. Not only did I get an A on
this project; it also became one of the strongest pieces
in my portfolio. I realized that few things can be done
successfully the first time. If I had given up after my
first try, I would never have captured the real me.

(Note: See p. 240 for a rough draft of this essay, before its final revisions.)

Learning to support your main ideas with vivid details is perhaps the most important goal you can accomplish in this course. Many writing problems are not really writing problems but *thinking* problems. Whether you're writing a research paper or merely an answer to a test question, if you take enough time to think, you'll be able to discover a clear thesis statement and support it with paragraphs full of meaningful details.

Writing Exercise 10

WRITE AN ESSAY ON ONE OF YOUR INTERESTS

Return to the thesis statement you wrote about one of your interests for Writing Exercise 6 on p. 217. Now write a thoughtful essay about it (using either the first-person or third-person approach, see p. 201). You can explain the allure of your interest, its drawbacks or its benefits. Don't forget to include details from the free writing or clustering you may have done on the topic beforehand and to use meaningful transitional expressions.

VII. Choosing and Using Quotations

Including quotations from another writer can add dimension and depth to your paragraphs and essays. Try to think of a reading as a friendly resource, inviting you to quote from it in order to present ideas beyond your own. Remember, you're in control of what any other writer "says" in your writing by choosing what to quote and where to include quotations in your paper.

Choosing Quotations

Imagine you've been asked to read a short selection and write a response that answers the following question: "Which is more important for success, talent or hard work?" You should have no trouble using the previously discussed methods to organize your ideas about talent vs. hard work and support them with details and observations of your own. But the assignment also requires that you include quotations from the reading prompt in your response.

Let's look at the sample reading below. It's about how hard work may have contributed as much to Mozart's music as his legendary talent did. As you read this brief excerpt from Geoff Colvin's book *Talent Is Overrated*, try to spot phrases or statements that you think would be particularly quotable in a paper about talent vs. hard work. Also notice that Colvin includes a quotation to support his own ideas:

> Mozart is the ultimate example of the divine-spark theory of greatness. Composing music at age five, giving public performances as a pianist and violinist at age eight, going on to produce hundreds of works, some of which are widely regarded as ethereally great and treasures of Western culture, all in the brief time before his death at age thirty-five—if that isn't talent, and on a mammoth scale, nothing is. . . .
>
> Mozart's method of composing was not quite the wonder it was long thought to be. For nearly two hundred years many people have believed that he had a miraculous ability to compose entire major pieces in his head, after which writing them down was mere clerical work. That view was based on a famous letter in which he says as much: "the whole, though it be long, stands almost finished and complete in my mind . . . the committing to paper is done quickly enough . . . and it rarely differs on paper from what it was in my imagination."
>
> That report certainly does portray a superhuman performer. The trouble is, this letter is a forgery, as many scholars later established. Mozart did not conceive whole works in his mind, perfect and complete. Surviving manuscripts show that Mozart was constantly revising, reworking, crossing out and rewriting whole sections, jotting down fragments and putting them aside for months or years. Though it makes the results no less magnificent, he wrote music the way ordinary humans do.

One way to begin quoting effectively is to highlight the details or phrasing that you respond to the most in a reading. Be choosy. Just as you would choose ring tones or clothes to reflect your personality, you can pick particular quotations from readings to enhance the effect of your writing. Remember that quotations must reproduce the original's exact wording, so transcribe them very carefully and place them within quotation marks. (See p. 185.)

Let's say you've chosen these four sentences to quote from in your essay:

"Mozart is the ultimate example of the divine-spark theory of greatness."

"For nearly two hundred years many people have believed that he had a miraculous ability to compose entire major pieces in his head, after which writing them down was mere clerical work."

"Surviving manuscripts show that Mozart was constantly revising, reworking, crossing out and rewriting whole sections, jotting down fragments and putting them aside for months or years."

"Though it makes the results no less magnificent, he wrote music the way ordinary humans do."

Using Quotations

The next step is to cut the quotations down to a manageable size so they won't overpower your ideas.

"Mozart is the ultimate example ~~of the divine-spark theory~~ of greatness."

"For nearly two hundred years many people have believed that he had a miraculous ability to compose entire major pieces in his head~~, after which writing them down was mere clerical work~~."

"~~Surviving manuscripts show that Mozart was~~ constantly revising, reworking, crossing out and rewriting whole sections, jotting down fragments and putting them aside for months or years."

"~~Though~~ it makes the results no less magnificent, ~~he~~ wrote music the way ordinary humans do."

Read on to see how these shortened quotations can be included in the paper using signal phrases and proper punctuation to let the reader know where you've left out or changed wording from the original.

Signal Phrases and Punctuation

A quotation by itself—even if it's a complete statement such as "I have a dream"—cannot function as a sentence in your paper without a signal phrase. The job of a signal phrase is to identify the writer or source of the quotation and to provide a subject and a verb to anchor the quotation within your paper. The italicized subject and verb in the following sentence make up its signal phrase:

In his famous speech, *Martin Luther King, Jr. declares*, "I have a dream."

A **signal phrase** should include the writer's name or other identification and a strong verb like the ones listed below. Avoid relying on the verb *says* or *writes* when so many more interesting verbs like the following are available:

explains	suggests	argues	feels
points out	asserts	illustrates	adds
believes	thinks	notes	insists
claims	observes	declares	reports
acknowledges	admits	states	concludes

A signal phrase can be placed *at the beginning, in the middle,* or *at the end* of the quotation to add variety to your sentences. Use commas to set off signal phrases and an **ellipsis** (. . .) to show where you have cut words from full-length quoted sentences. No ellipsis is necessary when quoting only phrases from the original. If an ellipsis ends the sentence, the period makes a total of four dots:

Signal phrase at the beginning of the quotation (a comma follows the signal phrase):

> **Geoff Colvin believes**, "Mozart is the ultimate example of . . . greatness."

Signal phrase in the middle of the quotation (commas surround the signal phrase):

> "For nearly two hundred years," **Colvin explains**, "many people have believed that he had a miraculous ability to compose entire major pieces in his head. . . ."

Signal phrase at the end of the quotation (a comma comes before the signal phrase):

> Mozart worked very hard, "constantly revising, reworking, crossing out and rewriting whole sections, jotting down fragments and putting them aside for months or years," **Colvin adds**.

You may have noticed that the previous examples use an ellipsis when words have been left out of the *middle* or the *end* of a shortened quote, but not the *beginning* of one. When leaving off the first words of a quotation, maintain the small letter that the quoted part begins with to show that the opening words have been cut.

When a quotation is introduced by "that," the signal phrase does *not* require a comma. Note that any change made to a quote should placed within **brackets** [ ]:

> **Colvin feels *that*** "it makes [Mozart's] results no less magnificent. . . ."

Once you've identified the single source writer's name in previous sentences, you can include *brief* quotations without a signal phrase:

> As a music major myself, I'm glad to know that Mozart "wrote music the way ordinary humans do."

A Sample Paragraph Using Quotations

The following paragraph answers the question about talent vs. hard work and uses quotations from the reading on p. 225 to support the writer's ideas and experiences:

> I always thought that talent was more important than hard work. I never tried anything for too long if I didn't have the talent to do it easily. For instance, I started learning the violin and gave up within two weeks because it didn't feel as natural for me as the guitar. After reading Geoff Colvin's information about Mozart, I wish I had tried harder. Many people think of Mozart when the word *talent* comes up. Colvin believes, "Mozart is the ultimate example of . . . greatness." Without even studying Mozart's life, everyone seems to know about his gifts. "For nearly two hundred years," Colvin explains, "many people have believed that he had a miraculous ability to compose entire major pieces in his head. . . ." However, Mozart worked very hard, "constantly revising, reworking, crossing out and rewriting whole sections, jotting down fragments and putting them aside for months or years," Colvin adds. I never pictured Mozart doing so much hard work. Colvin feels that "it makes [Mozart's] results no less magnificent. . . ." I agree with him. As a music major myself, I'm glad to know that Mozart "wrote music the way ordinary humans do." Next semester, I might give the violin one more try.

GUIDELINES FOR INCLUDING QUOTATIONS

1. Choose a sentence that you would like to quote from a reading.
2. Consider shortening the phrasing of the original sentence for clarity.
3. Put quotation marks around the other writer's words.
4. Write a signal phrase to identify the writer or source of the quotation.
5. Use a comma (or commas) to set off the signal phrase in your sentence.
6. No comma is necessary if the word "that" introduces the quotation.
7. Use brackets [ ] to identify a change made within a quotation.
8. Use an ellipsis . . . in place of words cut from the middle or end of a quoted sentence (but not when quoting just a phrase).

These methods for including quotations are not difficult to learn; with practice, they will become second nature. Understanding how to quote from a reading will help you complete more complex assignments in the future. Once you know how to include quotations from a single source effectively, you will be ready to learn how to quote from multiple readings and to document them using the Modern Language Association (MLA) format. For now, just practice the basic methods of quoting from one source.

Writing Exercise 11
WRITE A PARAGRAPH USING QUOTATIONS

Return to the excerpt on "Workaholism" on page 207 and find three quotations that you would like to use to support your own ideas in a short paragraph that answers the question "Why do some people work harder than others?" Be sure to follow the "Guidelines for Including Quotations" on page 228. Note that the excerpt on "Workaholism" has two authors, so you'll just need to use *and* in between their two last names in your signal phrases (*Fried and Hansson explain . . .*). Feel free to imitate the Sample Paragraph Using Quotations on page 228.

VIII. WRITING AN ARGUMENT

Writing assignments often ask you to take a stand on an issue or to share an opinion and prove that it is valid. This type of writing is called *argumentation*, but it doesn't involve "fighting" or "arguing" in the sense that these words might be used in everyday life. In fact, intense emotions can weaken an argument if they are not balanced by logic and fairness. The purpose of a written argument is to convince the reader to value your opinion and possibly to agree with it.

Taking a Stand and Proving Your Point

A strong written argument fulfills three basic requirements. First, it takes a clear stand on an issue or a controversial topic. Second, it provides logical and relevant support for the writer's position. And third, it discusses the issue or topic in a fair-minded way, taking other points of view into account. Let's look at some examples by both professional and student writers.

As an in-class assignment, students were asked to write a short essay in response to the following excerpts from Leon Botstein's book *Jefferson's Children: Education and the Promise of American Culture*. In Chapter III, "Replacing the American High School," Botstein argues that young people in America should enter the "real world" two years earlier than they do now. Here are the excerpts that the students read from Botstein's book:

> The American high school is obsolete. It can no longer fulfill the expectations we legitimately place on it. It offers an inadequate solution to the problem of how best to motivate and educate American adolescents . . . .

The key reason for reducing the total number of years in school before college is educational. Children and young adults can begin learning sooner and more quickly. Since they mature earlier, they need to be released from the obligations of compulsory education at an earlier age. The high school diploma as we define it, which is now given to Americans at age eighteen, could be awarded at age sixteen . . . .

Those interested in going to college will be able to exercise greater choice in the new system. For those who stay at home, the community college system is the most likely option. Already these institutions are dedicated to repairing the damage done in high school or doing what ought to have been done. The basic organization of the community college is more respectful of the incipient adult. Classes are selected and scheduled by the individual. There is a campus. The day is divided so that night classes are an option. The classes are run by faculty with better training in the subject matter. The presumption of the classroom is not rote fulfillment of state requirements, but rather teaching in response to the ambitions of students to learn and get ahead. Community colleges have large numbers of older students, well beyond the so-called traditional college age. As teachers know, nothing better serves the swaggering sixteen- and seventeen-year-old more obsessed with style and the peer group than being in classes with students in their late twenties and early thirties, for whom school has become truly voluntary and serious.

A Sample Argument

As you might imagine, Botstein's idea to shorten high school and to send sixteen-year-olds directly to college drew mixed reactions from student writers. In the short essay that follows, one student argues that the last two years of high school are extremely important based on her own high school experiences:

College at Sixteen? I Think Not!

I strongly disagree with Leon Botstein's idea to eliminate the American high school. I don't believe that all teenagers mature early enough to attend college at sixteen. Yes, there is a small percentage (that could be counted on the fingers of my left hand) who could indeed go off to college and do very well at sixteen years of age, but is it really worth letting the other ninety-five percent go, too?

When I think of my high school experience and the kids who attended with me, I think of just that—kids.

Most of the students at my high school sought pleasure in spitting over the third floor balcony onto the lunch crowd below. Half of the population of my school had not learned how to throw their trash into the trashcan five feet away from them. Most weren't mature enough to leave high school at eighteen, let alone sixteen.

How would my life have been without high school? Well, that would have been interesting, and Botstein's ideas do make me wonder if I might have accomplished more sooner. But I believe that if I had gone off to college at sixteen, I would have lost more than I gained. I learned a lot from my high school experience, not from the mandatory classes that were required for graduation, but from the classes that I chose to take and that I participated in with my teenage peers.

It may sound strange to say so, but my dance and drama classes taught me a lot of very important life skills. I learned responsibility by multitasking to be able to fit weekend rehearsals and practices into my full load of regular classes, homework, and after-school activities. I learned that it is possible to get out of bed before ten o'clock on Saturday because 3 a.m. roll calls, teamwork, dedication, and competition can take you anywhere you want to go.

Without my valuable high school experiences, I know I wouldn't be the well-rounded person I am today. If I had to compete with Botstein's thirty-year-old community college students and meet them at 3 a.m. on Saturdays for dance rehearsals as my introduction to responsibility, the effects would not have been the same. In high school, we matured together, and that was important.

This student's in-class essay fulfills the three requirements of a strong written argument by clearly stating her position in her opening sentences, by describing her own vivid high school experiences to support her position, and by fairly acknowledging that some people in high school would be better off in college and even wondering what would have happened if she had graduated earlier.

Obviously, the student's paper would have been longer and more developed if it had been an out-of-class essay with a two- or three-week deadline. Then this student could have read Botstein's whole book and included factual support with her personal experiences. She could have interviewed fellow students and included their comments. She might have found an expert who shares her opinion about high school and written her essay as a comparison-contrast of Botstein's and the other expert's opinions.

THREE REQUIREMENTS OF A STRONG WRITTEN ARGUMENT

1. Takes a clear stand on an issue or a controversial topic.
2. Provides logical and relevant support (personal experience, opinions of experts, facts and statistics, results of interviews).
3. Discusses the issue or topic in a fair-minded way, allowing for other points of view.

Writing Exercise 12

TAKE A STAND ON GRADES

Read and carefully consider the following paragraph proposing a few changes in education:

> Education at all levels should be changed so that it is completely grade-free and noncompetitive. All letter grades should be eliminated and replaced by a pass/fail system, and scores of any kind should be provided as information only, not for the purpose of ranking. Students should also receive credit for self-study and Internet-gained knowledge and skills. Attendance and completion of assignments should be the only requirements for moving ahead in a course of study. In addition, students should be allowed to repeat courses, even after successfully completing all of the assignments, if they so choose. Students should take charge of their own educations and learn at their own pace.

Do you agree or disagree with this hypothetical proposal to eliminate grades and give students total flexibility in their studies? Take care to consider the issue from all angles. How would such profound changes affect students, teachers, parents, school officials, and the public? Then use what you've learned about argumentation to write a brief essay in which you take a stand on one side of this issue or the other. Refer to the student sample "College at Sixteen? I Think Not!" as a model for using relevant experiences and observations to prove your point, and remember to be fair-minded in your presentation.

Reading Longer, More Challenging Works

See if you can spot all of the elements of strong written argument in the following professional sample from the book *Scientists Anonymous: Great Stories of Women in Science,* by Patricia Fara. This biographical reading about Rachel Carson and her work as a scientist and writer may require you to look up several words in the dictionary. Notice that Fara also quotes a bit of Carson's writing to give a clear example of its impact and importance.

Although you may feel challenged by the level of writing and the references to history, politics, and sociology in this excerpt, your own feelings about gender and about the environment should make it easy for you to relate to the issues that Fara addresses in her portrayal of Rachel Carson as "The Green Pioneer."

THE GREEN PIONEER

One common form of gender prejudice is to say that women are closer to nature than men, and are therefore (supposedly) better at studying plants and animals. At first Rachel Carson (1907–64) seemed to match this stereotype—she was a superb writer who won prizes for her poetic books about the oceans and marine life. But in her mid-fifties, she wrote a very different type of book, *Silent Spring*, which accused scientists of destroying the world.

Carson loved writing, and at university in America she studied English before switching to science. After her father died she had to support her family, and she combined her twin passions—literature and marine biology—by writing information booklets for the Bureau of Fisheries. While she continued to work for the government, she also became famous for her books about the sea, which she wrote in a lyrical style as if they were poems written in prose, even though they were scientifically accurate. Carson described the environment as harmonious and beautiful, and stressed the underlying unity of nature. For example, she described how a small worm normally washed up by the tide twice a day will spontaneously follow the same pattern in an aquarium, living "out its life in this alien place, remembering in every fiber of its small green body the tidal rhythm of the distant sea."

After the Second World War, people were appalled at the devastations caused by the atomic bombs dropped on Japan, and physicists were strongly criticized. Carson increased this scepticism about science by discussing the biological sciences. She had been planning a book about the origin of life, but then she realized that scientists were destroying the natural world she loved so much. Instead of writing about the beauty of nature, she decided to write a hard-hitting book exposing the dangers of chemicals. She attacked commercial companies, condemning them for sacrificing the health of the environment in order to make more profit.

Carson collected evidence from scientific experts to prove that the environment was being ruined forever. She explained how protecting crops with insect sprays was a short-sighted policy because the lethal chemicals were killing birds and also seeping higher and higher up the food chain to harm human beings.

She lashed out at hypocrisy. Why, she asked, were so many scientists researching into insecticides? The answer, of course, was money. . . . If they refused to accept that insecticides should be banned until absolutely solid evidence of their destructive effects had been found, then it would be too late to do anything about it.

After Carson's *Silent Spring*, the old-fashioned view that studying nature was a gentle female pastime disappeared forever. The book marks the beginning of a new type of environmental writing that focuses on the potentially horrific consequences of scientific progress. Issues such as global warming and genetically modified foods are no longer restricted to academic conferences, but have become urgent political problems.

From now on, try not to avoid reading essays, articles, or books that challenge you. Even if you don't understand every word and reference, you'll improve as a reader and a writer and will prepare yourself to succeed in future classes that deal with information about many different subjects and schools of thought.

IX. WRITING SUMMARIES

One of the best ways to learn to read carefully and write concisely is to write summaries. A summary is a brief piece of writing (a paragraph, usually) that presents the main ideas of a reading—a book chapter, an article, a speech, or a long essay—in your own words. It does not call for any reactions, opinions, or experiences of your own for support. Summaries contain only the most important points of the original and leave everything else out. Writing summaries strengthens your reading and writing skills. You have to understand the essence of a reading, gather its supporting points, and rephrase them in your *own* words (without including quotations from the original). Here's a tip: put the original away while you make a list of its four or five "big ideas." Then you can write sentences that express those ideas and combine them in paragraph form.

A summary, by definition, should always be much shorter than the original. Writing something *short* sounds easy, but actually it isn't. Rephrasing the main ideas of a reading in a short paragraph is a time-consuming task—not to be undertaken in the last hour before class. However, if you practice writing summaries conscientiously, you will improve as a reader and will be able to write concise, clear, smooth paragraphs. These skills will then carry over into your reading and writing for other courses.

A Sample Reading

Read the following excerpt from the book *Bollywood Crafts—20 Projects Inspired by Popular Indian Cinema*. It will be followed by a sample summary.

BOLLYWOOD FILM FACTS

Bollywood is the biggest film industry in the world. Approximately one thousand films are made in India under the "Bollywood" umbrella each year (that is double the amount of Hollywood films) and over 12 million Indians watch a Bollywood film every day. The films are also popular throughout the Middle East, Russia and Africa, and, increasingly, Western audiences are surrendering to the charms of Indian cinema.

Bollywood is also referred to as Hindi cinema—there are 22 official languages spoken in India; however, the major movies are made in Hindi as it is the country's dominant language, though films in other languages, such as Tamil and Urdu, are also made. Although the main hub of production companies are based in

Mumbai (Bombay), films are shot in locations all over the country and recent films have even been set abroad [in England, Europe, and America].

Like mainstream Hollywood movies, Bollywood films also fall into specific genres, such as action or romance, but most are multi-genre, family movies. In India, going to the movies is a family event, and often several generations watch a film together. This means the content has to appeal to all. It also means filmmakers have to be creative in their approach to telling narratives. How they express emotions is a key element. Emotions are represented not just through acting, but also through the use of spectacle—songs and dance.

The key to a successful [Bollywood] movie is to have a popular soundtrack, and for the choreography that accompanies it to be equally impressive. Song sequences usually start in the middle of a dialogue and are a break from the reality of the storyline. Characters are transported to different locations and their costumes become very significant; a leading lady can go through several costume changes per dance scene, which makes for compelling viewing! When you're watching a song from a film, it's best to ignore the subtitles and instead let yourself be entertained by the visuals. The choreography is a mixture of Indian dancing styles with global influences such as MTV. Extras play a key role in bringing the dances to life, and as a viewer, I often want to get up and join in!

Some Bollywood films are inspired by Hollywood tales, but most are original ideas, often based on moral or family dilemmas. Like Hollywood, the star system is an important part of Bollywood and the biggest actors and actresses are celebrities in their own right. Unlike Hollywood, however, Indian actors often work on several films at one time, even switching between movie sets in the same day. And while Hollywood left behind its musicals in the 1950s, Bollywood films always contain a performance element. Actors have to demonstrate impeccable dancing skills as well as acting ability.

If you have yet to watch a Bollywood movie, don't worry! They are far more accessible than you may think, with cinemas and rental stores responding to audience demands by showing and stocking new movies. Don't be alarmed by the length; Bollywood movies are longer than other films to allow for the songs, but there is always an interval [intermission].

Bollywood films are an exciting and original contribution to the filmmaking world and, as the popularity of Bollywood continues to spread around the globe, Indian filmmakers are getting more progressive with their plots, special effects and visuals. This means that films will develop stylistically even further and continue to get better—something I'm really looking forward to!

Source: From *Bollywood Crafts—20 Projects Inspired by Popular Indian Cinema*, by Momtaz Begum-Hossain, a freelance crafts maker and customized clothing designer (www.momtazbh.co.uk). Reprinted by permission of the author.

A good summary begins with a statement of the reading's "biggest" idea, written in your own words. An effective summary does not just translate or re-order the words of the original. Some single words from the original—"India," "Hollywood," and "Bollywood," in this case—may be used in a summary when they lack a substitute. However, as the writer of an effective summary, you must find new ways to phrase the original reading's ideas, present them in a condensed form, and reveal your understanding of the original in the process.

A Sample Summary

```
In "Bollywood Film Facts," Momtaz Begum-Hossain explains
that India has its own version of Hollywood—called
Bollywood—that produces movies that are growing in
popularity worldwide. Bollywood releases twice as many
movies a year as Hollywood does. Unlike Hollywood
movies, Bollywood movies can include different languages
besides India's main language, Hindi. These films also
include more music and dancing than Hollywood movies do.
Elaborate, well-performed songs are essential and unique
```

> to Bollywood films. Therefore, movie stars in India have
> to act well and dance well, too. Indian movies are longer
> than Hollywood movies and might require subtitles, but
> they continue to attract new audiences because of their
> high entertainment value and universal appeal.

Writing Exercise 13

WRITE A SHORT SUMMARY: ASK YOURSELF, "WHAT'S THE BIG IDEA?"

Return to Patricia Lara's biography of Rachel Carson on page 233, and read it carefully. Then follow the instructions below to write a practice summary:

A good way to begin the summary of a reading is to identify the most general idea that the author (in this case, Patricia Lara) wants to get across to the reader. Write your own sentence expressing the main idea of "The Green Pioneer" now.

You may have written a sentence like this:

> Rachel Carson challenged ideas about female scientists and began the fight to save our environment.

Next, it's important to add the author's name and the reading's title to identify what you are summarizing:

> In "The Green Pioneer," Patricia Fara explains that Rachel Carson challenged ideas about female scientists and began the fight to save our environment.

Now that you have your first sentence, summarize the rest of the reading by rephrasing only its "big ideas." Be sure to use your *own* words. It's not difficult if you remember to put the reading aside and write as if you're telling a friend the essay's main ideas in your own way. The first draft of your summary may be too long. Cut it down by including only the essential points and by omitting any of Lara's details or examples. Stay within a limit of 100–120 words.

When you have written the best summary you can, then compare it with the sample summary in the Answers section on page 318. If you look at the sample sooner, you'll cheat yourself of the opportunity to learn the valuable skill of writing summaries. If you read the sample summary before writing your own, it will be impossible not to be influenced by it. So do your own thinking and writing, and then compare.

SUMMARY CHECKLIST

Even though your summary is different from the sample, it may be just as good. If you're not sure how yours compares, consider these questions:

1. Have you included the writer's main ideas *without* adding your own reactions or opinions?
2. Have you written the summary in your own words *without* using any quotations?
3. Have you left out all of the writer's examples and supporting details?
4. Does your summary read smoothly?
5. Would someone who had not read the article get a clear overview of it from your summary?

X. REVISING, PROOFREADING, AND PRESENTING YOUR WORK

Great writers don't just sit down and write a final draft. They write and revise. You may have heard the expression, "Easy writing makes hard reading." True, it is *easier* to turn in a piece of writing as soon as you finish the first draft. But your reader (and eventually you) will probably be disappointed by the results. Try to think of revision as an opportunity instead of a chore, as a necessity instead of a choice.

Whenever possible, you should write a paper several days before it is due. Let it sit for a while. When you reread it, you'll see many ways to improve the organization, add more details, and clarify phrasing. After revising the paper, put it away for another day, and try again to improve it. Save all of your drafts along the way to see the progress you've made or possibly to find text deleted in an early draft that fits in again after revision.

Don't call any paper finished until you have worked through it several times. Revising is one of the best ways to improve your writing.

A Sample Rough Draft

Take a look at an early draft of the student essay you read on page 223 about learning to draw a self-portrait. Notice that the student has revised her rough draft by crossing out weak parts, correcting word forms, and adding new phrasing or reminders for later improvement.

Drawing a Blank

~~If at First You Don't Succeed . . . Try, Try Again~~

On the day ~~that~~ my drawing class started to learn about self-portrait last year, each of us had to bring a mirror to class. In backpacks and purses ~~There~~ were make-up mirrors, dressing table mirrors—large and small mirrors of every shape and kind. I was nervous about drawing a self-portrait, so I brought only a tiny plastic pocket mirror. That way if I didn't do a good job, it would be my mirror's fault. *Add a thesis

I had never done well on human figure drawing. First ~~Anyway,~~ our teacher, Ms. Newman, demonstrated ~~showed us how to do~~ the proportion of a human figure; she explained that ~~something like~~ a human body measures about seven times a human head. She used a tiny piece of chalk to draw on the board while she was talking. Then she ~~also~~ showed how to sketch ~~out~~ the face, from eyebrows to eyes, nose, mouth and ears. After her lecture ~~all that,~~ she told ~~led~~ us to begin ~~start our drawings~~ our self-portraits.

We all ~~Everyone in the class~~ set up our ~~their~~ mirrors; ~~and~~ The ceiling danced with ~~all of~~ the reflections they made, as we got to work. ~~Then we started to draw~~ I looked down at my little square of scratched-up plastic ~~mirror~~ and started to draw gingerly on my ~~drawing~~ paper. ~~I looked at my face, eyebrows, eyes, nose, mouth, and ears.~~ the eyes, nose, and mouth I tried to put ~~what~~ I had seen on the paper. When ~~Then~~ I finished, I wondered, ~~was like~~ "Who the heck is this?" The drawing didn't look anything ~~was totally bad. Nothing looked~~ like me. I was ~~so~~ frustrated and sank down in my chair. After a minute, I told myself, "Try again," ~~the next one will be better.~~ I drew another one, and it was a little better. ~~It looked a little like me. Nevertheless~~ But I could not really call ~~say that~~ it ~~was~~ a self-portrait because it did not look exactly like me.

I asked ~~my teacher to come over and help me out.~~ ms. Newman for help. She ~~saw~~ glanced at my previous ~~drawings~~ attempts and said, "A good self-portrait doesn't just look like you, it also shows your personality and ~~characteristics.~~ your feelings." ~~From my drawing~~ she did not see in my ~~other drawings.~~ any of these. So I tried again. I borrowed my friend's big glass mirror and stared into it; I was not only looking at my face, but also deep inside my face. This time, I freely sketched ~~out~~ the shape of my face ~~shape first.~~ Then I roughly placed my eyebrows, eyes, nose, mouth, and ears. ~~And~~ I looked into ~~at~~ the mirror ~~again and~~ ~~seeing my reflection closely. I~~ drew ~~what I felt to be like in the mirror.~~ the expression I saw there.

When my ~~drawing~~ Portrait was finished, I wondered at ~~what an~~ the amazing work I had done. Even though it did not perfectly look like me, it really showed my ~~characteristics~~ personality and emotions through the contrast of light and dark. When ~~my teacher~~ ms. Newman saw it, she applauded ~~my drawing and she really liked it.~~ Not only did I get an A ~~in~~ on this project; it also became one of the strongest pieces in my portfolio. I ~~recognized~~ realized that ~~nothing could~~ few things can be done successfully the first time. If I ~~gave~~ had given up after my first try, I would never have ~~known I could have done~~ captured the real me. ~~such a great job. Now I know I will succeed no matter how many times I must try.~~

Can you see why each change was made? Analyzing the reasons for the changes will help you improve your own revision skills.

Writing Exercise 14

IS THE GLASS HALF EMPTY OR HALF FULL?

The old test of optimism and pessimism is to look at a glass filled to the midpoint. An optimist, or positive thinker, would see it as "half *full*." But a pessimist, or negative thinker, would consider it "half *empty*." Is it better to be an optimist or a pessimist? What are the consequences of focusing on the bright side or on the dark side? Think about these questions, do some free writing or clustering about them, come up with a thesis statement, and organize your results into the structure of a brief essay.

Write a rough draft of the paper and set it aside. A day or two later, reread your paper to see what improvements you can make to your rough draft. Use the following checklist to help guide you through this or any other revision.

REVISION CHECKLIST

Here's a checklist of revision questions. If the answer to any of these questions is no, revise that part of your paper until you're satisfied that the answer is yes.

1. Does the introductory paragraph introduce the topic clearly and include a thesis statement that the paper will explain or defend?
2. Do all of the body paragraphs support the thesis statement?
3. Does each body paragraph begin with a clear topic sentence and focus on only one supporting point?
4. Do the body paragraphs contain relevant details, and are transitional expressions well used?
5. Do the final thoughts expressed in the concluding paragraph bring the paper to a smooth close?
6. Does your (the writer's) voice come through?
7. Do the sentences read smoothly and appear to be correct?
8. Are words well chosen and are spelling and punctuation consistent and correct?

Exchanging Papers (Peer Evaluations)

The preceding checklist can also be used if you exchange papers with another student. Since you both have written a response to the same assignment, you will understand what the other writer has been going through and learn from the differences between the two papers.

Proofreading Aloud

Finally, you should read your finished paper *aloud*. If you read it silently, your eyes will see what you *think* is there, but you are sure to miss some errors. Read your paper aloud slowly, pointing to—and listening carefully to—each word as you read it. When you *hear* your sentences, you will notice missing words and find errors in spelling and punctuation. Reading a paper to yourself this way may take fifteen minutes to half an hour, but it will be time well spent. You can also ask a friend or relative to read your paper to you. This method can be fun as well as helpful. If you don't like the way something sounds, don't be afraid to change it! Make it a rule to read each of your papers *aloud* before handing it in.

Presenting Your Work

Part of the success of a paper could depend on how it looks. The same paper written sloppily or typed neatly might even receive a completely different grade. It is human nature to respond positively to an object created and presented with care. Here are some general guidelines to follow.

Paper Formats

Following instructions and standard formats is essential. Your paper should be typed, double-spaced, or written neatly in ink on 8 1/2-by-11-inch paper. A 1-inch margin should be left around the text on all sides for your instructor's comments. The beginning of each paragraph should be indented.

Most instructors specify a particular format for presenting your name and the course material on your papers. Always follow such instructions and other formats carefully in preparation for following more complicated formats in the future.

Titles

You should spend some time thinking of a good title for any paper long enough to deserve one. Just as you're more likely to read a magazine article with an interesting title, so your readers will be more eager to read your paper if you give it a good title. Which of these titles from student papers would make you want to read further?

An Embarrassing Experience	Gone in a Flush!
American Beauty: Diversity	Paper on Immigration in America
Argument Essay	Got Elk?

Learn these three rules about titles, and you'll always write them correctly:

1. Capitalize only the first, the last, and the important words within a title. Don't capitalize articles (*a*, *an*, or *the*), prepositions (*to, at, in, around* . . .), or connecting words (*and, or, but* . . .) in the middle of a title.

   A Night on Eagle Rock   To the Limit of Endurance and Beyond

2. Don't use quotation marks unless your title includes a quotation or the title of an article, a poem, a song, or other short work.

   Mozart's "Divine" Talent   The Call of "The Raven"

3. Don't underline or use italics in your title unless it includes the title of a book, movie, magazine, or other long work.

   Promises in The Pact   *Avatar* Sinks *Titanic*

Remember that "Haste is the assassin of elegance." Instead of rushing to finish a paper and turn it in, take the time to give your writing the polish that it deserves.

Answers

SPELLING AND WORD CHOICE

GUIDELINES FOR DOUBLING A FINAL LETTER

EXERCISE 1 (PP. 6–7)

1. tinting
2. dressing
3. towing
4. stealing
5. discovering
6. splitting
7. sanding
8. quizzing
9. boxing
10. squinting

EXERCISE 2

1. shouting
2. mixing
3. dripping
4. deploying
5. referring
6. displaying
7. digging
8. enjoying
9. hemming
10. taxing

EXERCISE 3

1. getting
2. trusting
3. tripping
4. planning
5. playing
6. missing
7. reading
8. occurring
9. skimming
10. screaming

EXERCISE 4

1. creeping
2. subtracting
3. abandoning
4. drooping
5. saying

6. weeding
7. fogging
8. dropping
9. referring
10. submitting

EXERCISE 5

1. interpreting
2. fixing
3. betting
4. stooping
5. flipping

6. inferring
7. guessing
8. bugging
9. jogging
10. building

WORDS OFTEN CONFUSED, SET 1 (PP. 13–17)

EXERCISE 1

1. an, new
2. It's, its
3. already, accepted
4. except, its
5. a, it's

6. a, are, an
7. do, feel, are
8. conscience
9. hear
10. affect, its

EXERCISE 2

1. already, its
2. coarse
3. course, complement
4. know
5. A, it's

6. It's, an, effect
7. an, our
8. hear, choose, fill
9. except, a, a
10. advise

EXERCISE 3

1. our, an, are
2. It's, feel
3. clothes, know
4. due, do
5. conscious, an, effect, our

6. break, conscience
7. course, an, dessert, feel
8. advice, forth, conscious
9. it's
10. know, no, already, chose

EXERCISE 4

1. advice, accepted, our
2. are
3. an, desserts
4. course, chose, course, dessert
5. hear, feel

6. conscience, knew
7. effect, complemented
8. fourth, course, all ready
9. break
10. have

EXERCISE 5

1. It's, its, a
2. chose, do, an
3. Due, new, already
4. fill, clothes
5. its, a

6. knew
7. Conscious
8. clothes, have
9. complement, its
10. break

PROOFREADING EXERCISE

I've always wanted to ~~no~~ *know* what makes a person want to set or ~~brake~~ *break* a Guinness world record. For example, if someone ~~all ready~~ *already* has a record for collecting more than 2,500 rubber ducks, does another person really need to beat that record? Also, the objects that people ~~chose~~ *choose* to collect ~~our~~ *are* often strange. There are records for collecting the highest number of erasers from all over the world, tags from designer ~~cloths~~ *clothes*, and labels from water bottles, to name just a few. Of ~~coarse~~ *course*, it's nice to receive ~~complements~~ *compliments* and recognition for ~~a~~ *an* impressive collection. Maybe I should ~~of~~ *have* kept all those take-out menus I just threw away and tried to set a new record myself.

WORDS OFTEN CONFUSED, SET 2 (PP. 22–26)

EXERCISE 1
1. whose
2. woman, to
3. passed
4. wear
5. led, their
6. passed
7. then, women
8. write
9. through
10. Whether, quiet

EXERCISE 2
1. your, they're
2. their, who's, led
3. to, than, past
4. There, through
5. their, to
6. principal
7. quite
8. there
9. loose
10. where, to

EXERCISE 3
1. their
2. two
3. past, were
4. than
5. were, who's
6. through
7. women, wear
8. women, their
9. were, weather, where, were
10. than

EXERCISE 4
1. your
2. You're, right, they're, quite
3. through, to, right
4. Their, wear, loose, there
5. to, quite, to, peace
6. than, their
7. who's, they're
8. piece
9. two
10. their, there

EXERCISE 5
1. through
2. women, than
3. whose, who's
4. past, their
5. whether, they're, their
6. woman, wear
7. quite, they're
8. principle, you're, then
9. whether, right, personal
10. There, lose, than, there

PROOFREADING EXERCISE

When I was in high school, I ~~past~~ *passed* all my classes but didn't learn as much as I wanted ~~too~~ *to*. All of my teachers did ~~they're~~ *their* best, and the ~~principle~~ *principal* was an enthusiastic ~~women~~ *woman* ~~who's~~ *whose* love of education was contagious. ~~Their~~ *There* was no shortage of school spirit; I just wasn't paying enough attention to make the hard information stick. Since I ~~lead~~ *led* a carefree life at the time, I goofed off more ~~then~~ *than* I should have. If I had those high school years to live over again, I would listen in class, do my homework carefully, and make sure that I knew all of the ~~write~~ *right* answers on tests and that I didn't just forget the answers once the test was over.

THE EIGHT PARTS OF SPEECH (PP. 30–32)

EXERCISE 1

(Notice that this *exercise* includes several proper nouns that are made of two or more capitalized words acting as one noun.)

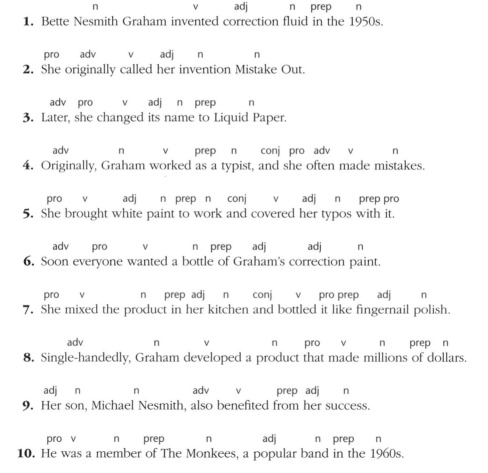

        n   v   adj   n prep   n
1. Bette Nesmith Graham invented correction fluid in the 1950s.

  pro   adv   v   adj   n   n
2. She originally called her invention Mistake Out.

  adv pro   v   adj n prep   n
3. Later, she changed its name to Liquid Paper.

  adv   n   v   prep   n   conj pro adv v   n
4. Originally, Graham worked as a typist, and she often made mistakes.

  pro   v   adj   n prep n conj   v   adj   n   prep pro
5. She brought white paint to work and covered her typos with it.

  adv   pro   v   n prep   adj   adj   n
6. Soon everyone wanted a bottle of Graham's correction paint.

  pro   v   n   prep adj   n   conj   v pro prep   adj   n
7. She mixed the product in her kitchen and bottled it like fingernail polish.

    adv   n   v   n   pro v   n   prep n
8. Single-handedly, Graham developed a product that made millions of dollars.

  adj   n   n   adv   v   prep adj   n
9. Her son, Michael Nesmith, also benefited from her success.

   pro v   n   prep   n   adj   n prep   n
10. He was a member of The Monkees, a popular band in the 1960s.

EXERCISE 2

(Notice that the word *exercise* is used as three different parts of speech in these sentences: verb, adjective, and noun.)

        n   v   prep adj   adj   n
1. Adults exercise in many different ways.

     adj   n   v   prep   n   conj v prep   n
2. Some people walk around the neighborhood or run in the park.

       pro   v   adj   n   prep conj prep   n   conj n
3. Others ride their bikes to and from work or school.

     adj   n   v   n   prep adj adj   adj   n
4. Many people join programs at their local fitness centers.

     adj   n   v   adj   adj   n
5. These centers have the latest exercise equipment.

        n   conj adj   n   v adv   adj
6. Treadmills and weight machines are very popular.

       n   v   v prep n   conj   pro   v
7. People can listen to music while they exercise.

       n   v   adv   v adj
8. Exercise should always be fun.

   adj   n prep adj   adj   n   v   n
9. One secret to a good exercise program is flexibility.

      n   pro v adv adj   adv   v prep n
10. A schedule that is too strict often leads to failure.

EXERCISE 3

      n   v   n   conj   n
1. Plants need water and sunlight.

     adv   adj   n   v   adv
2. Sometimes house plants die unexpectedly.

     adv   n   v   pro adv adj   n conj adv adj   n
3. Often people give them too much water or not enough water.

   pro v   n   prep   adj   n   adv

4. I saw an experiment on a television show once.

   pro   v   adj   n

5. It involved two plants.

      adj   n   v   adj   n   prep   n   conj   n

6. The same woman raised both plants with water and sunlight.

      n   v prep   adj   n

7. The plants grew in two different rooms.

   pro   v   prep adj n conj v   adj   n   prep   pro

8. She yelled at one plant but said sweet things to the other.

      adv   adj   n   v   adv

9. The verbally praised plant grew beautifully.

      adv   adj   n   v

10. The verbally abused plant died.

EXERCISE 4

   interj   n   v   adj   n   prep adj   n

1. Wow, pigeons have a built-in compass in their brains!

   adj   n   v   pro prep   adj   n   conj pro   v

2. This compass points them in the right direction as they fly.

    adv   adj   n   prep   n   v   n   prep adj   n

3. Recently, pigeon experts in England conducted a study of these birds.

      n   v   n   prep adj   n   prep adj   n

4. The study tracked the flights of certain pigeons for two years.

      n   v   adv   adj

5. The results were very surprising.

    adj   n   adv   v   adj adj   n

6. Modern pigeons usually ignored their inner compasses.

   pro   v   prep adj   n   adv

7. They navigated by other methods instead.

      n   adv   v   adv conj   v   adj   n

8. The pigeons simply looked down and followed human highways.

     pro   v   n   prep   adj   n   conj v   adj   n   adv

9. They remembered roads from previous flights and took the same roads home

   adv

again.

       n   adv   v   adj   n   n   conj   n   conj pro   v

10. The pigeons even traced the roads' turns, curves, and roundabouts as they flew.

EXERCISE 5

    adj   adj   n   v   adv   adj   n

1. Wild Quaker parrots are also interesting birds.

    pro   adv   v   prep   n

2. They originally came from Argentina.

    pro v   adj   n   prep   n   prep   n

3. They are noisy inhabitants of neighborhoods across North America.

    adj   n   v prep adj   n   prep   n prep adj   n

4. These birds live in large nests at the top of tall trees.

    adv   adj   n   v   n

5. Only Quaker parrots build nests.

    adj   n   v   adj   n

6. These nests have three compartments.

    adj   n   v   n   prep   n

7. The back part offers protection for the eggs.

     adj   n   v   n

8. The middle section houses the adults.

     n   prep   adj   n   v   n   prep   n

9. Parrots in the front compartment guard the entrance to the nest.

    adj   n   v   adj   n prep n

10. Some people raise Quaker parrots as pets.

PARAGRAPH EXERCISE

conj pro v adv prep adj n conj n prep adj n pro adv v conj
When I look back over my life and the lives of my friends, I also see that

n prep adj conj adj n v pro conj pro v
involvement in school and community activities helped us [when we felt] the

adj n prep adj n pro v n prep adj n
negative pull of our peers. I joined the Shakespeare Club in elementary school

conj n prep adv adj n conj pro v n
and the Police Athletic League in junior high school, and I played baseball

prep adj n n v adj n prep adj n prep adj adj n
in high school. Sam took karate lessons from grade school through his early years

prep adj n conj adv v prep adj adj adj n conj n v
in high school and also played on our high-school baseball team. And Rameck took

adj n prep adv adj n conj prep adj n pro v adj n
drama lessons in junior high school, and in high school he joined the drama club.

ADJECTIVES AND ADVERBS (PP. 36–39)

EXERCISE 1

  1. adverb adding to the verb *attract*

  2. adjective adding to the noun *entrance*

  3. adjective adding to the noun *paperbacks*

  4. adjective adding to the noun *topics*

  5. adverb adding to the verb *discovered*

  6. adverb adding to the adjective *straightforward*

  7. adjective adding to the noun *subtitle*

  8. adverb adding to the adjective *pink*

  9. adverb adding to the verb *considered*

  10. adverb adding to the verb *took*

EXERCISE 2

  1. adjective adding to the noun *dollar*

  2. adverb adding to the adjective *one*

  3. adjective adding to the pronoun *I*

  4. adverb adding to the verb *paints*

5. adjective adding to the noun *buildings*

6. adjective adding to the noun *shingles*

7. adjective adding to the noun *French*

8. adverb adding to the verb *speak*

9. adjective adding to the noun *child*

10. adjective adding to the pronoun *one*

EXERCISE 3

1. close	**6.** bad
2. closely	**7.** very happily
3. close	**8.** very happy
4. badly	**9.** good
5. bad	**10.** well

EXERCISE 4

1. largest	**6.** ugliest
2. larger	**7.** uglier
3. large	**8.** friendliest
4. ugly	**9.** friendly
5. ugly	**10.** friendlier

EXERCISE 5

(Notice that *online* is used as both an adjective and an adverb in this exercise.)

        adj   adv
1. I took a helpful class online in the spring.

      adj   adj
2. An Internet specialist taught me research skills.

       adv adj   adj
3. I discovered very useful tools for Web research.

        adv   adj   adj
4. The instructor clearly explained various kinds of online resources.

       adj   adj   adj
5. She gave me several optional topics for each assignment.

            adv   adj   adj

6. I especially enjoyed the articles from my two projects about world music.

      adv   adv   adj

7. Now I fully understand the benefits of online classes.

           adj   adj   adj   adj

8. They are fun and rewarding because students work at their own pace.

          adv   adv   adj   adj

9. I am definitely less confused about online sources.

                       adv   adv

10. I can do research online and enjoy the process completely.

PROOFREADING EXERCISE

                    adj   adj   adj

My ~~most favorite~~ *favorite* movie of all time is <u>The Matrix</u>. This movie is

         adv   adj   adj   adj   adj

~~intenser~~ *more intense* than any other movie about the future. Neo, the main

         adj   adj   adj   adj

character, is smart and creative. He feels ~~badly~~ *bad* about the emptiness of his life

      adj   adj   adj

He has a dull, unsatisfying job, and he wants some excitement. Eventually, a team

  adj   adv

of real people from outside the Matrix find Neo and try ~~repeated~~ *repeatedly* to

                    adj

recruit him. Neo joins their team and fights against the agents in the Matrix.

                    adv   adj   adj   adv

<u>The Matrix</u> may be just the first part of a trilogy, but in my opinion, it's still the

      adj

~~better~~ *best* movie of the three.

CONTRACTIONS (PP. 41–45)

EXERCISE 1

1. aren't
2. haven't
3. don't
4. they're
5. she'd
6. they'd
7. aren't
8. who've
9. there's
10. who's

EXERCISE 2

1. What's
2. You're, you're
3. no contractions (The word *its* is possessive; it does not mean *it is* or *it has*.)
4. it's, it's, it's (The third *its* is possessive; it does not mean *it is* or *it has*.)
5. there's
6. don't, they're
7. There's
8. doesn't, won't
9. It's, isn't
10. They'll, won't

EXERCISE 3

1. aren't, they're
2. they've
3. They're, you're
4. we've, they're
5. They're
6. they're
7. There's, who's, they've
8. shouldn't
9. doesn't, it's
10. that's

EXERCISE 4

1. I'm, you've
2. didn't
3. she's, he's, they're, who's
4. that's
5. didn't
6. That's, we've, she's, don't
7. wasn't
8. didn't, she's
9. no contractions
10. didn't, she's

EXERCISE 5

1. they're	**6.** we're, I'm
2. they've	**7.** he's
3. they're	**8.** he's, it's
4. I've	**9.** isn't, they're
5. it's, that's	**10.** there's

PROOFREADING EXERCISE

I bought a ~~knew~~ *new* car last week. It was the first time I had ~~too~~ *to* deal with car salespeople. I ~~did'nt~~ *didn't* believe all those stories about the pressure they make you feel. However, now that I have gone ~~threw~~ *through* the experience, I ~~no~~ *know* that ~~its~~ *it's* true. Whether I was alone or with my family, the salespeople were at my elbow the whole time. Even when I asked them to give me time to look around, they were still ~~quiet~~ *quite* persistent. The only one ~~who's~~ *whose* sales pitch wasn't annoying was a ~~women~~ *woman*. Out of all the salespeople, she was the ~~calmer~~ *calmest*, so I bought my car from her.

POSSESSIVES (PP. 50–51)

EXERCISE 4

1. Jagger's	**6.** London's
2. couple's	**7.** characters'
3. Hall's	**8.** theaters', actress's
4. no possessives	**9.** role's, Hall's
5. Hall's	**10.** judges', character's

EXERCISE 5

1. Manning's	**6.** studio's
2. critic's, Columbia Pictures'	**7.** Manning's
3. Manning's, *Knight's*	**8.** public's
4. writer's	**9.** no possessives
5. Manning's	**10.** films'

PROOFREADING EXERCISE

The Martins are a family that has lived next door to me for eighteen years. I have grown up with the ~~Martin's~~ *Martins'* son, Milo, as my best friend. My family is smaller than Milo's family, but I've never been close to anyone but him. The funny thing about the Martins is their names. They all begin with the letter "M." ~~Milos'~~

Milo's ~~parent's~~ *parents'* names are Michael and Maureen. His ~~brother's~~ *brothers'* names are Monty and Mike; his sister's name is Marie. Unlike the Martins, my family ~~member's~~ *members'* names all begin with different letters, and I'm glad.

REVIEW OF CONTRACTIONS AND POSSESSIVES (PP. 52–53)

1. *I Love Lucy's*, today's

2. Lucy's, Ethel's

3. can't, it's

4. it'll

5. Lucy and Ethel's, agent's

6. factory's, candies'

7. Lucy's, can't, doesn't

8. don't

9. Ricky and Fred's, haven't, Lucy and Ethel's, it's

10. We've, men and women's, *I Love Lucy's*, it's

I consider my friend Alexis to be one of the smartest people I know. Alexis is a twenty-five-year-old film student at a nearby university. ~~Shes~~ *She's* presently in her senior year, but ~~thats~~ *that's* just the beginning for Alexis. She plans to take full advantage of her ~~universitys~~ *university's* resources to learn what she needs before starting her own filmmaking career. She has access to her fellow ~~students~~ *students'* talent, her different ~~teachers~~ *teachers'* equipment and experience, and the film ~~schools~~ *school's* many contacts. Alexis ~~doesnt~~ *doesn't* agree with a lot of the advice she gets from people in the film industry. They try to discourage her sometimes, but she ~~wont~~ *won't* let anything distract her from her goal of making great movies. ~~Ive~~ *I've* always been impressed by ~~Alexis~~ *Alexis'* (or *Alexis's*) self-confidence, and ~~its~~ *it's* inspired me to believe in myself more than I ever have before.

PROGRESS TEST (P. 54)

1. A. *candidates'*

2. B. *its* performance

3. B. training me *well*

4. A. *an* abandoned cat

5. B. *through* all of their luggage

6. A. *a* unicycle

7. A. network has *already* gone out

8. B. a better lecturer *than* the other

9. B. sweets can *affect* the brain's ability

10. A. to accept *advice*

SENTENCE STRUCTURE

FINDING SUBJECTS AND VERBS (PP. 59–62)

EXERCISE 1

1. Morpheus is a new kind of robot.

2. His creators named him after the character in *The Matrix* and gave him Moe as a nickname.

3. Scientists at the University of Washington in Seattle developed Moe's hardware and software.

4. They designed Moe for a very useful purpose.

5. Some disabled people have limited movement and need physical help at times.

6. Only a person's thoughts control Moe's movements and tasks.

7. The thoughts reach Moe through sensors in a cap on the person's head.

8. Moe requires no physical contact.

9. Currently, Moe is still in his experimental stages.

10. The possibilities for thought-controlled robots are almost endless.

EXERCISE 2

1. All U.S. presidents give speeches as a part of their duties.

2. They deliver different styles of speeches, however.

3. In U.S. history, there are many famous presidential speakers.

4. Their unique voices, phrases, and mannerisms contribute to their fame.

5. *Presidential Voices* is a book about the speaking styles of the presidents.

6. John Adams included a 700-word sentence in his Inaugural Address.

7. The first speech of William Henry Harrison lasted for two hours and partially caused his death.

8. Harrison developed pneumonia from the cold, wet weather on his inaugural day.

9. Surprisingly, the book places Thomas Jefferson on the list of poor speakers.

10. At times, Jefferson avoided important speeches, even the State of the Union.

EXERCISE 3

1. Ancient Egyptians worshipped cats of all sizes.

2. Archeologists find many mummies of cats in Egyptian tombs.

3. Carvings in the tombs reveal a strong belief in the god-like powers of large cats.

4. Scientists always look for new evidence of ancient beliefs.

5. Archaeologists recently discovered the mummy of a lion in a tomb in Saqqara, Egypt.

6. It is the first discovery of a lion skeleton in an Egyptian tomb.

7. There were no bandages around the lion.

8. But there were other signs of mummification.

9. The lion rested in the tomb of King Tutankhamen's nurse.

10. Archaeologists now have real evidence of lion worship in Egypt.

EXERCISE 4

1. I never knew much about curses and magic spells.

2. According to *Smithsonian* magazine, the ancient Greeks and Romans used them all the time.

3. There were magicians for hire back then.

4. These magicians made money through their knowledge of the art of cursing.

5. Some citizens took revenge on their enemies with special curses for failure.

6. Others wanted only love and placed spells on the objects of their desire.

7. The magicians wrote the commissioned curses or love spells on lead tablets.

8. Then they positioned these curse tablets near their intended victims.

9. Archaeologists found one 1,700-year-old curse tablet over the starting gate of an ancient race course.

10. It named the horses and drivers of specific chariots and itemized the specifics of the curse.

EXERCISE 5

1. Human beings are creatures of habit.

2. They visit predictable places and do predictable things.

3. In their work, scientists study such behavior.

4. George Karev is a member of the Bulgarian Academy of Sciences.

5. Karev studied the habits of people in movie theaters.

6. Karev's results about moviegoers make a lot of sense.

7. Most people prefer seats on the right side of the theater and always sit there.

8. Therefore, their left eye sees most of the movie.

9. The left eye generally reports to the right hemisphere of the brain.

10. The right hemisphere connects people with their own feelings and with the emotions of others.

PARAGRAPH EXERCISE

Al Levis invented the popular snack Slim Jims. Slim Jims are stick-shaped meat snacks. Levis was a high-school dropout but eventually made a fortune from his snack product. Slim Jims originally came in jars full of vinegar. In the 1940s and 50s, bar customers ate Slim Jims with their cocktails. Then Levis's company offered Slim Jims in individual packages. People ate them on camping trips and at sporting events. Levis sold his invention in the late 1960s but continued his good work. Before his death in March of 2001, Levis donated millions of dollars to worthy causes.

LOCATING PREPOSITIONAL PHRASES (PP. 65–68)

EXERCISE 1

1. Viganella is a tiny village (at the bottom) (of the Alps) (in Italy).

2. Due (to its physical position) (between the mountains), the town (of Viganella) suffered (from an unusual problem).

3. The sun's rays never reached the village (from the middle) (of November) (to the first week) (in February).

4. The mountains kept the little town (in shadow) (without any direct sunlight) (for several months) each year.

5. Then <u>Giacomo Bonzani</u> <u>found</u> a high-tech solution (to Viganella's dreary situation).

6. (In 2006), <u>engineers</u> <u>installed</u> a huge mirror thousands (of feet) (above Viganella) (on the side) (of one) (of the mountains) (around it).

7. A <u>computer</u> (at the mirror's location) <u>keeps</u> track (of the sun's movements).

8. The computer's <u>software</u> <u>rotates</u> the mirror (into the perfect position) to reflect sunlight (into the village square). [Note: "To reflect sunlight" is a verbal, not a prepositional phrase.]

9. The <u>mirror</u> <u>began</u> its work (in December) (of 2006).

10. Now the <u>sun</u> <u>"shines"</u> (on the town) (of Viganella) (during all months) (of the year).

EXERCISE 2

1. The many <u>cases</u> (of food poisoning) (in America) each year <u>alarm</u> people.

2. Some food <u>scientists</u> <u>point</u> (to food irradiation) (as one possible solution).

3. The <u>irradiation</u> (of food) <u>kills</u> bacteria (through exposure) (to gamma rays).

4. (With irradiation), <u>farmers</u> <u>spray</u> fewer pesticides (on their crops).

5. And irradiated <u>food</u> <u>lasts</u> longer (on the shelf) or (in the refrigerator).

6. However, many <u>scientists</u> and <u>consumers</u> <u>worry</u> (about the risks) (of food irradiation).

7. <u>Irradiation</u> <u>reduces</u> vitamins and <u>changes</u> nutrients (in the food).

8. The radioactive <u>materials</u> (at the irradiation plants) <u>are</u> also potentially dangerous.

9. <u>Critics</u> <u>predict</u> accidents (in the transportation and use) (of these radioactive substances).

10. (In the United States), the <u>controversy</u> (about food irradiation) <u>continues</u>.

EXERCISE 3

1. *Romeo and Juliet* <u>is</u> a famous play (by William Shakespeare).

2. <u>It</u> <u>remains</u> one (of the most popular love stories) (in the world).

3. Many <u>movies</u> <u>use</u> aspects (of it) (in their plots).

4. One <u>thing</u> (about Shakespeare's version) (of the story) <u>surprises</u> people.

5. Both <u>Romeo</u> and <u>Juliet</u> <u>have</u> other love interests (in the play).

6. <u>Romeo</u> <u>has</u> a crush (on Rosaline) (before Juliet).

7. Juliet elopes (with Romeo) (in secret).

8. Then Juliet accepts a marriage proposal (from another man) (against her will).

9. Friar Lawrence helps Romeo and Juliet (with a plan) (for their escape).

10. However, the complicated timing (of his plan) has tragic results (on the lives) (of the famous couple).

EXERCISE 4

1. (As a change) (of pace), I shopped (for my Mother's Day gift) (at an antique mall).

2. I found old Bakelite jewelry (in every shade) (of yellow, brown, red, blue, and green).

3. There were even linens (from the pioneer days).

4. One booth sold drinking glasses (with advertising slogans and cartoon characters) (on them).

5. Another stocked old metal banks (with elaborate mechanisms) (for children's pennies).

6. (In the back corner) (of the mall), I found a light blue pitcher (with a familiar dark blue design).

7. My mother had one (like it) (in the early years) (of my childhood).

8. My sisters and I drank punch (from it) (on hot days) (in the summer).

9. I checked the price (on the tag) (underneath the pitcher's handle).

10. I reached (for my credit card) (without hesitation).

EXERCISE 5

1. (Over the weekend), I watched a hilarious old movie, *Genevieve,* (on late-night television).

2. The story takes place (in the countryside) (of England).

3. It is a black-and-white movie (from the 1930s or 1940s).

4. The clothes and manners (of the characters) (in *Genevieve*) are very proper and old-fashioned.

5. Two young couples enter their cars (in a road rally) (for fun).

6. They participate (in the race) strictly (for adventure).

7. Genevieve is the name (of the main couple's car).

8. (During the road rally), the polite manners (of the two couples) disappear (in the rush) (for the finish line).

9. Predictably, <u>they</u> <u>fight</u> (with each other) and <u>sabotage</u> each other's cars.

10. (Like all good comedies), <u>Genevieve</u> <u>has</u> an ending (with a surprise) (in it) (for everyone).

PARAGRAPH EXERCISE

HEARSAY (ON Q-TIPS)

(In 1922), Leo Gerstenrang, an immigrant (from Warsaw, Poland), who had served (in the United States Army) (during World War I) and worked (with the fledgling Red Cross Organization), founded the Leo Gerstenrang Infant Novelty Co. (with his wife), selling accessories used (for baby care). (After the birth) (of the couple's daughter), Gerstenrang noticed that his wife would wrap a wad (of cotton) (around a toothpick) (for use) (during their baby's bath) and decided to manufacture a ready-to-use cotton swab. [Note: "To manufacture" and "to use" are verbals, not prepositional phrases.]

(After several years), Gerstenrang developed a machine that would wrap cotton uniformly (around each blunt end) (of a small stick) (of carefully selected and cured nonsplintering birch wood), package the swabs (in a sliding tray-type box), sterilize the box, and seal it (with an outer wrapping) (of glassine)—later changed (to cellophane). The phrase "untouched (by human hands)" became widely known (in the production) (of cotton swabs). The *Q* (in the name Q-Tips) stands (for *quality*) and the word *tips* describes the cotton swab (on the end) (of the stick).

UNDERSTANDING DEPENDENT CLAUSES (PP. 71–75)

EXERCISE 1

1. Tina, my twin sister, got a job that requires late-night hours.

2. The hours that I like the best are between six and eleven in the morning.

3. Now Tina sleeps until noon because she works all night. [Note: "Until noon" is a prepositional phrase, not a dependent clause.]

4. When she comes home from work, our whole family is asleep.

5. Since Tina is at work all night, I rarely see her.

6. Our dad thinks that Tina works too hard.

7. Our mom believes that Tina's new hours are a good challenge for her.

8. Yesterday, Tina's boss asked me if I want a job like Tina's.

9. I am not sure when I will find the right job for me.

10. Whenever I do find a good job, it will be during the day.

EXERCISE 2

1. Although it happened several years ago, one news story stays in my mind.

2. It was the story of a puppy that shot his owner in self-defense.

3. The man decided to kill the large litter of puppies because he could not find anyone to adopt them.

4. As he held this special little dog in his arms, the man fired a revolver at the other puppies.

5. The hero puppy pawed at the man's hand that held the gun.

6. The puppy fought and struggled so hard that the gun turned and fired a shot into the man's wrist.

7. After the incident, many people wanted to adopt the puppies that escaped.

8. I remember this story because it is so incredible.

9. The sad part of the story is that a few of the puppies died.

10. The man recovered from the shot that the hero puppy fired to save himself and several of his litter mates.

EXERCISE 3

1. People who need glasses often wear contact lenses.

2. Clear contact lenses maintain a person's appearance because they fit over the eye and have no frames.

3. But there are contact lenses that change a person's eye color.

4. Someone who has green eyes makes them blue or brown with colored contact lenses.

5. Now even people who don't need glasses change their eye color with contact lenses.

6. Colored lenses are fashion statements that are especially popular with young people.

7. Unless a doctor fits them, contact lenses that people buy or trade with friends invite injuries.

8. Ill-fitting lenses squeeze or scratch the eyes as they move around under the eyelids.

9. After a scratch occurs, germs easily infect the eyes' surface.

10. Such infections sometimes lead to damage that is permanent.

EXERCISE 4

1. I am not very talkative when I'm in school.

2. Whenever my teacher asks a question in class, I get nervous.

3. If I know the answer, I usually look straight ahead.

4. When I forget the answer, I check my shoes or a note in my notebook.

5. Usually, the teacher chooses someone else before I finish my fidgeting.

6. Obviously, when I take a speech class, I talk sometimes.

7. In my last speech class, we all demonstrated some sort of process that we knew.

8. The speech that I gave explained how I make crepes.

9. Since I work at a French restaurant, I borrowed a crepe pan for my demonstration.

10. The crepes cooked so quickly that the teacher and students passed the plates around before I said anything at all.

EXERCISE 5

1. Many people remember when microwave ovens first arrived in stores.

2. People worried about whether they were safe or not.

3. Before they had the microwave oven, people cooked all food with direct heat.

4. At first, microwave ovens seemed strange because they heated only the food.

5. And microwave ovens cooked food so much faster than ordinary ovens did.

6. Eventually, people welcomed the convenience that microwave ovens offered.

7. Since they are fast and cool, microwave ovens work well almost anywhere.

8. People who are on a budget bring lunch from home and heat it up at work

or school.

9. Now that microwave ovens are here, people make a lot more popcorn.

10. As each new technology arrives, people wonder how they ever lived without it.

PARAGRAPH EXERCISE
We have numbered the dependent clauses in the excerpt for clarity's sake.

We don't exist (1) unless there is someone (2) who can see us existing, (3) what we say has no meaning (4) until someone can understand, (5) while to be surrounded by friends is constantly to have our identity confirmed; their knowledge and care for us have the power to pull us from our numbness. In small comments, many of them teasing, they reveal (6) [that] they know our foibles and accept them and so, in turn, accept (7) that we have a place in the world. We can ask them "Isn't he frightening?" or "Do you ever feel that . . . ?" and be understood, rather than encounter the puzzled 'No, not particularly'— (8) which can make us feel, even when in company, as lonely as polar explorers.

True friends do not evaluate us according to worldly criteria; it is the core self (9) [that] they are interested in; like ideal parents, their love for us remains unaffected by our appearance or position in the social hierarchy, and so we have no qualms in dressing in old clothes and revealing (10) that we have made little money this year. The desire for riches should perhaps not always be understood as a simple hunger for a luxurious life; a more important motive might be the wish to be appreciated and treated nicely. We may seek a fortune for no greater reason than to secure the respect and attention of people (11) who would otherwise look straight through us. Epicurus, discerning our underlying need, recognized (12) that a handful of true friends could deliver the love and respect (13) that even a fortune may not.

CORRECTING FRAGMENTS (PP. 78–82)

EXERCISE 1

Possible revisions to make the fragments into sentences are *italicized*.

1. Correct

2. Improvements in fabric coatings *are* making it possible.

3. Clothes *are* treated with certain chemicals.

4. Correct

5. *They have already been tested* by the military for soldiers' uniforms.

6. Correct

7. Correct

8. *They* helped cure soldiers' skin problems, too.

9. Correct

10. *It could also* be used for hospital bedding, kitchen linens, and sport-related clothing.

EXERCISE 2

Possible revisions to make the fragments into sentences are *italicized*.

1. Correct

2. *Duct tape* holds objects together firmly.

3. *It also* patches holes in backpacks and tents.

4. Correct

5. Books *have been* written about the unique uses for it.

6. *The makers of Duck Brand duct tape hold a yearly contest.*

7. Correct

8. Strips of duct tape *form* tuxedos, cummerbunds, gowns, hats, and corsages.

9. A $3,000 prize *goes* to the couple with the best use of duct tape and another $3,000 *goes* to their high school.

10. Correct

EXERCISE 3

Answers may vary, but here are some possible revisions.

1. We shopped all day at the mall, looking for the perfect suitcases.

2. We knew of a specialty store selling hard and soft luggage, large and small sizes, and lots of accessories.

3. Walking from store to store and getting tired, we gave up after a while and sat down.

4. Resting on a bench for a few minutes, we enjoyed ourselves by "people-watching."

5. Crowds of people filled the mall in every shop and at the food court, too.

6. Crowding the walkways and window shopping, our fellow consumers circulated in every direction.

7. Teenagers gathered in groups, laughed at each other, and ignored the other shoppers.

8. Using the mall as an exercise facility, pairs of older people walked briskly around the balconies.

9. We finally found the perfect luggage at a little store near the elevators at the end of the mall.

10. Because of all the interesting people and the final outcome, our shopping trip was a complete success.

EXERCISE 4

Answers may vary, but here are some possible revisions.

1. Thrift stores, yard sales, and flea markets are popular places to shop because they sell items that aren't available anywhere else.

2. Since most thrift stores help charities, they are there to assist people in need.

3. Although the objects in thrift stores are often five to thirty years old, many people prefer their vintage designs.

4. For instance, thrift stores sell old metal shelving units, which are much better than modern ones made of cheap wood or plastic.

5. There are many famous stories of people becoming rich because they shopped at flea markets and yard sales.

6. When one man bought a framed picture for a few dollars at a flea market, he liked the frame but not the picture.

7. As he removed the picture from the frame, he found one of the original copies of the "Declaration of Independence."

8. At a yard sale, a woman bought a small table that she later discovered was worth half a million dollars.

9. Of course, collectors always shop at these places, where they hope to find historical treasures and other objects of value.

10. In a way, shopping at thrift stores, yard sales, and flea markets is a kind of recycling, which is something that benefits everyone.

EXERCISE 5
Answers may vary, but here are some possible revisions.

1. As the players congratulated each other, they walked off the field.

2. My favorite television show has been canceled.

3. Cell phones are distracting when you drive.

4. No one knows where the technology of cloning will be in ten years.

5. The government protects people's property with laws.

6. Since that car costs too much, I will buy a different one.

7. An understanding of math is a requirement for most students.

8. She was tired of voting in most elections but never feeling represented.

9. Put my keys on the desk between my computer and my golfing trophy.

10. A keen sense of smell makes the dog a perfect detective.

PROOFREADING PARAGRAPH
Here is one possible revision to eliminate the five fragments.

Shark attacks have been on the rise. We've all heard the heartbreaking news stories of people on their honeymoons or children playing in only a few feet of water being attacked by sharks. Movies like *Jaws* and *Open Water* make us wary and scared when we watch them. But their effects fade over time, and we forget about the risks of entering the habitats of dangerous animals. Experts try to convince us that sharks and other powerful species are not targeting human beings on purpose. To a shark, a person is no different from a seal or a sea turtle. Facts such as these prompt many of us to think twice before we take a dip in the ocean.

CORRECTING RUN-ON SENTENCES (PP. 85–89)

EXERCISE 1
1. In early 2007, a mobile phone company sponsored a new kind of contest; it wanted to find the fastest text-messager in the United States.

2. To participate in the LG National Texting Championship, contestants had to be U.S. residents, and they had to be at least thirteen years old.

3. The first qualifying round of the texting contest was held on the West Coast in March; a separate qualifying round was held on the East Coast in April.

4. The West Coast participants competed in Hollywood, and the East Coast contestants battled in New York City.

5. Both the Hollywood and New York Regional Champions won $10,000. The Hollywood winner also received a trip to New York to participate in the National Championship.

6. Eli Tirosh, a 21-year-old woman from Los Angeles, won the West Coast title; Morgan Pozgar, a 13-year-old girl from Claysburg, Pennsylvania, won the East Coast title.

7. The sentence is correct.

8. The two contestants were shown phrases on a screen, and they had to type the phrases on their tiny keypads quickly and perfectly.

9. Pozgar beat Tirosh by typing several lines of the lyrics to the song "Supercalifragilisticexpialidocious." Pozgar typed 151 characters in just 42 seconds.

10. The sentence is correct.

EXERCISE 2

Your answers may differ depending on how you choose to separate the two clauses.

1. Nearly everyone yawns, but few understand the dynamics of yawning.

2. The sentence is correct.

3. The sentence is correct.

4. The sentence is correct.

5. Groups of people do similar things, for they are acting somewhat like herds of animals.

6. The sentence is correct.

7. The yawning helps the group act as one, so it minimizes conflict.

8. There are a few misconceptions about yawns. One of them has to do with oxygen levels.

9. The sentence is correct.

10. Surprisingly, studies show no changes in yawning patterns due to levels of oxygen; in fact, research subjects inhaling pure oxygen yawned the same number of times as those breathing normally.

EXERCISE 3

Your answers may differ since various words can be used to begin dependent clauses. The dependent words we have added are *italiziced*.

1. On summer evenings, people around the world enjoy the sight of little lights *that* are flying around in the air.

2. *Although* most people know the glowing insects as fireflies, they are also called lightning bugs and glowworms.

3. Glowworms are unique *since* they don't fly.

4. The term "fireflies" may be a little misleading *because* they are not technically flies.

5. Lightning bugs are beetles *that* have special substances in their bodies.

6. The substances *that* make them glow are luciferin and luciferase.

7. *When* the luciferin and luciferase combine with oxygen, they produce a greenish light.

8. The light can be *so* intense *that* people in some countries use caged fireflies as lamps.

9. The sentence is correct.

10. Incredibly, *even though* groups of fireflies blink out of order at first, they seem to coordinate their blinking within a few minutes.

EXERCISE 4

Your answers may differ since various words can be used to begin dependent clauses. The dependent words we have added are *italiziced*.

1. The sentence is correct.

2. The calls are made by companies *whose* salespeople try to interest us in the newest calling plan or credit card offer.

3. They don't call during the day *when* nobody is home.

4. I feel sorry for some of the salespeople *because* they are just doing their job.

5. *When* my father tells them to call during business hours, they hang up right away.

6. The sentence is correct.

7. *When* my mother answers, she is too polite, so they just keep talking.

8. *Although* we try to ignore the ringing, it drives us all crazy.

9. The sentence is correct.

10. *Since* we never buy anything over the phone, maybe these companies will all get the message and leave us alone.

EXERCISE 5
Your answers may differ depending on how you chose to connect the clauses.

1. In 2001, American businessman Dennis Tito did something *that* no one had done before.

2. Tito became the world's first tourist in space *when* he paid twenty million dollars for a ride to the International Space Station.

3. Tito wanted the United States to take him into space, but NASA said no.

4. NASA declined Tito's offer; however, Russian space officials accepted it gladly.

5. In early May 2001, Tito boarded a Russian Soyuz rocket, and he blasted off into outer space.

6. Tito could talk to the cosmonauts on board *because* he studied Russian for six months before his trip.

7. Dennis Tito's first-of-its-kind vacation was just the beginning of civilian travel into outer space; more and more individuals will want to follow Tito's example.

8. Soon there will be travel agents *who* will specialize in space travel.

9. Other countries besides Russia will welcome the income from such trips; for example, China may soon have the ability to take people into space.

10. In 2001, NASA chose not to let Tito on one of its space shuttles; in the future, NASA may welcome space tourists.

REVIEW OF FRAGMENTS AND RUN-ON SENTENCES (P. 90)

Your revisions may differ depending on how you chose to correct the errors.

In 2001, a writer named Terry Ryan published a book about her mother, and it later became a movie. The title of the book was *The Prize Winner of Defiance: How My Mother Raised 10 Kids on 25 Words or Less*. Ryan had already written two poetry books and was busy writing a comic strip for a San Francisco newspaper when she decided to tell her mom's story. Terry's mother, Evelyn Ryan, was a remarkable woman who entered contest after contest in the 1950s and won most of them. In those days, companies sponsored competitions, and they gave prizes to the writers of the best slogan, poem, or song about their product. Evelyn Ryan was such a naturally good writer that she won countless prizes, ranging from small appliances to large cash awards. She earned all of them through skill and perseverance. Terry Ryan clearly described her mother's organizational skills and generosity. Evelyn Ryan, her daughter explained, was also motivated by her circumstances as the wife of an alcoholic. Evelyn did it all for her family. Winning such contests was her way of staying at home, supporting ten children, and keeping the family together.

IDENTIFYING VERB PHRASES (PP. 92–96)

EXERCISE 1

1. Scientists of all kinds <u>have been learning</u> a lot lately.

2. Those who <u>study</u> traffic safety <u>have</u> recently <u>discovered</u> a puzzling truth.

3. People <u>drive</u> more safely when they <u>encounter</u> fewer traffic signs and traffic lights.

4. The reason behind the "Shared Space" theory <u>is</u> easy to explain.

5. Drivers <u>will regulate</u> their speed and <u>pay</u> closer attention to other drivers when they <u>are</u> not <u>told</u> to do so by signs and lights.

6. Traffic signs and signals <u>give</u> drivers a false sense of security that often <u>leads</u> to recklessness.

7. When no signs or signals <u>exist</u>, drivers <u>think</u> about their own safety and <u>drive</u> more cautiously.

8. Many towns in Europe and America <u>have</u> already <u>taken</u> steps to test the truth of this theory.

9. In some cases, all lights, signs, and barriers <u>have been removed</u> so that all drivers and pedestrians <u>must negotiate</u> with each other to proceed through the town.

10. These changes <u>have</u> usually <u>resulted</u> in lower speeds, fewer accidents, and shorter travel times.

EXERCISE 2

1. Shopping for holiday items <u>has changed</u> in recent years.

2. Before one celebration <u>has arrived</u>, another holiday's decorations <u>are</u> on display in stores.

3. In early July, for instance, shoppers <u>will</u> not <u>find</u> banners to celebrate Independence Day.

4. Instead, they <u>will see</u> Halloween items for sale.

5. And by October, store owners <u>will have placed</u> turkeys and pilgrims in their windows.

6. Of course, Kwanzaa, Hanukah, and Christmas sales <u>begin</u> in September on their own special aisles.

7. What <u>can</u> people <u>do</u> about this trend?

8. Shoppers <u>could protest</u> and <u>boycott</u> early displays.

9. They <u>could tell</u> store managers about their concerns.

10. But they <u>might miss</u> the spring-fever sales in January.

EXERCISE 3

1. Felix Hoffmann, a chemist, <u>was trying</u> to ease his own father's pain when he <u>discovered</u> aspirin in 1897.

2. Although aspirin <u>can cause</u> side effects, each year people around the world <u>give</u> themselves fifty billion doses of the popular pain killer.

3. But different countries <u>take</u> this medicine in different ways.

4. The British <u>dissolve</u> aspirin powder in water.

5. The French <u>have insisted</u> that slow-release methods <u>work</u> best.

6. Italians <u>prefer</u> aspirin drinks with a little fizz.

7. And Americans <u>have</u> always <u>chosen</u> to take their aspirin in pill form.

8. However it <u>is taken</u>, aspirin <u>surprises</u> researchers with benefits to human health.

9. It <u>has been</u> a benefit to people with heart problems, colon cancer, and Alzheimer's disease.

10. Where <u>would</u> we <u>be</u> without aspirin?

EXERCISE 4

1. I <u>have</u> recently <u>read</u> about the life of Philo T. Farnsworth.

2. Thirteen-year-old Philo T. Farnsworth <u>was plowing</u> a field in 1922 when he <u>visualized</u> the concept that <u>led</u> to television as we <u>know</u> it.

3. Others <u>were working</u> on the idea of sending images through the air, but Farnsworth actually <u>solved</u> the problem in that open field.

4. He <u>looked</u> at the rows that the plow <u>had made</u> in the earth.

5. And he <u>reasoned</u> that images <u>could be broken</u> down into rows and <u>sent</u> line by line through the air and onto a screen.

6. Farnsworth's idea <u>made</u> television a reality, but historically he <u>has</u> not <u>been</u> fully <u>recognized</u> for this and his other accomplishments.

7. In 1957, he <u>was featured</u> as a guest on *I've Got a Secret,* a television show that <u>presented</u> mystery contestants.

8. The panelists on the show <u>were supposed</u> to guess the guest's secret, which the audience <u>was shown</u> so that everyone <u>knew</u> the answer except the people asking the questions.

9. They <u>asked</u> if he <u>had invented</u> something painful, and he <u>replied</u> that he <u>had</u>; the panelists never <u>guessed</u> that he <u>was</u> the inventor of television.

10. Farnsworth <u>did receive</u> a box of cigarettes and eighty dollars for being on the show.

EXERCISE 5

1. On December 16, 2000, the London stage production of Agatha Christie's play *The Mousetrap* <u>marked</u> a milestone.

2. On that night, actors <u>were performing</u> Christie's play for the twenty-thousandth time.

3. In fact, *The Mousetrap* <u>broke</u> the record as the world's longest running play.

4. The play <u>opened</u> in London on November 25, 1952, and <u>had been running</u> continually ever since.

5. More than ten million people <u>had attended</u> the London performances.

6. Here <u>are</u> some other interesting facts about this production.

7. Two pieces of the original set—the clock and the armchair—<u>had survived</u> on stage for half a century.

8. The cast, however, <u>changed</u> more often.

9. Some actors <u>had remained</u> in the show for years while others <u>had played</u> parts for a short time.

10. One actress <u>understudied</u> for over six thousand performances, but she <u>was needed</u> on stage only seventy-two times.

REVIEW EXERCISE

Sometimes when the <u>moon</u> <u>is</u> a thin crescent, <u>you</u> <u>can see</u> the dim reddish structure (of the rest) (of the moon) filling out the circle. <u>It</u> <u>is</u> the rest (of the moon), and not some other body, because the <u>moon</u> <u>has</u> certain visible markings (on it), and the dim reddish <u>structure</u> <u>has</u> those same markings. <u>People</u> still <u>call</u> this effect "the old moon (in the new moon's arms)". . . .

When the <u>moon</u> <u>is</u> (in a thin crescent stage), <u>it</u> <u>is</u> almost exactly (between us and the sun) so that <u>we</u> <u>see</u> only a little bit (of its lighted surface) (along one edge). If <u>you</u> <u>were</u> (on the moon) (at this time), however, <u>you</u> <u>would see</u> the sun shining (over the moon's shoulder) and lighting up the entire face (of the Earth) that <u>happens</u> to be pointed (toward the moon). In short, when <u>you</u> <u>see</u> a new moon (from Earth), <u>you</u> <u>see</u> a *full Earth* (from the moon). . . .

The unlit <u>side</u> (of the moon) <u>is</u> therefore <u>receiving</u> the light (of the full Earth). *Earthlight* <u>is</u> far feebler than <u>sunlight</u> <u>is</u>, but <u>it</u> <u>is</u> enough to light up the dark side (of the moon) measurably, and <u>it</u> <u>allows</u> us to see the moon's dark side very faintly (at the time) (of the new moon). <u>Galileo</u> <u>was</u> the first to advance this explanation (of the "old moon) (in the new moon's arms"), and <u>it</u> <u>made</u> so much sense that few <u>have</u> <u>doubted</u> it since.

USING STANDARD ENGLISH VERBS (PP. 99–102)

EXERCISE 1
1. walk, walked
2. is, was
3. have, had
4. do, did
5. needs, needed
6. am, was
7. has, had
8. are, were
9. does, did
10. works, worked

EXERCISE 2
1. is, was
2. do, did
3. have, had
4. asks, asked
5. have, had
6. learn, learned
7. are, were
8. does, did
9. plays, played
10. am, was

EXERCISE 3
1. started, like
2. offers
3. are, have
4. finished, needed
5. run, do
6. advise, comfort
7. enjoy, are
8. completed, expected
9. have
10. thank

EXERCISE 4
1. do, don't
2. am, is
3. need, explains
4. help, does
5. works, hope
6. did, dropped
7. was, do
8. work, check
9. learn, learns
10. expect, don't

EXERCISE 5
1. The sentence is correct.
2. The sentence is correct.
3. It *takes* a lot of time and effort to produce a musical.
4. Fifty actors and musicians *have* to coordinate their schedules to practice.
5. The results *are* going to be worth the effort.

6. When our lead actress *sings*, the people in the theater *go* completely quiet.

7. Our dance numbers *are* also impressing everyone who *comes* to rehearsals.

8. The final song definitely *has* the best choreography in the show.

9. The sentence is correct.

10. The sentence is correct.

PROOFREADING EXERCISE

Every day as we drive though our neighborhoods on the way to school or to work, we see things that ~~needs~~ *need* to be fixed. Many of them cause us only a little bit of trouble, so we forget them until we face them again. Every morning, drivers in my neighborhood ~~has~~ *have* to deal with a truck that someone ~~park~~ *parks* right at the corner of our street. It ~~block~~ *blocks* our view as we try to turn onto the main avenue. We need to move out past the truck into the oncoming lane of traffic just to make a left turn. One day last week, I ~~turn~~ *turned* too soon, and a car almost hit me. This truck ~~do~~ *does* not need to be parked in such a dangerous place.

USING REGULAR AND IRREGULAR VERBS (PP. 107–111)

EXERCISE 1
1. looked

2. look

3. looking

4. look

5. looked

6. look

7. looked

8. looking

9. looks

10. look

EXERCISE 2
1. drive, driven

2. thinking, thought

3. take, takes

4. told, telling

5. wrote, written

6. knew, know

7. teach, taught

8. torn, tearing

9. ridden, rode

10. made, make

EXERCISE 3
1. were, heard

2. seen, begun

3. flown, eaten

4. got, did

5. take, eating

6. written, coming, lost

7. swore, felt

8. bought, paid

9. getting, thought

10. saw, told, lay

EXERCISE 4

1. used, supposed
2. catch, came, heard
3. were, left
4. read, draw, build
5. felt, drew

6. did, slept
7. knew, spent
8. went, were
9. woke, stayed
10. forget, spent, were

EXERCISE 5

1. laid, lying, felt
2. know (or knew), been
3. broke, had
4. became, thought
5. was

6. read, frightened
7. kept, shook
8. worked, rose, snuck
9. left, go
10. lose, stung

PROGRESS TEST (P. 112)

1. B. run-on (*Needs a semicolon:* Online, books can be less expensive; however, they are often older editions.)

2. A. fragment (*Combine A and B:* Although I don't like the taste of pineapple and coconut, I do like shampoos that smell like pineapple and coconut.)

3. B. wrong word (I don't *know* how to get there, but my friend does.)

4. B. wrong word (She should *have* gone to the library last week.)

5. A. incorrect verb form (The last student to leave was *supposed* to lock the door. . . .)

6. B. run-on (*Needs a comma:* They're going away for spring break, but I'm staying at home.)

7. B. incorrect verb form (We were *surprised* that it was delivered to us on time.)

8. A. wrong word (In my math class, *there* have already been three quizzes.)

9. B. incorrect apostrophe (However, *Janet's* was the clearest one of all.)

10. B. incorrect verb form (As soon as I wrote my final answer, the bell *rang*.)

MAINTAINING SUBJECT-VERB AGREEMENT (PP. 116–119)

EXERCISE 1

1. are
2. has
3. are
4. is
5. involves, are

6. enter
7. includes
8. set, receive
9. has, have
10. is

EXERCISE 2

1. are
2. are
3. is
4. comes
5. ranks

6. put
7. is
8. are
9. is
10. fill

EXERCISE 3

1. has
2. have, have
3. love
4. makes
5. says

6. thinks
7. is, haven't
8. has
9. looks
10. knows

EXERCISE 4

1. have
2. is
3. is
4. is, is
5. are

6. has
7. represent
8. are
9. comes
10. shine

EXERCISE 5

1. is

2. surprise

3. aren't

4. is

5. shines

6. speak

7. talk

8. is

9. enjoys

10. waits

PROOFREADING EXERCISE

My teachers for this school year are really interesting. Each of their personalities ~~are~~ *is* different. Some of them ~~requires~~ *require* us to be on time every day and follow directions to the letter. Others ~~treats~~ *treat* students almost as casual friends. The expectations of my geography teacher ~~is~~ *are* higher than I expected. Students in that class ~~has~~ *have* to do just what the teacher says, or they risk failing. Most of my other professors ~~takes~~ *take* a more lenient approach. But two of them ~~has~~ *have* an odd grading technique; at least it seems odd to me. These two teachers ~~wants~~ *want* us to turn in all of our papers over the Internet. We can't turn in any handwritten work. I guess there ~~is~~ *are* good reasons behind their demands. My friends ~~says~~ *say* that turning in work over the Internet makes the teachers' jobs easier because it ~~eliminate~~ *eliminates* the possibility of plagiarizing.

AVOIDING SHIFTS IN TIME (P. 121)

PROOFREADING EXERCISES

Corrected verbs are *italicized*.

1. I am taking an art history class right now. Every day, we ~~watched~~ *watch* slide shows of great pieces of art throughout history. We ~~memorized~~ *memorize* each piece of art, its time period, and the artist who created it. I enjoy these slide shows, but I ~~had~~ *have* trouble remembering the facts about them. I always get swept away by the beautiful paintings, drawings, and sculptures and ~~forgot~~ *forget* to take notes that I ~~could~~ *can* study from at home.

2. The paragraph is correct.

3. I enjoyed traveling by plane to Texas. Even though I ~~have~~ *had* to arrive three hours early at the airport, it didn't bother me. I ~~watch~~ *watched* all the people taking off their shoes for security. And once I ~~am~~ *was* through to the boarding gates, I bought some food and ~~relax~~ *relaxed* until it was time to enter the plane. Before I ~~board~~ *boarded* the plane, the passengers who were arriving walked off the ramp with all of their carry-on luggage. They ~~look~~ *looked* tired but happy to be at their destination. Both of my flights were comfortable, and the flight attendants ~~are~~ *were* so nice and cheerful. I liked the way they said, "Y'all come back to Texas real soon."

RECOGNIZING VERBAL PHRASES (PP. 123–127)

EXERCISE 1

1. Parents who <u>like</u> [to go clubbing] can now <u>take</u> their children along—well, sort of.

2. On weekend afternoons, nightclubs around the country <u>childproof</u> their facilities [to allow children] [to dance the day away].

3. An organization [called Baby Loves Disco] <u>orchestrates</u> these events, [offering real drinks for the parents and juice boxes and healthy snacks for the kids].

4. The nightclubs <u>try</u> [to keep the club atmosphere realistic] for the families while [making sure that the volume of the music <u>is</u> not too loud for the children's ears].

5. They <u>keep</u> the music real, too, [playing songs] by the best-[known] bands of the 1970s and '80s.

6. Kids up to eight years old <u>have</u> fun [dancing], [dressing in disco styles], [wearing fake tattoos], [jumping around], and [yelling with other kids and parents].

7. Baby Loves Disco <u>provides</u> special areas for parents [to change their children's diapers] or [to treat themselves to a massage].

8. Baby Loves Disco <u>has</u> its own Web site, [posting videos, news stories, and future events] [taking place in cities across the country].

9. [To attract parents who don't like disco music], the BLD home page <u>includes</u> links to a kids' version of hip hop—[called "Skip Hop"]—and jazz for kids.

10. Videos and testimonials on the site <u>show</u> that kids love [dancing at nightclubs] as much as adults do.

EXERCISE 2

1. Many people <u>dislike</u> [speaking in front of strangers].

2. That <u>is</u> why there <u>is</u> an almost universal fear of [giving speeches].

3. [Feeling exposed], people <u>get</u> dry mouths and sweaty hands.

4. Note cards <u>become</u> useless, [rearranging themselves in the worst possible order].

5. [To combat this problem], people <u>try</u> [to memorize a speech], only [to forget the whole thing] as the audience <u>stares</u> back at them expectantly.

6. And when they <u>do remember</u> parts of it, the microphone <u>decides</u> [to quit at the punch line of their best joke].

7. [Embarrassed] and [humiliated], they <u>struggle</u> [to regain their composure].

8. Then the audience usually <u>begins</u> [to sympathize with and encourage the speaker].

9. Finally [used to the spotlight], the speaker <u>relaxes</u> and <u>finds</u> the courage [to finish].

10. No one <u>expects</u> [giving a speech] [to get any easier].

EXERCISE 3

1. I <u>have learned</u> how [to manage my time] when I <u>am</u> not <u>working</u>.

2. I <u>like</u> [to go to the movies on Friday nights].

3. [Watching a good film] <u>takes</u> me away from the stress of my job.

4. I especially <u>enjoy</u> [eating buttery popcorn] and [drinking a cold soda].

5. It <u>is</u> the perfect way for me [to begin the weekend].

6. I <u>get</u> [to escape from the deadlines and pressure of work].

7. I <u>indulge</u> myself and <u>try</u> [to give myself a break]—nobody <u>is</u> perfect, and everybody <u>has</u> setbacks.

8. All day Saturday I <u>enjoy</u> [lounging around the house in my weekend clothes].

9. I <u>do</u> a little [gardening] and <u>try</u> [to relax my mind].

10. By Sunday evening, after [resting for two days], I <u>am</u> ready [to start my busy week all over again].

EXERCISE 4

1. [Choosing a major] <u>is</u> one of the most important decisions for students.

2. Many students <u>take</u> a long time [to decide about their majors].

3. But they <u>fear</u> [wasting time on the wrong major] more than indecision.

4. They <u>spend</u> several semesters as undecided majors [taking general education classes].

5. [Distracted by class work], students <u>can forget</u> [to pay attention to their interests].

6. Finally, a particular subject area <u>will attract</u> them [to study it further].

7. One student <u>might find</u> happiness in [doing a psychology experiment].

8. [Writing a poem in an English class] <u>may be</u> the assignment [to make another decide].

9. [Attracted by telescopes], a student <u>might choose</u> [to major in astronomy].

10. [Finding a major] <u>takes</u> time and patience.

EXERCISE 5

1. What <u>would cause</u> a television [to send out an SOS signal]?

2. After [moving into his own apartment], Chris van Rossman <u>received</u> a Toshiba television as a present from his parents.

3. [Positioned safely in the [living] room], van Rossman's TV <u>had</u> a [built]-in VCR, DVD, and CD player.

4. Not [subscribing to a cable service], however, van Rossman <u>could watch</u> only four broadcast channels.

5. On October 2, 2004, van Rossman's TV <u>started</u> [to do something very unusual].

6. [Sending out an SOS, the international distress signal], the television <u>called</u> for help.

7. An [orbiting] satellite [designed [to pick up such calls]] from [downed] planes or [sunk] boats <u>heard</u> the distress signal and <u>alerted</u> Air Force officials.

8. After [receiving the information], local Civil Air Patrol authorities in van Rossman's town <u>traced</u> the signal to his apartment complex.

9. Van Rossman <u>opened</u> his door to a team of [uniformed] officers [dispatched [to rescue his television]].

10. [Surprised by the discovery of the source of the call for help], authorities <u>told</u> van Rossman [to turn off the TV] [to avoid a $10,000 fine] for [emitting a false distress signal].

PARAGRAPH EXERCISE

Feather colors <u>are</u> not the only things that <u>help</u> [to camouflage owls]. They <u>have</u> other neat tricks [to conceal, or hide, themselves]. Many <u>stand</u> tall and <u>pull</u> their feathers in tightly, [making the owls skinnier and harder [to see]]. When [trying [to conceal themselves]], owls <u>raise</u> the whitish feathers [surrounding the bill]. [Tufted] owls also <u>raise</u> their tufts, and round-[headed] owls <u>lift</u> their facial and "eyebrow" feathers.

When an owl <u>tries</u> [to hide itself] by [changing its shape], it <u>is</u> in concealment posture. In this posture, the owl's [rounded] outline <u>is broken</u> up and <u>is</u> less likely [to be seen by humans or predators].

SENTENCE WRITING

Your sentences may vary, but make sure that your verbals are not actually the main verbs of your clauses. You should be able to double underline your real verbs, as they are here.

1. I enjoy [speaking Italian].

2. [Typing on a small keyboard] hurts my wrists.

3. [Driving to the beach from here] takes about three hours.

4. I spent the day [reading the final chapters of my textbook].

5. I love [to ski in the winter].

6. We were invited [to go out to dinner].

7. I always like [to chat with you].

8. [To cook like a real gourmet] takes practice.

9. [Impressed by my grades], my parents bought me a new car.

10. [Taken in small doses], aspirin helps prevent heart attacks.

CORRECTING MISPLACED OR DANGLING MODIFIERS (PP. 129–132)

Corrections are *italicized*. Yours may differ slightly.

EXERCISE 1

1. After *I watched* TV for half an hour, the pasta was ready.

2. I found a dollar *as I jogged* around the block.

3. *Sitting in their chairs, the children* ate the cupcakes.

4. One year *after I became manager,* the company closed the store.

5. The sentence is correct.

6. My *mom smiled as she handed me* a bouquet of flowers for my birthday.

7. The usher slipped *on someone's program and fell.*

8. *Through the window,* they gave directions to the driver.

9. The sentence is correct.

10. I bought a new shirt *that has* silver buttons.

EXERCISE 2

1. *I proudly display my new parking pass, hanging from my rearview mirror.*

2. The students *took a train* to the museum.

3. After driving around the block three times, *I found a parking space* right in front of the restaurant.

4. The sentence is correct.

5. *Drivers swerved to avoid the old car that was stalled in the middle of the freeway.*

6. She sent us *her dog's picture mounted in a gold frame.*

7. *As I looked through my backpack,* the police officer waited for me to find my driver's license.

8. The sentence is correct.

9. After shouting, "Surprise!" *they presented the TV in a huge wrapped box.*

10. *The sun can do real damage to people's eyes if they don't wear sunglasses.*

EXERCISE 3

1. The sentence is correct.

2. *Taking careful notes,* the applicants listened to each of the employers.

3. The sentence is correct.

4. *After I gave the waiter my order in a low voice,* he asked me to speak louder.

5. The sentence is correct.

6. We received an invitation to their party; *it arrived in a pink envelope.*

7. *Since our car had a full tank of gas,* we were able to drive all the way to San Francisco.

8. *After we set the table,* our guests started eating.

9. I wrote a note *that said* I would return shortly, *and I taped it to the door.*

10. *Wearing gloves and safety goggles,* the student workers built a nice wall.

EXERCISE 4

1. I saw a parking ticket *clamped down on my windshield.*

2. The sentence is correct.

3. Using red ink, *teachers can mark mistakes* more clearly.

4. *Reading their policy very carefully,* they noticed a loophole.

5. *As they entered the arena,* she kicked her friend by accident.

6. The *frowning* teacher handed the tests back to the students.

7. *As I talked with the other students,* class finally started.

8. We bought a *cat with a fluffy tail* for our friend.

9. *Dressed in farmer outfits,* the pre-schoolers planted seedlings.

10. At the age of sixteen, *a person can easily obtain* a driving permit.

EXERCISE 5

1. One day *after I turned forty,* my new car broke down on the freeway.

2. *My brother lets his dog hang out the window of the car because the dog likes the rush of fresh air on his face.*

3. The sentence is correct.

4. Studying in the writing lab, *I eliminated* my comma problems.

5. The sentence is correct.

6. *We saw a pair of squirrels chasing each other up and down a tree.*

7. The sentence is correct.

8. The sentence is correct.

9. Lifting the heavy television, *she became red in the face.*

10. The sentence is correct.

PROOFREADING EXERCISE

Corrections are *italicized.* Yours may differ slightly.

I love parades, so last year my family and I traveled to Pasadena, California, to see one of the biggest parades of all—the Tournament of Roses Parade on New Year's Day. It turned out to be even more wonderful than I expected.

Although we arrived one day early, the city was already crowded with people. Lots of families were setting up campsites on Colorado Boulevard. We didn't want to miss one float in the parade, so we found our own spot and made ourselves at home. When the parade began, I had as much fun watching the spectators as the parade itself. I saw children *sitting on their fathers' shoulders* and pointing at the breathtaking horses and floats. *The floats were decorated completely with flowers or plant material.* I couldn't believe how beautiful they were and how good they smelled.

The crowd was overwhelmed by the sights and sounds of the parade. Everyone especially enjoyed hearing the school bands, *marching and playing their instruments with perfect precision.* They must have practiced for the whole year to be that good.

My experience didn't end with the parade, however. After the last float had passed by, I found a twenty dollar bill *as I walked down Colorado Boulevard. I framed it as a souvenir of my trip to the Rose Parade, and now it hangs on my wall at home.*

FOLLOWING SENTENCE PATTERNS (PP. 135–139)

EXERCISE 1

    S L V   Desc
1. I am a fan (of televised golf).

    S   AV   Obj
2. Golf eases my mind.

                                  S AV   AV
3. (During a weekend tournament), I sit (in my office) (at home) and watch
      Obj
the action (on a portable TV).

                                    S   AV   AV
4. (With the soft sound) (of the announcer's voice), I can relax and participate
(at the same time).

    S AV   Obj
5. I use the ongoing competition (as a distraction).

                             S   AV   Obj   AV
6. (By the middle) (of the tournament), I have finished the bills and have started
            Obj
next month's budget.

      S AV   Obj
7. Then I pay closer attention (to the leaders).

              S   LV   Desc
8. Occasionally, the competition becomes really intense.

  S   AV   Obj   Obj
9. I especially love tied scores and extra rounds.

  S   LV   Desc
10. I will always be a golf fan.

EXERCISE 2

    S   AV
1. People often travel (with their dogs, cats, or other pets).

     S   AV   Obj
2. Veterinarians offer some suggestions (about traveling) (with pets).

          S   LV Desc
3. First, a <u>pet</u> <u>should be</u> old enough to travel. [*To travel* is a verbal phrase.]

        S   AV
4. All <u>pets</u> <u>should travel</u> (in special carriers) (with food and water dishes).

           S   AV
5. Ordinary <u>water</u> (in a pet's dish) <u>spills</u> easily.

          S   AV
6. But ice <u>cubes</u> (in the water dish) <u>will melt</u> slowly.

                    S   AV   Obj   Obj
7. (During long car rides), <u>pets</u> <u>should have</u> enough shade and fresh air.

        S   AV
8. Small <u>pets</u> <u>can ride</u> (with passengers).

            S   AV   Obj
9. However, a loose <u>pet</u> <u>could cause</u> an accident.

         S   LV Desc   Desc
10. <u>Sedatives</u> (for pets) <u>are</u> risky but sometimes necessary.

EXERCISE 3

      S AV
1. <u>We</u> <u>live</u> (in a world) (with photocopiers, scanners, and fax machines).

       S   AV   Obj   S   AV   Obj
2. If <u>we</u> <u>need</u> copies (of documents), these <u>machines</u> <u>make</u> them (for us).

                      S   AV   Obj
3. (During the late 1800s), <u>people</u> still <u>copied</u> all documents (by hand).

                                S   AV   Obj
4. (As a solution) (to this problem), <u>Thomas Edison</u> <u>invented</u> an electric pen.

                             S   AV   Obj   S   LV
5. (Unlike ordinary pens), Edison's electric <u>pen</u> <u>made</u> stencils; the <u>pen</u> itself <u>was</u>
   Desc
inkless.

          S   AV   Obj   S   AV   Obj
6. Its sharp <u>tip</u> <u>poked</u> holes (in the paper), and later a <u>roller</u> <u>spread</u> ink (over the holes).

            S   AV

7. The ink went (through the holes) (onto another sheet) (of paper) underneath.

         S   LV   Desc   S   AV   Obj

8. And an exact copy was the result; in fact, one stencil produced many copies.

           S   S   AV   LV

9. The first documents [that] Edison reproduced (with his electric pen) were a

    Desc   Desc

speech (from *Richard III*) and the outline (of a photograph) (of Edison's wife,

Mary). [*That Edison reproduced with his electric pen* is a dependent clause that

comes between the subject and verb of the independent clause.]

          S   AV   Obj

10. Although Edison sold many thousands (of his electric pens) (at the time), only

 S   AV

six (of them) have survived.

EXERCISE 4

                                S   AV   Obj

1. (On November 4, 1922), archaeologist Howard Carter discovered the tomb
(of King Tutankhamen).

 S   AV

2. Carter had been excavating (in Egypt) (for years) (without success).

     S   AV   Obj

3. Then he made his famous discovery.

                  S   AV   Obj

4. (With the help) (of his workers), Carter found the top step (of a stone stairway).

   S   AV   Obj

5. They followed the staircase (down a total) (of sixteen steps).

            S   S   AV   Obj

6. (At the bottom), Carter and his team encountered a sealed door.

   S   AV   Obj

7. They had found a tomb undisturbed (for thousands of years). [*Undisturbed* is
a verbal.]

S   AV   Obj

8. It held the personal belongings (of a young Egyptian king).

S   LV   Desc   S   LV

9. Some (of the objects) were precious; others were just ordinary household

Desc

effects.

S   AV   Obj

10. The job (of cataloging and removing the items) took ten years. [*Cataloging* and *removing* are verbals.]

EXERCISE 5

S   AV   Obj

1. (In 1993), Sears discontinued its famous catalog.

S   AV   Obj

2. (For 97 years), a person could buy almost anything (through the Sears catalog).

S   AV   Obj

3. People called it "The Big Book."

S   AV   Obj

4. The final issue contained 1,500 pages (of merchandise) (for sale).

S   AV   Obj   S

5. (In 1897), before the government regulated such things, even medicines (with

LV   Desc

opium) were available (through the catalog).

S   AV   Obj   S   AV

6. (In 1910), Sears manufactured its own motor car; the Sears catalog advertised

Obj

the automobile (for sale) (at a cost) (of just under four hundred dollars).

S   AV   Obj S

7. (From the 1918 version) (of the catalog), people could purchase a kit that

AV   Obj   Obj

included building instructions and the materials (for an entire house); the

S   LV   Desc

price was fifteen hundred dollars.

S   AV   Obj
8. Sears sold more than 100,000 houses (through its catalog).

                                S   AV   Obj
9. (Before 1992), all customers used mail order forms, not phone calls, to place
their orders. [*To place their orders* is a verbal phrase.]

                    S   AV   S   AV
10. When the merchandise arrived (at the catalog center), customers went and

        AV   Obj   S   AV   Obj
picked it up; (for most) (of its history), the catalog offered no delivery service.

PARAGRAPH EXERCISE

The Earth's Motions and Weather

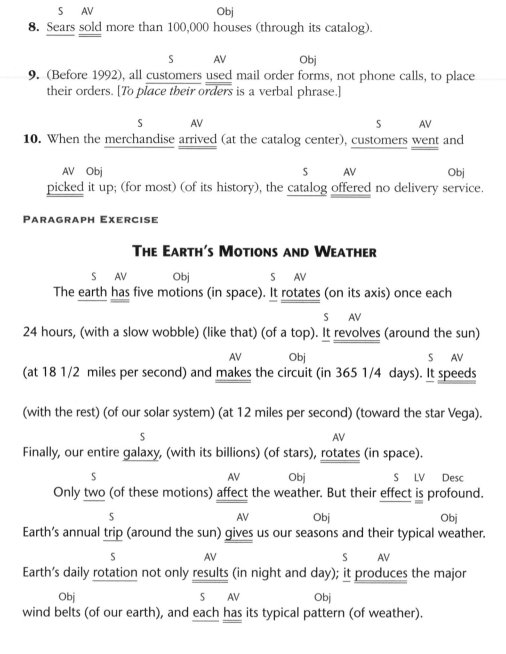

          S   AV   Obj   S   AV
The earth has five motions (in space). It rotates (on its axis) once each

                                                      S   AV
24 hours, (with a slow wobble) (like that) (of a top). It revolves (around the sun)

                              AV   Obj   S   AV
(at 18 1/2 miles per second) and makes the circuit (in 365 1/4 days). It speeds

(with the rest) (of our solar system) (at 12 miles per second) (toward the star Vega).

                    S   AV
Finally, our entire galaxy, (with its billions) (of stars), rotates (in space).

          S   AV   Obj   S   LV   Desc
Only two (of these motions) affect the weather. But their effect is profound.

          S   AV   Obj   Obj
Earth's annual trip (around the sun) gives us our seasons and their typical weather.

          S   AV   S   AV
Earth's daily rotation not only results (in night and day); it produces the major

    Obj   S   AV   Obj
wind belts (of our earth), and each has its typical pattern (of weather).

AVOIDING CLICHÉS, AWKWARD PHRASING, AND WORDINESS (P. 143)

Your revisions may differ.

1. Because popular technologies are advancing, all of my friends now have cell phones with cameras. Camera phones have become essential. For instance, when my friend was robbed, he took a picture of the robber and his truck as he was driving away. When the police arrived and saw the pictures, they sent out a description of the truck and the robber. The police arrested the criminal in just a few hours. Also, if my friend hadn't had his camera phone, he would not have been able to submit such strong evidence at the trial.

2. My favorite movie is *Back to the Future* because it is funny and because it is based on the idea of traveling back to the past without changing the future. I especially enjoy the performances of Michael J. Fox and the other actors in the movie. [Note: The writer of this paragraph would need to provide more details from the movie to support the topic sentence of this short paragraph.]

3. My son has trouble finishing his first-grade homework every night. As his parent, I think that he is smart, but he doesn't always show it. He works for a few minutes on his workbooks and then runs off to play. I tell him how strict teachers were about homework when I was his age. Unfortunately, my son's teacher uses stickers to keep track of his progress, and they just don't motivate him. I hope that my son will learn the value of keeping up in school.

CORRECTING FOR PARALLEL STRUCTURE (PP. 145–149)

Your answers may differ from these possible revisions.

EXERCISE 1

1. Taking driving lessons was exciting but nerve-wracking.

2. At first, I learned how to start, steer, and stop the car smoothly.

3. Between driving lessons, I studied the manual, watched driving videos, and practiced emergency hand signals.

4. My instructors taught me, tested me, and encouraged me.

5. The sentence is correct.

6. Finally, my teachers decided that I had learned enough and that I was ready to take the test for my driver's license.

7. I arrived at the testing location, waited in the lobby for a few minutes, and heard someone call my name.

8. The sentence is correct.

9. The man who tested me said that I knew the rules and that I must have had good teachers.

10. The sentence is correct.

EXERCISE 2

1. If I had a choice to live in the country or the city, I would choose the city.

2. I like being surrounded by people and having privacy at the same time.

3. The country is too quiet and peaceful for me.

4. The country has dirt and flies everywhere.

5. The city has pollution, smog, and noise, but it just feels like home.

6. The sentence is correct.

7. Most country houses seem to be small and red or white.

8. The country also has many animals that look and smell the same.

9. In the city, I enjoy visiting the zoo and seeing all sorts of exotic animals anytime I want.

10. For these reasons, choosing between country life and city life is easy for me.

EXERCISE 3

1. The sentence is correct.

2. They taught us the joy of reading and getting good grades in school.

3. They told us that we should work hard in school and that we should always think about the future.

4. Throughout our childhood, our parents were there, but they were always working.

5. I remember my parents working day and night to support our family.

6. The sentence is correct.

7. I loved to see their work on the walls of their classrooms and to read their names on their desks.

8. The teachers seemed to be so friendly and to care about their students.

9. Since that time, I never saw school as a stressful place or as a waste of time.

10. By making us care for and encourage each other, our parents taught us the value of an education.

EXERCISE 4

1. The sentence is correct.

2. The article is written for adults, but it is about children.

3. It explains that many kids have become frightened by information about global warming and other environmental concerns.

4. Children are watching the same scary news stories and upsetting images that adults see.

5. The sentence is correct.

6. Some children suffer very strong reactions of fear and helplessness when they encounter such information.

7. Others ignore or disregard the same troubling information.

8. The *Newsweek* article makes an interesting point: as kids, some of today's parents were panicked by the idea of nuclear war; now their children worry about climate change.

9. The sentence is correct.

10. Adults can take certain steps to help kids cope: point out the positive aspects of nature, limit exposure to frightening images or information, and find ways to help them take positive action.

EXERCISE 5

1. I've been learning to cook lately, but I keep making the same mistakes.

2. I always add too much salt or too much sugar.

3. The sentence is correct.

4. If I use too much salt, I could add a little sugar.

5. If soups or stews have too much salt, I could add a slice of raw potato.

6. If the salt is still too overpowering, I could double the dish's ingredients and not add any salt to the new batch.

7. Then, if there's too much food, I could put half in the freezer for later.

8. If I use too much sugar when baking, I could add a little salt.

9. If vegetables and entrees are too sweet, I could add some vinegar.

10. The sentence is correct.

PROOFREADING EXERCISE

Your revisions within the paragraph may differ. This paragraph is just one possibility.

Carry A. Nation was an American woman who lived from 1846 to 1911. She is most famous for two things: her name, which helped inspire her to be an activist, and her habit of wrecking any saloon or bar in sight. Carry Nation hated alcohol and any place that sold it. She was a powerful woman who was almost six feet tall. During her adult life, she went on a mission to destroy saloons across the country one at a time. Her crusade began in Wichita. She used a hatchet to smash windows, chop up furniture, crack mirrors, and break as many liquor bottles in a saloon as possible. Carry A. Nation repeated this offense from east to west. Whenever she landed in jail, this enterprising American sold toy replicas of her hatchet and gave speeches to raise money for her bail. Carry Nation took action based on her beliefs. She caused trouble for some people but helped other people. She donated funds to the poor and founded a shelter for the wives of alcoholics.

USING PRONOUNS (PP. 152–156)

EXERCISE 1

1. I

2. she

3. she and I (or *we*)

4. I

5. she and I (or *we*), me

6. she

7. I

8. I

9. her and me (or *us*)

10. me, her

EXERCISE 2

1. its

2. its

3. their

4. their

5. their

6. its

7. his

8. Everyone in the class sold the books back to the bookstore.

9. their

10. Either the employees or the employer gets a settlement notice after a dispute.

EXERCISE 3

1. me

2. He and she (or *They* are alike in many ways.)

3. I

4. their

5. their

6. I

7. Each of the new teachers has *a* set of books.

8. their

9. Everyone at the polling place had *an* opinion and expressed it with *a* vote.

10. he

EXERCISE 4

1. I

2. she

3. *Students need* to buy *their* textbooks before classes begin.

4. she

5. their

6. their

7. I

8. me

9. its

10. its

EXERCISE 5

1. The Hascoms or their neighbor on the right will need to relocate *a* driveway.

2. its

3. me

4. their

5. their

6. they

7. he

8. us

9. Every person has to use *a* password to access the computers in the lab.

10. its

PROOFREADING EXERCISE
Corrections are *italicized*.

I gave my friend James some advice at work the other day. The boss assigned James and ~~I~~ *me* to different supervisors, and I advised James to ask his supervisor for a raise. Right before I gave him the advice, I said, "You and ~~me~~ *I* have been friends for a long time, and you're not going to blame me if my advice doesn't work, right?" He assured me that the only person whose advice he would follow was ~~me~~ *I*. I made the mistake of believing him. Later I noticed that ~~him~~ *he* and his supervisor were talking in the lounge. James was following my advice, and I knew that the one that would be responsible for the outcome was ~~me~~ *I*. Unfortunately, my advice backfired when James followed it. As a result, James and ~~me~~ *I* are still coworkers, but we are no longer friends.

AVOIDING SHIFTS IN PERSON (PP. 158)

PROOFREADING EXERCISES
Your revisions may differ depending on your choice to begin in first, second, or third person.

1. ~~We have all~~ *You have probably* seen images of astronauts floating in their space capsules, eating food from little silver freeze-dried cube-shaped pouches, and sipping Tang out of special straws made to function in the weightlessness of space. Now you can buy that same food and eat it yourself on earth. NASA has gone online with a site called thespacestore.com, and all ~~one has~~ *you have* to do is point and click and get these space munchies delivered to your door. If ~~people~~ *you* want NASA souvenirs or clothing, ~~they~~ *you* can purchase them at the same site. [Note that we chose to revise this paragraph in second person.]

2. ~~People~~ *Those of us* who drive need to be more aware of pedestrians. We can't always gauge what ~~someone~~ *people* walking down the street will do. ~~You~~ *We* might think that all pedestrians will keep walking forward in a crosswalk, but ~~one~~ *they* might decide to turn back if ~~he or she~~ *they* forgot something. ~~You~~ *We* could run into ~~him or her~~ *them* if that happens. ~~A person's life could be affected~~ *We could affect other people's lives* in an instant. We all should slow down and be more considerate of others. [Note that we chose to revise this paragraph in first person. We also changed the singular pronouns referring to "pedestrians" to plural pronouns for consistency in number.]

3. This paragraph is correct.

REVIEW OF SENTENCE STRUCTURE ERRORS (PP. 159–160)

Your corrections may differ slightly.

1. B. incorrect verb form (They're *supposed* to be relaxing for parents and exciting for children.)

2. A. incorrect pronoun (My speech professor is much luckier than *I*.)

3. B. awkward phrasing (I have taken day and night classes but *have never given up my weekends*. or *will never give up my weekends*.)

4. B. run-on sentence (He put them on the podium, and he immediately started lecturing.)

5. B. fragment (Too many people wander in if we don't.)

6. A. wordy and cliché (People today don't usually get involved in strangers' lives.)

7. A. incorrect pronoun (The library renewed the books that my friend and *I* had checked out.)

8. A. wordy (The store was offering a free coffee maker.)

9. A. shift in time (My essay is full of interesting details and *has* a strong thesis.)

10. B. pronoun agreement (*People* at the party had a shocked look on *their* faces.)

11. A. subject-verb agreement error (Some of the new furniture *has* scratches on it already.)

12. B. fragment and wordy (They can be as small as a baby bottle or as large as a magnum of champagne.)

13. B. misplaced modifier (We saw a beautiful metallic *kite hanging from the top of a tree*.)

14. B. run-on sentence (However, there is one big difference between them; Shawn is not as ambitious as Sharon is.)

15. A. wordy (Whenever I plan a *meal* around a single ingredient, the *different dishes* don't taste good.)

PROOFREADING EXERCISE

Corrections are *italicized*. Yours may differ.

LET'S GET TECHNICAL

In my child development classes, I'm learning about ways to keep girls interested in technology. Studies *show* that girls and boys begin their school years equally interested in technology. After elementary school, *girls lose interest*. Because boys keep up with computers and other technology throughout their educations, *boys* get ahead in these fields. Experts have come up with some suggestions for teachers and parents to help *girls stay involved in technology.*

Girls need opportunities to experiment with computers. Girls spend time on computers, but they usually just do their *assignments; then* they log off. Since computer games and programs are often aimed at *boys, parents* and teachers need to buy computer products that will challenge girls not only in literature and art, but also in math, science, and *business.*

Another suggestion is to put computers in places where girls can socialize. One reason many boys stay interested in technology is that *they can do it on their own.* Girls tend to be more interested in working with others and *sharing* activities. When computer terminals are placed close to one another, girls work at them longer.

Finally, parents and teachers need to *provide positive role models. They need to teach girls* about successful women in the fields of business, *science*, and technology. And the earlier *girls get interested* in these fields, the better.

PUNCTUATION AND CAPITAL LETTERS

PERIOD, QUESTION MARK, EXCLAMATION POINT, SEMICOLON, COLON, DASH (PP. 164–169)

EXERCISE 1

1. My friend Kristine and I arrived early for work yesterday; it was a very important day.

2. We had worked late the night before, perfecting our presentation.

3. The boss had given us an opportunity to train our colleagues in the use of a new computer program.

4. I wondered how the other workers would react when they heard that we had been chosen to teach them.

5. Would they be pleased or annoyed?

6. Kristine and I worked hard on the visual aid to accompany our workshop: a slide show of sample screens from the program.

7. Kristine thought our workshop should end with a test; however, I didn't think that was a good idea.

8. I knew that our fellow employees—at least *some* of them—would not want us to test them.

9. By the time we ended our presentation, we both realized that I had been right.

10. Now our co-workers see us as a couple of experts—not a couple of know-it-alls. (or !)

EXERCISE 2

1. People in Australia have been asking themselves a question: why are some dolphins carrying big sponges around on their heads?

2. First, it was just one dolphin; now many dolphins are doing it.

3. Marine biologists all over the world have been trying to understand this unusual sponge-carrying behavior.

4. They wonder about whether the sponges decrease the dolphins' ability to maneuver under water.

5. If they do, then why would the dolphins sacrifice this ability?

6. The dolphins might be using the sponges for a very important reason: to help them find food.

7. Some scientists think that the sponges may protect the dolphins' beaks in some way.

8. The sponges might indicate position in the social order; that's another explanation.

9. Or the dolphins could be imitating each other—a kind of dolphin "fad," in other words.

10. Only one group of experts knows whether these sponges are hunting tools or just fashion statements; that is the dolphins themselves.

EXERCISE 3

1. Ralph Waldo Emerson gave us this famous bit of advice: "Build a better mousetrap, and the world will beat a path to your door."

2. People have not stopped inventing mousetraps; in fact, there are more U.S. patents for mousetraps than for any other device.

3. Some are simple; some are complicated, and some are just weird.

4. Nearly fifty new patents for machines to kill mice are awarded every year— perhaps thanks to Mr. Emerson's advice.

5. The most enduring mousetrap was designed by John Mast; it is the one most of us picture when we think of a mousetrap: a piece of wood with a spring-loaded bar that snaps down on the mouse just as it takes the bait.

6. John Mast's creation received Patent #744,379 in 1903; since then no other patented mousetrap has done a better job.

7. There is a long list of technologies that other inventions have used to trap mice: electricity, sonar, lasers, super glues, etc.

8. One patented mousetrap was built in the shape of a multilevel house with several stairways; however, its elaborate design made it impractical and expensive.

9. In 1878, one person invented a mousetrap for travelers; it was a box that was supposed to hold men's removable collars and at night catch mice, but it was not a success.

10. Who would want to put an article of clothing back into a box used to trap a mouse?

EXERCISE 4

1. The sentence is correct.

2. This young woman—a very controversial figure in Washington, D.C.—began her career as a sculptor in 1863 at the age of sixteen.

3. Miss Ream was a student of the famous sculptor Clark Mills; he is perhaps best known for his statue of Andrew Jackson located across from the White House.

4. Vinnie Ream started to work with Mills in his studio in the basement of the Capitol building; soon members of Congress were volunteering to sit for Miss Ream, and she sculpted busts of them.

5. Her fame and reputation grew in the late 1860s; that's when she was awarded a ten-thousand-dollar commission to create a life-size statue of Abraham Lincoln.

6. Vinnie Ream had known Lincoln; in fact, before his assassination, President Lincoln would allow Miss Ream to sit in his office within the White House and work on a bust of him as he carried out the business of running the country.

7. The sentence is correct.

8. Vinnie Ream's relationships and the works she produced were not accepted by everyone; Ream's youth and physical beauty led to much of this harsh criticism.

9. Some people questioned her motives; others even questioned her abilities.

10. The sentence is correct.

EXERCISE 5

1. I just read an article that connected two things that I would never have thought went together: the Old West, with its miners and saloon life, and Shakespeare, with his poetry and politics.

2. People who had traveled out West on the Oregon Trail brought their Shakespeare books and shared them with a willing audience: the unruly population of the mining camps and tiny towns of the West.

3. Mountain men like Jim Bridger paid others who could read to act out Shakespeare's plays; then he memorized the speeches and performed them for others.

4. Theaters staged productions of the tragedies of *Hamlet, Othello,* and *Romeo and Juliet* to the delight of the Western crowds; however, if they weren't pleased with an actor, theatergoers threw vegetables—as large as pumpkins at times—to get the actor off the stage.

5. Crowds likewise rewarded good acting, which was lively and not overly refined; spectators in gold mining camps threw nuggets and bags of gold on stage if they liked a performance.

6. Oral storytelling had always been popular in the West; therefore, people of the time embraced Shakespeare's language without thinking of it as intellectual or sophisticated.

7. In the mid-1800s, people across the country had strong opinions about how Shakespeare should be performed; there was a riot at one New York City theater concerning a particularly snobby performance of *Macbeth.*

8. The fight moved from the theater into the streets; more than twenty people were killed, and a hundred were injured.

9. The casting of characters in Western performances included everything from all-male casts in the mining camps to a female Juliet performing without a real Romeo; a stuffed dummy played his part.

10. There was even a little girl named Anna Maria Quinn—just six years old—who played *Hamlet* at the Metropolitan Theatre in San Francisco in 1854.

PROOFREADING EXERCISE
Your punctuation choices may differ slightly.

Who hasn't seen one of those inflatable jumping rooms at a park or in the front yard of a house hosting a child's birthday party? These jumpers are popular for several reasons: children can have fun playing with their friends; adults can keep an eye on many children at once, and everyone gets a lot of exercise. In 2007, a freak accident occurred on a beach in Hawaii; it involved an inflated castle-shaped bouncer, a few brave adults, and several lucky children. As the kids bounced around as usual, a strong gust of wind—a whirlwind, according to one witness—lifted the castle straight up into the air and knocked all but two of the children out instantly. Then the castle bounced on the sand once before flying fifty yards out into the ocean. As the castle flew, another child dropped out of it; luckily, he was unhurt. Many adults—both lifeguards and others—jumped in to save the two-year-old girl who remained inside the castle. One man was able to reach her; incredibly, she was not seriously injured!

COMMA RULES 1, 2, AND 3 (PP. 171–175)

EXERCISE 1
1. Scientists have been studying the human face, and they have been able to identify five thousand distinct facial expressions.

2. The sentence is correct.

3. Winking is action number forty-six, and we do it with the facial muscle that surrounds the eye.

4. The sentence is correct.

5. These facial expressions are universally understood, but different societies have different rules about showing their emotions.

6. The smile is one of the most powerful expressions, and it can change the way we feel.

7. A real smile is someone's way of showing genuine happiness, and our brains react by producing a feeling of pleasure.

8. In contrast, people give us polite imitation smiles all day, and our brains show no change.

9. The sentence is correct.

10. A smile also wins the long-distance record for facial expressions, for it can be seen from as far away as several hundred feet.

EXERCISE 2
1. An eleven-year-old boy from Kansas City, Missouri, recently took an unplanned 200-mile trip in the family car.

2. The sentence is correct.

3. On October 5, 2004, he got in the family's 1995 Chevrolet and took off.

4. He started in Kansas City, drove to Bethany, continued through Macon County, and ended up in Callao.

5. The boy's adventures along the way included driving 85 miles-an-hour, running out of gas, getting help from a group of construction workers, and finally locking himself out of his car.

6. The sentence is correct.

7. The boy's family had meanwhile noticed that their son, their car, and their keys were missing.

8. The sentence is correct.

9. The sentence is correct.

10. Soon the police called to say that the boy had been located, that he was unharmed, and that the parents could pick him up in Callao.

EXERCISE 3

1. Whenever I ask my friend Wendy a computer-related question, I end up regretting it.

2. Once she gets started, Wendy is unable to stop talking about computers.

3. When I needed her help the last time, my printer wasn't working.

4. Instead of just solving the problem, Wendy went on and on about print settings and font choices that I could be using.

5. When she gets like this, her face lights up, and I feel bad for not wanting to hear the latest news on software upgrades, e-mail programs, and hardware improvements.

6. Even though I feel guilty, I know that I am the normal one.

7. I even pointed her problem out to her by asking, "You can't control yourself, can you?"

8. With a grin, she just kept trying to fix my printer.

9. Since Wendy always solves my problem, I should be grateful.

10. When I ask for Wendy's help in the future, I plan to listen and try to learn something.

EXERCISE 4

1. I've been reading Helen Keller's autobiography, and I have learned a lot more about her.

2. I originally thought that Keller was born deaf and blind, but I was wrong.

3. When she was about two years old, Keller developed a terrible fever.

4. The sentence is correct.

5. Not long after the doctor shared his fears with her family, Keller recovered from her fever.

6. Unfortunately, the high fever left Keller without the ability to see, to hear, or to speak.

7. The only tools that Keller had left were her sense of touch, her active mind, and her intense curiosity.

8. With her teacher Anne Sullivan's constant assistance, Keller eventually learned to read, to write, and to speak several languages.

9. The sentence is correct.

10. Helen Keller never stopped learning, and her story inspires me to do my best.

Exercise 5

1. Gold is amazing, isn't it?

2. Unlike metals that change their appearance after contact with water, oil, and other substances, gold maintains its shine and brilliant color under almost any circumstances.

3. When a miner named James Marshall found gold in the dark soil of California in 1848, the gold rush began.

4. The piece of gold that Marshall discovered was only about the size of a child's fingernail, but it meant that there was more to be found.

5. Before the gold rush, San Francisco was a small town called Yerba Buena.

6. The sentence is correct.

7. Gold is actually present all over the world, but the biggest nugget to be found so far came from a location on the Potomac River.

8. This chunk of gold is as big as a yam, and it is on display at the National Museum of Natural History.

9. Some people have become rich directly because of gold, and some have become rich indirectly because of gold.

10. For example, if it had not been for California's gold rush, Levi Strauss would not have had any customers, and the world would not have blue jeans.

Proofreading Exercise

Like other people who surf the Web regularly, I like to keep up with important and interesting world events. In April 2010, an online friend told me about a contest that was going on in Europe. It's a yearly song contest called Eurovision, and countries from across Europe participate in it. It began in 1956 as a way for European nations to come together, share their songs, and celebrate their unique cultural styles. To participate in the Eurovision contest, countries pick a song and a singer to represent them. Then they make song videos to show to the other countries. All participating countries can vote during the competition, but they can't vote for their own country's song. That seems fair, doesn't it? On May 29, 2010, the Eurovision Song Contest Final was held in Oslo, Norway, and the winning country was Germany with its song called "Satellite," sung by 19-year-old Lena Meyer-Landrut. Because Germany won in 2010, it will host the Eurovision Song Contest in 2011. People who don't live in Europe can watch the competition and learn more about the Eurovision Song Contest on www.eurovision.tv.

Sentence Writing

Here are some possible combinations. Yours may differ.

I drive to school alone every day, but I would consider carpooling.

When my car alarm goes off, I don't even look out the window anymore.

Although Melanie and Kurt are currently software developers, they used to be dancers, and now they both want to get back in shape.

Because I was born, got married, and graduated from high school on the twenty-fifth of May, I have a special fondness for that date.

COMMA RULES 4, 5, AND 6 (PP. 179–182)

EXERCISE 1

1. The sentence is correct.

2. The sentence is correct.

3. Cats become confused when their owners react angrily, not happily, to these "presents."

4. Desmond Morris, a renowned animal expert, explains this misunderstood behavior in his book *Catwatching*.

5. The sentence is correct.

6. The sentence is correct.

7. In the absence of kittens, these cats treat their owners as the next best thing, kitten replacements.

8. The first step in the process of teaching "kittens" how to hunt, the one cat owners hate most, is sharing the results of the hunt with them.

9. The owners' reaction, which usually involves yelling and disappointment, should include praise and lots of petting.

10. The sentence is correct.

EXERCISE 2

1. Paula, who left at intermission, missed the best part of the play.

2. The sentence is correct.

3. The sentence is correct.

4. Our teacher posted the results of the midterm, which we took last week.

5. The sentence is correct.

6. Mr. Simon, the math teacher, looks a lot like Mr. Simon, the English teacher.

7. My clothes dryer, which has an automatic shut-off switch, is safer than yours, which doesn't.

8. The sentence is correct.

9. The sentence is correct.

10. John and Brenda, who ask a lot of questions, usually do well on their exams.

EXERCISE 3

1. This year's photo directory, I believe, turned out better than last year's.

2. The sentence is correct.

3. There were, I think, still a few problems.

4. The sentence is correct.

5. The sentence is correct.

6. My supervisor, whose picture is at the top of our page, is wearing his name tag, but he's not listed at the bottom.

7. Ms. Tracy, the photographer who took the pictures, needed to help people with their poses.

8. The sentence is correct.

9. And no one, it seems, had time to look in a mirror.

10. The sentence is correct.

EXERCISE 4

1. We hope, of course, that people will continue to vote in elections.

2. The sentence is correct.

3. The sentence is correct.

4. The Fosters, who usually volunteer their house as a polling place, may have to install new equipment.

5. You may leave the sentence alone, or you may use commas around *therefore*.

6. You may leave the sentence alone, or you may use a comma after *Therefore*.

7. The voting booth, a small cubicle where each person casts a vote, will probably become more high-tech.

8. The sentence is correct.

9. The sentence is correct.

10. No one, we trust, will attempt to influence our thoughts there.

EXERCISE 5

1. Jim Henson, creator of the Muppets, began his television career in the mid-1950s.

2. He was, it seems, eager to be on TV, and there was an opening for someone who worked with puppets.

3. Henson and a buddy of his quickly fabricated a few puppets, including one called Pierre the French Rat, and they got the job.

4. Henson's next project, *Sam and Friends*, also starred puppets.

5. *Sam and Friends* was a live broadcast lasting only five minutes; however, it was on two times a day and ran for six years.

6. Kermit the Frog, the character which we now associate with *Sesame Street*, was part of the cast of *Sam and Friends*.

7. Henson provided the voice and animated the movements of Kermit and a few others from the beginning, and he worked with Frank Oz, who helped round out the cast of Muppet characters.

8. In 1969, the Muppets moved to *Sesame Street*; however, they graduated to their own prime-time program, *The Muppet Show,* in the late 1970s.

9. The sentence is correct.

10. The sentence is correct.

PROOFREADING EXERCISE

Two types of punctuation, internal punctuation and end punctuation, can be used in writing. Internal punctuation is used within the sentence, and end punctuation is used at the end of a sentence. Commas, the most important pieces of internal punctuation, are used to separate or enclose information within sentences. Semicolons, the next most important, also have two main functions. Their primary function, separating two independent clauses, is also the most widely known. A lesser-known need for semicolons, to separate items in a list already containing commas, occurs rarely in college writing. Colons and dashes, likewise, have special uses within sentences. And of the three pieces of end punctuation—periods, question marks, and exclamation points—the period, which signals the end of the majority of English sentences, is obviously the most common.

SENTENCE WRITING

Here are some possible combinations. Yours may differ.

The 5,000 Fingers of Dr. T., a live-action film with outrageous sets and costumes from the 1950s, is a great old movie written by Dr. Seuss.

Dr. Seuss's *The 5,000 Fingers of Dr. T.* is a great old live-action movie with outrageous sets and costumes from the 1950s.

The songs in *Dr. T.,* I believe, are better than in any other musical I have seen.

I believe that the songs in *Dr. T.* are better than in any other musical I have seen.

Dr. Terwilliker, a crazy piano teacher, wants to rule the world by forcing 500 little boys to play an enormous piano with 5,000 keys.

Dr. Terwilliker is a crazy piano teacher whose plan to rule the world involves forcing 500 little boys to play an enormous piano with 5,000 keys.

COMMA REVIEW EXERCISE (P. 184)

I am writing you this note, Michael, to ask you to do me a favor. [4] Before you leave for work today, would you take the turkey out of the freezer? [3] I plan to get started on the stuffing, potatoes, and desserts as soon as I wake up. [2] I will be so busy, however, that I might forget to thaw out the turkey. [5] It's the first time I've cooked all the food for Thanksgiving by myself, and I want everything to be perfect. [1] The big enamel roasting pan, the one that is in the cupboard above the refrigerator, will be the best place to keep the turkey as it thaws. [6]

Thanks for your help.

QUOTATION MARKS AND UNDERLINING/*ITALICS* (PP. 186–190)

EXERCISE 1

1. After all these years, <u>Friends</u> is still a popular TV series.

2. "It is better to deserve honors and not have them," said Mark Twain, "than to have them and not deserve them."

3. Twain continued, "When people do not respect us, we are sharply offended, yet in his private heart no man much respects himself."

4. My roommate left an ominous note on the front door; all it said was, "Fix plumbing."

5. In his book <u>Crying: The Natural & Cultural History of Tears,</u> Tom Lutz explains that "Weeping is a human universal."

6. Whenever I see a new copy of <u>People</u> magazine, I buy it.

7. In Shakespeare's play <u>Henry V,</u> the French ambassador brings Henry a gift; when the king asks what it is, the ambassador replies, "Tennis balls, my liege."

8. The bus driver shouted "Hold on!" right before we hit the curb.

9. The movie version of <u>The Da Vinci Code</u> was not as popular as the book.

10. Every issue of <u>Smithsonian</u> magazine has amazing pictures in it.

EXERCISE 2

1. "The Raven" is a poem by Edgar Allan Poe.

2. "Once you complete your test," the teacher said, "please bring it up to my desk."

3. I have a subscription to several magazines, including <u>The New Yorker</u>.

4. Pablo Picasso perceived that "Everything exists in limited quantities, even happiness."

5. "How many times," she asked, "are you going to mention the price we paid for dinner?"

6. After Babe Ruth's death, his wife remarked, "I don't even have an autographed ball. You don't ask your husband for an autographed ball. He'd probably think you were nuts."

7. Sophocles, the Greek playwright, wrote the tragedy <u>Oedipus Rex</u> in the fifth century BCE.

8. Edward Hopper remarked, "When you go by on a train, everything looks beautiful. But if you stop, it becomes drab."

9. A famous Mexican proverb says, "Whoever sells land sells his mother."

10. When Fiorello La Guardia, who was just over five feet tall, was asked what it felt like to be short, he answered, "Like a dime among pennies."

EXERCISE 3

1. In his book <u>Catwatching</u>, Desmond Morris has this to say about their–preferences: "Cats hate doors."

2. Phil Hartman was the voice of Troy McClure and many other memorable–characters on the animated TV series <u>The Simpsons</u>.

3. Langston Hughes wrote about his childhood in a short essay called "Salvation."

4. Langston Hughes' essay is part of his full-length autobiography <u>The Big Sea</u>.

5. Joan Didion describes her relationship with migraine headaches in her essay "In Bed."

6. "Where can I buy some poster board?" the student asked.

7. "There is a school-supply store around the corner," his friend replied, "but I don't think that it's open this late."

8. Sylvia asked the other students if they had seen the Alfred Hitchcock movie called <u>The Birds</u>.

9. "I don't remember," James answered.

10. "It's not something you could ever forget!" she yelled.

EXERCISE 4

1. Kurt Vonnegut begins his futuristic short story "Harrison Bergeron" by stating, "The year was 2081, and everybody was finally equal."

2. "Now he belongs to the ages!" cried Edwin M. Stanton after Abraham Lincoln's assassination.

3. In her book <u>The Mysterious Affair at Styles</u>, Agatha Christie wisely observes that "Every murderer is probably somebody's old friend."

4. "Swear not by the moon," says Juliet to Romeo.

5. John F. Kennedy told the U.S. Congress, "The human mind is our fundamental resource."

6. Abraham Lincoln stated that "Public opinion in this country is everything."

7. "Writers are always selling somebody out," Joan Didion observed.

8. The expression "All animals are equal, but some animals are more equal than others" can be found in George Orwell's novel <u>Animal Farm</u>.

9. A Swahili proverb warns, "When a person seizes two things, one always slips from his grasp!"

10. Groucho Marx once remarked, "I wouldn't want to belong to any club that would accept me as a member."

EXERCISE 5

1. Ovid reminded us that "We can learn even from our enemies."

2. "We know what a person thinks not when he tells us what he thinks," said Isaac Bashevis Singer, "but by his actions."

3. The Spanish proverb "El pez muere por la boca" translated means "The fish dies because it opens its mouth."

4. "Ask yourself whether you are happy, and you cease to be so," John Stuart Mill wrote.

5. A Russian proverb states, "Without a shepherd, sheep are not a flock."

6. William Faulkner felt that "Some things you must always be unable to bear."

7. St. Jerome had the following insight: "The friendship that can cease has never been real."

8. Oscar Wilde observed that "In this world there are only two tragedies. One is not getting what one wants, and the other is getting it."

9. Henry Ford warned, "You can't build a reputation on what you're going to do."

10. "Choose a job you love," Confucius suggested, "and you will never have to work a day in your life."

PARAGRAPH EXERCISE

I admire the way that Helen Keller describes her feelings in her autobiography, <u>The Story of My Life</u>. Being totally blind and deaf, Keller tries to explain how she can experience something like moonlight. She writes, "I cannot, it is true, see the moon climb up the sky behind the pines and steal softly across the heavens." Then she continues, "But I know she is there, and . . . I feel the shimmer of her garments as she passes." Keller feels light rather than sees it. She explains that a certain combination of air and light makes her feel loved, or as she puts it, "A luminous warmth seems to enfold me. . . . It is like the kiss of warm lips on my face." I really like Keller's writing style. When I read her descriptions, I feel very calm.

CAPITAL LETTERS (PP. 192–196)

EXERCISE 1

1. Many consider *The Diary of Anne Frank* to be one of the most important books of the twentieth century.

2. Anne Frank wrote her famous diary during the Nazi occupation of Holland in World War II.

3. The building in Amsterdam where the Frank family and several others hid during the two years before their capture is now a museum and has been recently renovated.

4. Visitors to the Anne Frank House can stand before her desk and see pictures of movie stars like Greta Garbo on her wall.

5. They can climb the stairs hidden behind a bookcase that led to the annex where Anne lived with her mother, Edith; her father, Otto; and her sister, Margot.

6. One of the others hiding with the Franks was Peter van Pels, who was roughly the same age as Anne.

7. Anne writes of her relationship with Peter in her diary.

8. Visitors to the museum can enter the room where Peter gave Anne her first kiss just a few months before the Nazis discovered their hiding place in 1944.

9. Anne's family and Peter's were both sent to concentration camps in Germany.

10. Only Anne's father lived to see the Anne Frank House open as a museum for the first time on May 3, 1960.

EXERCISE 2

1. Dad and I have both decided to take college classes next fall.

2. Fortunately, in Los Angeles we live near several colleges and universities.

3. Classes at the community colleges usually begin in late August or early September.

4. Within twenty minutes, we could drive to Los Angeles Valley College, Los Angeles City College, Glendale Community College, or Pasadena City College.

5. I want to take credit classes, and my dad wants to sign up for community education classes.

6. For instance, I will enroll in the academic courses necessary to transfer to a university.

7. These include English, math, science, and history classes.

8. My father, on the other hand, wants to take noncredit classes with titles like "Learn to Play Keyboards," "Web Pages Made Easy," and "Be Your Own Real Estate Agent."

9. Dad already has a great job, so he can take classes just for fun.

10. I know that if I want to go to one of the University of California campuses later, I will have to be serious from the start.

EXERCISE 3

1. I grew up watching *The Wizard of Oz* once a year on TV before video stores like Blockbuster rented movies to watch at home.

2. I especially remember enjoying it with my brother and sisters when we lived on Topeka Drive.

3. Mom would remind us early in the day to get all of our homework done.

4. "If your homework isn't finished," she'd say, "you can't see the Munchkins!"

5. My favorite part has always been when Dorothy's house drops on one of the wicked witches and her feet shrivel up under the house.

6. The Wicked Witch of the West wants revenge after that, but Dorothy and Toto get help from Glinda, the Good Witch of the North.

7. Glinda tells Dorothy about the Emerald City and the Wizard of Oz.

8. On their way, Toto and Dorothy meet the Scarecrow, the Tin Man, and the Cowardly Lion.

9. Together they conquer the witch and meet Professor Marvel, the real man who has been pretending to be a wizard.

10. The ruby slippers give Dorothy the power to get back to Kansas and to her Aunt Em and Uncle Henry.

EXERCISE 4

1. Oscar Wilde was an Irish-born writer who lived and wrote in England for much of his life during the late 1800s.

2. He was famous for his refined ideas about art and literature.

3. While still a young man, Wilde traveled to America.

4. Contrary to what many people expected, he was well received in rough mining towns such as Leadville, Colorado.

5. He gave one particularly long speech to the miners who lived in Leadville.

6. Wilde spoke on the following topic: "The Practical Application of the Aesthetic Theory to Exterior and Interior House Decoration, with Observations on Dress and Personal Ornament."

7. During his stay in Leadville, Wilde had gained the miners' respect by visiting them down in the mines and by proving that he could drink as much whiskey as they could without getting drunk.

8. Wilde wrote about one incident that took place in Leadville.

9. Before giving a lecture he called *The Ethics of Art,* Wilde was told that two criminals accused of murder had been found in town.

10. Earlier that evening on the same stage where Wilde was about to give his speech, the two men were convicted and executed by Leadville officials.

EXERCISE 5

1. The southern writer known as Flannery O'Connor was born with the name Mary Flannery O'Connor.

2. O'Connor lived much of her life in Milledgeville, Georgia.

3. She attended Peabody High School, Georgia State College for Women (currently Georgia College), and the State University of Iowa (currently the University of Iowa).

4. While at college in Georgia, O'Connor edited the campus newspaper, *The Colonnade,* and its literary magazine, *The Corinthian*.

5. When she began publishing her writing, O'Connor left off her first name, Mary.

6. Students in literature classes study O'Connor's short stories, including "Revelation," "Good Country People," "A Good Man Is Hard to Find," and "The Life You Save May Be Your Own."

7. O'Connor's stories received the O. Henry Award many times.

8. Organizations such as the Ford Foundation and the National Institute of Arts and Letters awarded O'Connor with grants to support her writing.

9. She also wrote the novels *Wise Blood* and *The Violent Bear It Away*.

10. In 1962, Notre Dame's St. Mary's College made Flannery O'Connor an honorary Doctor of Letters.

REVIEW OF PUNCTUATION AND CAPITAL LETTERS (P. 197)

1. The Empire State Building is one of the most famous locations in New York City.

2. Have you ever read Gary Soto's narrative essay "The Pie"?

3. We traveled to many European cities with our high school band; it was an experience that we'll never forget.

4. How much would someone pay for an autographed script from the original <u>Star Wars</u> movie?

5. We received your résumé, Ms. Clark, and will contact you if we have any openings.

6. The participant who guessed the correct number of golfballs won an iPad.

7. Prof. Mitchell teaches the beginning French class.

8. Whenever I go there, I leave something behind; then I have to drive back and get it.

9. We brought the food, but we forgot the plates, forks, and plastic cups.

10. Roy Scheider came up with the famous line in the movie <u>Jaws</u>: "We're gonna need a bigger boat."

11. I love solving Sudoku puzzles in the newspaper; it's my favorite thing to do on Sundays.

12. Packing for a short trip should be easy; however, it's not.

13. Our English instructor taught us the following rhyme about commas: "When in doubt, leave them out."

14. I wonder if I needed to bring my math book with me today.

15. <u>The Simpsons</u> is the only TV series that my whole family still thinks is funny.

COMPREHENSIVE TEST (PP. 198–199)

Your revisions may vary slightly.

1. (ro) The tennis players put their gear away and grabbed a towel; then they met with reporters.

2. (adj) I felt *bad* about turning my paper in late.

3. (s-v agr) Each of the tutors *has* a different area of expertise.

4. (ww) On the final day of my art class, we critiqued all of *our* projects.

5. (verb) Students are *supposed* to use filtered water in the biology lab.

6. (ww) *They're* going to visit London, Paris, and Rome this summer.

7. (apos) Why are *men's* locker rooms always bigger than *women's* locker rooms?

8. (cs) A thunderstorm was on its way; we decided to stay at school until it passed.

9. (cliché) Our hands were *very cold* when we left the hockey game.

10. (c) Whenever I give a party, the guests always stay later than I expect.

11. (wordy) The trunk of her car was empty.

12. (ro) At the charity fundraiser, the adults washed the cars, and the kids dried them.

13. (p) I wonder how some people save so much money for their vacations.

14. (pro) The president of the college presented a special certificate to my friend and *me*.

15. (cap) "In and of *Ourselves We* Trust" is the title of an essay by Andy Rooney.

16. (frag) Increasing gas prices *have caused* people to take fewer car trips.

17. (adv) They missed a *really* important quiz when they were absent.

18. (// and wordy) To see the zoo animals, we drove to the parking lot, rode a bus to the front gate, and took a tram to the animal viewing area.

19. (shift in person) We ordered soup and salad, and *we* couldn't believe how small the portions were.

20. (pro agr) Everyone was allowed to drop *the* (to avoid *his or her*) lowest grade.

WRITING

ORGANIZING IDEAS (P. 217)

EXERCISE 1 TOPIC, FACT, OR THESIS?

1. THESIS

2. TOPIC

3. FACT

4. FACT

5. THESIS

6. THESIS

7. FACT

8. THESIS

9. TOPIC

10. THESIS

WRITING EXERCISE 8 ADDING TRANSITIONAL EXPRESSIONS (P. 221)

When I moved into my own apartment for the first time last month, I discovered the many hidden expenses of entering "the real world." *First* (or *At first*), I had no idea that utility companies needed a security deposit from anyone who hasn't rented before. Each utility required a thirty-dollar to fifty-dollar deposit. *Therefore,* my start-up costs just for gas, electricity, and phone used up all the money I had saved for furnishings. *Next,* I found out how expensive it was to supply a kitchen with the basic staples of food and cleaning supplies. My initial trip to the grocery store cost $225, and I hadn't even bought my curtains at that point. *Finally* (or *With practice*), I was able to budget my money and keep a little aside for any other unexpected expenses of living on my own.

WRITING EXERCISE 13 WRITE A SHORT SUMMARY (P. 238)

In "The Green Pioneer," Patricia Fara explains that Rachel Carson challenged ideas about female scientists and began the fight to save our environment. Some people believe that the influence of women in science is limited. Rachel Carson's early works didn't challenge those views. She succeeded in two areas: observing positive truths about nature and recording her unique observations in her writing. After WWII, however, Carson could not continue to write supportively about the future of nature. The use of chemicals at nature's expense had changed everything. She wrote *Silent Spring* as a warning to her fellow scientists and human beings. With that book, Carson started the fierce environmental debate that continues today.

Index

Notes

Notes

Notes